A WINDOW ON ETERNITY

The Life and Poetry of
JANE HESS MERCHANT

A WINDOW ON ETERNITY

Foreword by
RUTH BELL GRAHAM

SARAH JORUNN OFTEDAL RICKETTS

ABINGDON PRESS
Nashville

A WINDOW ON ETERNITY

Copyright © 1989 by Abingdon Press

This book is printed on acid-free paper.

Library of Congress Cataloging-in-Publication Data

Ricketts, Sarah Jorunn Oftedal. 1933–
  A window on eternity : the life and poetry of Jane Hess
Merchant / Sarah Jorunn Oftedal Ricketts.
    p. cm.
  ISBN 0-687-45603-7 (alk. paper)
    1. Merchant, Jane. 2. Poets, American—20th
century—Biography. I. Title.
  PS3525.E54Z87   1989
811'.54—dc20
[B]   89-36470
                                                                   CIP

Scripture quotations, unless otherwise specified, are from the King James Version of the Bible. Those noted JBP are from *The New Testament in Modern English*, by J. B. Phillips. Copyright © 1958, 1959, 1960, 1972 by J. B. Phillips. LETTERS TO YOUNG CHURCHES © 1947, 1957 by Macmillan Publishing Co., Inc. Those noted RSV are from the Revised Standard Version of the Bible, copyright 1946, 1952, 1971 by the Division of Christian Education of the National Council of Churches of Christ in the USA. Used by permission.

The author gratefully acknowledges the following for permission to reprint Jane Merchant's work:

Elizabeth Merchant, for all poems not noted here or on pages 335-36 and for the use of Jane Merchant's letters, diaries, and scrapbooks.

The Christian Science Monitor, for "Exception," copyright © 1953, and for "A Parade of One," copyright © 1970, by the Christian Science Publishing Society. All rights reserved.

Christianity Today, for "Of Marred Creation." Copyright © 1968 by *Christianity Today*.

David C. Cook Publishing Company, for "Lazarus," copyright © 1946; "Sunset in December," copyright © 1948; "Pine Bough at My Bedside," copyright © 1952; "Dawn," copyright © 1953; "On a Biography," copyright © 1956; "Quest," copyright © 1959; "Friends," copyright © 1960; and "Christ Has Conquered," copyright © 1973.

The Knoxville *News-Sentinel*, for "Measured." From a column by Bert Vincent in the August 5, 1952, Knoxville (Tenn.) *News-Sentinel*.

The New York Times, for "Song for April." Copyright © 1948 by The New York Times Company.

The Progressive Farmer, for "No Other Acres" and "Plowing Song." Copyright © 1945 by *The Progressive Farmer*.

additional copyright information is on pages 335-36.

MANUFACTURED IN THE UNITED STATES OF AMERICA

"In the wall of time Thou hast made windows that open on eternity."
Jane Hess Merchant

To Elizabeth, sister and faithful friend.

CONTENTS

FOREWORD

Many years ago I discovered the poetry of Jane Merchant in popular magazines—*Good Housekeeping, Saturday Evening Post,* and others. Old scrapbooks are enriched by them—from the poignant to the humorous—to me they were delightful.

Then I learned that she was a cousin of a dear local friend, Jean Merchant, who told me of Jane's background and physical handicaps.

From then on Jane's poems took on special meaning.

This book is deeply absorbing, an inspiration and a challenge, and an eye opener in how Jane worked at her poetry.

It is a book that will stretch your mind and your heart and leave you the richer for having read it.

Ruth Bell Graham

ACKNOWLEDGMENTS

This work could not have been undertaken without the help of Elizabeth Merchant, who graciously welcomed me to the family home on Emoriland Boulevard in Knoxville, Tennessee, where she and Jane once lived with their mother. Elizabeth shared her memories—as well as Jane's diaries, letters, papers, books, and pictures—and provided introduction to other family members and Jane's friends. Through ten years of research and writing, she gave patient counsel and encouragement.

Grateful acknowledgment must also be made to Jane's many faithful friends and fans who kept her letters and allowed me to read them. To John Dobson, Special Collections Librarian at the University of Tennessee, Knoxville, who made available the May Justus–Jane Merchant and the Dr. Alwin Thaler–Merchant letters.

Special thanks are due Shirley Whitney Kerr, Pat Lassen, Eva Venable (now deceased), Carolyn Ruth Reynolds, Frances Winter, Bruffie Connor, Carl Arneson, Gurre Noble, Kay Gudnason, Dorothy Brown Thompson, Webb Dycus, Betty Washer, Eleanor Stanford, Ruth Hunt, Dorothy Carol Barton, Corrine Erwin, June Arnold, Gerald Fisher, Irma Lidner, Ann Samson, Marilu Terral Jeans, Margaret Jean Jones, Patricia Stone Rogers, Tess Hovde (now deceased), Billie McKinney, Rita Snowden, Josephine Breeding, Mildred Thompson, Wallen Bean, Frank Bird, Robert Roy Wright, Dr. Thomas F. Chilcote, Wayne Chilcote, Fred Strathdee, and Gordon A. Sterchi, many of whom turned over their Jane Merchant correspondence, and all who took time to answer questions and supply insights.

I am particularly grateful to Elizabeth Merchant, Pat Lassen, Shirley Whitney Kerr, Ruth Bell Graham, who first suggested the project, and Shirley Brown, who read the manuscript at various stages and provided encouragement and criticism. To Bunny Graham Dienert, who went through the manuscript with an editor's eye and pencil, and to members of the San Diego County Christian Writers' Guild critique group who exhorted and disciplined me through the long, dry stretches!

Special thanks to my friends Harriet Molloy and Vicki Burgermeister and to members of my family—Anne, Alexandra, and Christa Ricketts, who helped index more than 3,000 poems, 2,000 letters, and Jane's diary and scrapbook.

To all who loved me and believed in the work through these long years, thank you for being there, I could not have made it alone.

S.J.O.R.

INTRODUCTION

In her diary Jane Merchant wrote: "It would be especially impossible, I think, for any highly improbable biographer to know 'how it feels to be Jane.' I don't, of course, have any special public image to confuse a biographer, except that some who haven't met me seem to think I'm a plastic [synthetic] saint" (June 27, 1966).

With that warning, it seemed wise to let Jane speak for herself, as far as possible, through letters, diaries, and poetry. Inevitably the selection and treatment of material reveals more of the bias of a biographer than of the subject. So it is fortunate that only synthetic saints can be contained in pre-cast molds. Live ones have a way of defying precise description.

Jane was neither plastic nor synthetic. I had not heard of her before a friend quoted a poem in 1976, four years after Jane's death. I was immediately captivated by its lively candor. Then I read her books and "met" her in diaries, letters, and the memories of family and friends. Something about her—an aura of authenticity, of wholeness, of laughter—touched me and drew me. She seemed to be one of the most *alive* humans I had ever encountered.

The question that invariably presented itself was how did Jane come by this wisdom, this insight, this joy, this faith, this love, this ability to cope, this aliveness? What was her secret? Her strength? What pilgrim journey had her soul traveled?

Now, after researching, writing, and rewriting—immersing myself in her life—I would not dare presume to say precisely "how it feels" to be Jane. But all along the conviction has grown; Jane somehow knew "how it feels" to be me, to be human. She was no stranger to failure, to darkness and despair. She knew intimately the suffering and joy of the human condition—the "gloom and glory" she called it—and the dull dreariness in between.

As closely as I could, I followed her journey of soul from childhood to maturity, from certainty through the darkness of unknowing, to faith. Inevitably it became my own journey. I wanted to discover Jane and found that in the process she helped me discover more of myself. She became for me a window, opening outward on regions I had never dared explore, and letting light into inner rooms that had long been closed off.

From her friends I learned that Jane had done the same for them. She does it still for those who encounter her in poetry today, inviting us on the inward and outward journey of discovery, deeper into the love of God and all of his creation.

I hope you will meet Jane in these pages and see in her, as I did, the truth of Augustine's words: "The glory of God is man fully alive."

S.J.O.R.

1

THE WALL WITH A WINDOW

In a certain sullen wall
That shuts the spacious world from view
Chance—or miracle—has made
A space for looking through;

A little blessed window space
Through which imprisoned eyes may see
An upward-going leafy road,
A tiny flowering tree;

And, growing close and pressing inward
Through the window in the wall,
Sprays of blossoms shaped to music,
White and sweet and small.

In whatever walls surround us,
Stubborn walls of grief or pain,
Barred by gates that will not open
While our lives remain,

God's love is a window, showing
Us a wide and leafy land,
And his mercy, bell-like, blossoms,
Sweetly close at hand.

A cold wind blew across Bookwalter cemetery in Knoxville, Tennessee, on January 5, 1972, when a small crowd gathered to lay the body of Jane Hess Merchant, poet, to rest.

During the graveside service, the sun broke through low clouds, and robins played in the thin snow. Jane had loved the sight of robins in the snow.

Her death, at fifty-two, had been sudden and stunned all who knew her. An editorial in the Knoxville *Journal* later noted: ''When the best minds of the universe ponder that rare quality of creativity, they should consider the moving example of the late Knoxville poet Jane Merchant . . . her work will live on.''

In the Knoxville *Sentinel,* a columnist wrote: "Jane Merchant was a great poet, and a great woman of indomitable courage.''

Her accomplishments were remarkable by any standard, but to those who knew something of her circumstances, they were extraordinary. Jane's influence reached around the globe, though she had never traveled more than a few hundred miles from the place where she was born. A multitude of fans and friends knew her as an overcomer, possessed of wisdom, humor, compassion, understanding, and faith. She had been a light-bringer in darkness, an encourager, a comforter, a guide, and a steadfast friend.

Outwardly, Jane's life had seemed uneventful. For most of her adult years, she had lived quietly with her widowed mother and nurse sister in a small gray house with a bright red door on Emoriland Boulevard in Knoxville. The room she shared with her mother looked out on a small, well-tended garden. The view was winter bleak now, except for birds flocking to the feeder by the window.

The bookshelf, with its well-worn volumes, and the small walnut table by Jane's bed still held her things as she had left them two days before. In her file box were copies of poems submitted to editors the day she died. More than two thousand had been printed in magazines; Jane had clipped and pasted them in seven scrapbooks. Some were included as well in the ten slender volumes bearing her name. Two large scrapbooks held reviews of her work and biographical articles, though Jane had disliked and avoided publicity.

The bulging portfolio on her table contained personal correspondence waiting to be answered. Jane's "peculiar circumstances" had prevented all but a few of her friends from meeting her in person. Instead there had flourished deep and treasured relationships by mail with individuals of an amazing diversity of backgrounds and interests. Jane did not take the commitment to friendship lightly. Her letters were a dependable source of cheerful empathy. Few of her friends knew the lonely depths she had plumbed at times within the "narrow walls" or how much she needed *them.*

Friends—and books—were somewhat like "windows" to Jane, a "blessed space for looking through" beyond confining walls of self and circumstance. There were times when she had nearly despaired of reaching her destination, times when a companion along the way had provided the only glimmer of hope that darkness would one day yield to light.

The soul of a poet is finely tuned to the heights and depths of living, and Jane had come precariously close to destruction, to giving up. The pilgrim road had seemed steep and bleak, and the treadmill of resignation less hazardous. It was tempting to lock herself within defensive walls instead of remaining vulnerable and open to pain. She could have taken refuge in self-pity and bitterness, numbing her heart, a living death.

Often her eyes had followed the flight of a bird, winging joyously and free, and her heart had longed to fly away, to escape the stubborn walls. She had tried to find release in the romance of daydreaming, and the lesson was hard won; illusion was deceptive comfort.

She had found true joy close at hand in living fully the life that was given her. Joy was like blossoms by her window, petals of light in dark places, like the sheen of tiny grasses bending in the wind along a narrow, uphill road.

She had kept on going when she did not think she could. She had kept the faith, and now the journey was done. The end determines the story; now hers could be told. The pilgrim was home. In "Pedestrian" Jane wrote:

> To be pedestrian is to be
> Profoundly intimate
> With earth scent and grass sheen
> And the sun's light and weight.
>
> It's scorched dust and brambles
> And pebbles in the shoe,
> And violets surprising
> The near, perceptive view.
>
> Oh, wings are wildly lovely
> In blue, alluring sky,
> But who would live at standstill
> Because he cannot fly?

2
FIRST THINGS
1936

Never return
To the towering hill,
The enormous river,
The mighty mill.

Whoever returns
Is apt to see
A dwindling homestead,
An outgrown tree.

But the love first given you,
The love first known,
Is always larger—
If you have grown.

The two-story frame house stood with wide porches on a small rise near the road. Tall maples gave shade and a shield against curious travelers, who were few on this farm road miles from the nearest town. The house faced a wide expanse of fields and low hills, but the better view was in the back, from the kitchen. There to the south ran the French Broad River on its way toward Knoxville from the distant Blue Ridge mountains.

On summer days, the front porch was coolest, and the young girl in a white hospital bed on wheels liked to be where she could watch for the mailman and keep an eye on her father's dairy herd grazing across the road.

It was June 1936 and the third month of drought in East Tennessee. The fields were brown, and farmers prayed for rain, fearing it would soon be too late. The girl prayed, too, but her fear was lessened by trust. The danger of losing the farm was real—they had lost one before—but other things were more certain. She had never known her parents defeated. Their God, and hers, would not fail them.

Her father's face was deeply lined and browned by the sun, but his blue eyes held a hint of laughter to dispel all gloom. Her mother knew to fill the house with the fragrance of baking bread when things looked darkest.

Their daughter had inherited some of the sensibilities of both, along

18

with an exuberance for living and an apparently boundless curiosity about nearly everything. Her dark blue eyes missed little. A pair of glasses perched on a rather prominent nose, which added to her eager look. The chin was firm and the clear forehead high under a "carefully cherished wave" of short dark hair. It was a pretty face, with an impish smile apt to soften the look of intense concentration she wore when a task or a thought absorbed her.

Life was no casual undertaking. Were it not for the irrepressible humor of it—and her faith that all things were bound to end well—she would have dreaded the future more.

Jane was the youngest of four children born to Clarence and Donia Merchant, and the only one still living at home. The place was quiet without her brother and two sisters, but Jane had always done much of her living by imagination and on paper. Words on a page or an image in her mind could be transformed into experience as vividly as if she had lived it. In a sense, she had.

Sitting still, gazing at trees, birds, flowers, earth, and sky, her being absorbed the life of them and the memories of all that had been there before her time. The old house had been used as a field hospital during the Civil War, and the tales of terror haunted her. Years later she wrote to a friend: "Even if one doesn't dwell on such facts as the finding of Civil War bullets in the fields, or on the knowledge that [Army] doctors threw amputated arms and legs on the porch where I used to lie and watch the sky, such memories, latently in the earth, may explain why the South didn't forget the War as easily as did the North'. . . . [Do] people breathe in, unconsciously, memories of events that happened years before on soil where they were born?"[1]

Jane was sixteen the year of the drought, but she would remember it as "the year when I first became aware of myself as a person, even though for a long time it seemed as though the ambitions awakened then were never going to bear any fruit."[2] It was the year she first dared reach out and expose herself to the world of strangers, risking their response. And it happened through words she put on paper.

She had always loved words. She could produce jingles, stories, or poems in her secret journal and voluminous letters to cousins and aunts. But now the potency and awesome power of words excited her as never before, flooding her mind with images and ideas faster than she could write them down. She longed to share them with others, to touch the world with them.

The first response to what she later called "the most significant thing I ever did"[3] came on a hot, dry day that would remain forever etched in her memory. She looked up from her notepad to scan the horizon for hint of a rain cloud, when puffs of dust churned up by the mailman's car swelled along the road in the distance. Always the sight set her heart to racing. The "struggle-buggy" progressed at a maddeningly slow pace, "pausing at mailboxes like a gigantic bee droning from one metallic flower to another."[4]

Jane tried to calm herself as the blue sedan stopped at the driveway where her mother was waiting already. There was a promising bundle destined for the Merchant household, but the mailman was in no hurry. A friendly chat with Donia was part of his daily routine. Jane searched their faces for a clue; was there mail for her? At last he was off with a smile and a wave, and Donia climbed the porch steps carrying the yet unexamined "treasure." She always brought the mail to Jane's bedside, and they would scan each item together, examining stamps and postmarks, putting the personal mail aside for private scrutiny before sharing the contents, reading excerpts out loud for extra pleasure. It was a ritual they both loved, highlighting their day.

A personal letter for Jane was rare, and it always made her acutely self-conscious. Today there was a bulky envelope addressed in an unfamiliar handwriting to Miss Jane Merchant, Dandridge, Tennessee, from Miss Carolyn Ruth Kiddoo of Creston, Iowa. The surprise of its presence made Jane nearly numb with excitement. And Donia, sensing something quite out of the ordinary, excused herself and went into the house. Privacy was a gift she could only offer her daughter in limited measure.

The Merchants were a close-knit family with a strong sense of loyalty, but they shared the fierce independence of the hill farmers of the Great Smoky Mountains. Both Donia and Clarence came from North Carolina, where they had first met at the Presbyterian Vocational College in Asheville. Donia's parents were Henry Nichols Swann and his wife Emma Clark, both of Irish and English descent. Clarence's father, John, had come to America as a boy with his parents from Gloucestershire, England. He grew up to be a school teacher and farmer, and he married Eliza Jane Hess, the daughter of German immigrants.

Perhaps Jane had inherited a love of words and writing from her paternal grandparents. John kept a journal that was continued after his death by his widow. They raised their six children on a rocky ridge farm in the Smokies and taught them hard work and to love God and creation, books and music.

Clarence was the youngest of the six. Among his brothers and sisters were a preacher, a teacher, a social worker, and two builders. He alone chose to farm, and he crossed the mountains to East Tennessee in a covered wagon, hoping to find richer soil there. Donia followed a year later. They were married in Knoxville in 1911 and settled in Inskip, not many miles from town.

There their children were born: Nelson first, then Elizabeth, then Ruth. The fourth arrived November 1, 1919, and was named after her grandmother, Jane Hess Merchant. It was the year her grandfather John died.

> My father's father died
> The year that I was born
> And never have I seen his house,
> Broad beamed and weather worn,
> That sat upon a lonesome ridge
> With widely welcoming door.
> Its sunny rooms and hallways
> Were not mine to explore.
>
> My father's father lived
> A life of faithful prayer
> And there is gentle fellowship
> That we may always share.
> Wherever I may go,
> Wherever I may be
> My father's father's dwelling place
> Will always welcome me.
>   "In All Generations"

Baby Jane was frail at birth, and the doctor feared she would not live long. Clarence and Donia hoped to prove him wrong. World War I had ended. Food shortages at the end of the war had caused Donia's inadequate diet during the pregnancy. They were sure it was to blame for the baby's weakness. Proper nutrition and care would be the remedy.

Jane was quick and alert, if tiny for her age. Blond curls framed her pretty face, and in the wind she clasped her flying hair with both hands and laughed with delight, "Wind's gonna blow my curls away!"

The cherished curls soon had to be shed. When Jane was eighteen months old, she stumbled and fell on the kitchen floor. Her cries of pain persisted; her right leg was broken. The family doctor came to set the bone and suspend the leg in traction over Jane's small bed. Her curls tangled and matted on the pillow, and with a heavy heart Donia cut them.

Through a long, hot summer, the family took turns away from their outdoor chores to stay with Jane. They read and sang nursery rhymes to occupy her, and Grandma Merchant sent a doll to be her cherished companion. Jane promptly named her Jane-Jane.

When the break mended, Jane tried to walk again, but the horror recurred: the other leg snapped under her. The doctor could only surmise that his small patient suffered from "brittle bones," as easily broken as pencil lead. No cure was known.

Jane drank the rich milk from her father's dairy cows and was given calcium supplements, bottled water, and an exercise bike, but her bones continued breaking under the least strain with "dreadful regularity."

Walking was too perilous. It was safer to be carried in her parents' arms. Outdoors she could be pulled in a small wagon or placed on a blanket on the grass, where she could watch her father drive the cows home from pasture or her mother at work in the garden. Higher on the hill was the peach orchard. Over all arched the wide sky she had loved since she first saw it.

> I always owned the sky; the sky was mine
> From the moment I first looked up at it, and felt
> All the enormous tender brilliance shine
> Into my wondering heart, where it has dwelt
> Unceasingly. I own uncounted millions
> Of stars, though using only two or three,
> And as for clouds, of course, I've many trillions,
> And the sun is my peculiar property.
> My ownership of sky does not preclude
> Others enjoying it; I'm glad to share
> My glad possession of infinitude,
> But any who come between us must beware,
> Since, whether lightning-lashed or rainbow-lit,
> The sky belongs to me, and I to it.
>
> "Possession"

The farm required much hard work, and the children each had chores. When Jane wasn't mending bones, she was expected to do her part. Her nimble fingers were adept at shelling peas or stringing beans, and her hands slipped easily through the narrow mouth of a canning jar to place the peach halves just right. No one else could accomplish that feat as well, and her mother's satisfaction was Jane's best reward. It seemed to prove that "having small hands was a most remarkable accomplishment."[5]

Jane learned early the satisfaction of doing the best she could with what she had and not wasting time fussing over what she didn't have. Grandma Merchant had made a scrapbook of bird and animal pictures from labels, baking soda boxes, and magazines, and Jane decided to make one like it for a small cousin. She asked for store-bought paste in place of the flour and water concoction Donia had prepared, but her mother was firm: "Grandma didn't have anything like that. She just used what she had" ("Two Scrapbooks").

Donia's sayings could be trusted. They had been tested in living and found true.

"Can't never did do nothing," she would say,
Whenever I complained, "I can't do this."
And always I would find there was a way
To do it well, helped onward by her kiss.

"Cheer up, the worst is yet to come!" she'd laugh,
Whenever I bemoaned tomorrows woes,
And ever since I've cut my grief in half,
Enjoying present good before it goes.

"Look at the little grass blooms," she would smile,
"Look at the baby sparrow, honey, look,"
And so I learned to pause and gaze awhile
Observing things not found in any book.

And when my world collapsed about my head
She built it back. "We love you, dear," she said.
"My Mother's Sayings"

Clarence and Donia were not given to wordiness. "Dad and Mother taught us by simply being what they were, living their values and expecting us to have gumption enough to know and to do right without a great deal of talk about it. I remember Dad writing once, concerning giving advice to children, that he never saw any use in hollering at a mule as long as it was going along steadily."[6]

The sun does not admonish grass
To drink its rain and stand up straight.
Earth finds no need, as calm hours pass,
To lecture and expostulate.

A warm expectant atmosphere
Without injunction or command
Or words too numerous to hear—
How tall and straight the grasses stand!
"Hint to Parents"

The parents seldom rested, but the four children were given time to swim in the pond (Jane paddled on a float) and read in the shade. When dusk deepened and the fireflies came out, they spread an old quilt on the grass and watched the stars.

We tried to count the stars
Three sisters and a brother,

We'd lie, computing stars,
    At ease with one another.

Our totals never tallied,
    We never did succeed
In numbering stars; but found
    Enough for every need.

And we were always four,
    We learned the number thus:
While we were counting stars,
    The stars were counting us.
                "Tally"

Some of Jane's best memories were of going with her father on his milk route or to market in Knoxville. "I do remember how very beautiful the drive in the early morning was, with the sun shining through the mists on the new green leaves, and especially on the weeping willow trees. . . . It would not have occurred to me to try to express the beauty of it in words, then, and probably I didn't even consciously feel it or think of it, but just absorbed it unthinkingly as children do, without realizing how much material for green thoughts these earliest impressions will give them later on."[7]

How many times we traveled
The weeping-willow road,
My Dad and I together,
Carrying a load

Of peaches to the market,
Or peas, or beans, or corn—
I must have started traveling it
As soon as I was born.

We'd ride along together
And both of us were shy
And neither of us mentioned
The weeping-willow sky,

The green and tremulous mystery
We traveled under all
The way into the city;
But though I don't recall

A word I said about it
Or one he said to me,
I like a weeping willow
As well as any tree.
              "The Willow Road"

24

Clarence was deacon and Sunday school superintendent at Inskip Methodist Church, and until she was nine, Jane was carried to Sunday school and took piano lessons from the pastor's daughter. That ended her "formal" schooling. At home she had studied with her brother and sisters from the age of five and had surprised them all by learning to read a book of favorite nursery rhymes on her own. From then on she was ready at the kitchen table when the others sat down to do homework; she had a way of asking eager questions until she was satisfied they had told her all they had learned in school that day.

Reading opened a new world to Jane. She read everything she could find, including the Bible and a one-volume edition of Shakespeare's plays. The best loved volumes were covered in sturdy oil cloth, lest they be worn to tatters. Among her favorite authors were Dickens and Sir Walter Scott, and on the family shelf of classics were anthologies of poetry, fairy tales and adventure stories, Greek mythology, and American history.

Stacks of books from the school library or the Knoxville public library rounded out Jane's early adventures, and on a few memorable occasions she was allowed to visit the library herself. "I would be carried in and placed on a hard chair at a hard table to stare at shelves of books too numerous to believe. . . . My memories of books I read during seemingly endless childhood summers are full of sky, the scent of clover and taste of peaches."[8]

> What trips to Troy and Camelot
> And Asgard I have had
> With just a grassy garden spot
> And a book for a launching pad.
>   "Excursions"

But best were the summer days when rain brought her father in from his work in the fields.

> Just what bad weather is I had to learn.
> It wouldn't have occurred to me that gray
> Storm clouds that wouldn't leave and not return
> Were reason for condemning any day,
> For days of pouring weather, on the farm,
> In childhood years, were simply days when Dad
> Stayed round the house, and it was with alarm
> I heard the grown-ups call such weather "bad."
> Grown-ups had curious notions, that I knew,
> But popping corn with Daddy, beating him
> At checkers while the laughing moments flew
> As bright as all outdoors was drenched and dim,
> I didn't see how anybody could
> Call rainy weather anything but good.
>   "Concerning Rainy Weather"

25

At home with her family, Jane did not feel it strange that she could not do all the things they did. "It seems to me that I always accepted the fact that walking and running, playing games, going to school; all the things my brother and sisters did, were pleasant natural things that had nothing whatever to do with me. I was one sort of person, and they another, and that, to me, was all there was to it. There didn't seem anything at all strange about my not being able to walk, and it seems to me perfectly true to say that I never felt at all sorry for myself because of it."[9]

It was different among strangers. The rare family outings—to the annual fair, where Nelson won blue ribbons for his calves and pigs, or trips over the mountains for happy visits with relatives—were mixtures of delight and torture. Curious strangers stared at her thin, useless legs and hunched, misshapen back. Even visitors to their farm could thoughtlessly ask for an explanation, and Jane hid her face, suddenly "horribly ashamed" of breaking her bones so often.

"I was most painfully, agonizingly shy, and quite irrationally afraid of being laughed at. . . . Part of my shyness was due to my hearing not at all well—anything that was not said directly to me—I was always so completely dumb in the presence of outsiders (and I'm sure a great many of them thought I was dumb in both senses of the word) that they often asked whether I *could* talk; such questions and Mother's explanations about my being 'shy' naturally making me shyer than ever. I wonder why perfectly kind, well-meaning people never seem to realize what pure brutality it is to discuss a child, and especially a child's peculiarities, in the child's presence."[10]

> I was the one who never learned to walk.
> I was the one who had to be explained.
> Strangers inquired if I could even talk.
> I could, when they weren't eyeing me with pained
> Commiserating glances. No one can
> Hold conversation with a pitying look.
> So while the other children played and ran,
> I was the one who hid behind a book.
>
> And yet, I wondered why they pitied me.
> My father's arms were always strong and sure,
> My mother's smile was always sweet to see,
> And with them I was perfectly secure,
> And it was many years before I knew
> I was the one who broke their hearts in two.
>   "The Odd One"

Occasionally she questioned "why I hurt so much so often, when I tried so hard to be good. The idea that it was God's doing or desire that I should hurt, does not seem to have much more than crossed my mind. I knew very well that my earthly father would not willingly have hurt me, even if I had been very naughty, and I usually wasn't. It seemed unlikely that my Heavenly Father would be less gentle. At Sunday school and at home we sang, 'Jesus loves me, loves me still, though I'm very weak and ill,' and that seemed to be answer enough to my theological questions."

The story of Job from the Bible was a favorite, "because it proved, I felt, that one could suffer without being wicked. So probably I wasn't being punished. . . . I made some sort of distinctive difference between the things God wanted to happen, like Mother smiling at me tenderly when I hurt, and the things that happened . . . because people weren't wise enough to prevent them, like my hurting. At any rate, I decided I would trust in Him and be polite about it—not ask rude questions—even when I hurt badly."[11]

Her greatest fear was not of breaking bones, but of being helpless and alone. It began with one of her earliest memories: she was in bed one summer afternoon with one leg strung high in traction. Seeing her safely asleep, the entire family had gone to the orchard to harvest peaches. Jane awoke to an empty house. No one answered her cries. The terror of abandonment struck deep. For years she dared not nap in the daytime without someone beside her. At night she prayed secretly that the family would not leave her for good while she slept.

All the love and care could not dispel her secret dread. Only prayer made it endurable, but she would wake from a nightmare to terrifying darkness, crying out till her mother came with light.

> My parents carried light with them, for they
> Lived in the days when people made their own
> Or did without. The lantern's frosty ray,
> When Dad came late from milking, always shone
> As if a star were coming home to us,
> And if I called at midnight, goblin-harried,
> The shadows fled and night grew luminous
> Before the little lamp that Mother carried.
>
> Folk have small need of lamps and lanterns now;
> Even on farms the darkness will withdraw
> By swift electric magic, but somehow
> I always shall be grateful that I saw
> My parents' coming make the darkness bright
> And knew them as the carriers of light.
>
> "Lanterns and Lamps"

Jane was twelve when another crisis struck the family. Crop failure and the Great Depression forced the sale of their farm and the home Clarence had built with his own hands. Nelson found work in construction, while the rest of the family moved their dairy herd to Dandridge, northeast of Knoxville. The upheaval was difficult, and things got worse when Jane suffered another break. She had gained weight, and the extra pounds may have put more strain on her bones. As Donia lifted her one day from wheelchair to bed, Jane's right arm and both legs broke simultaneously. Now she was flat on her back for a long and painful recovery. When her bones mended, she leaned on her right elbow in bed, and the arm broke again. It appeared that her future would have to be spent in the horizontal.

It was a radical reduction of mobility. It was difficult to write or do handwork lying down. But she could read, listen to the radio, and look out her window at scurrying clouds.

> Even with little else to see
> Of the world's bewildering array
> Of form and color, one might be
> Well occupied, day after day,
> Observing clouds. Enormous black
> And silver clouds ballooning by,
> And gray outrider clouds that crack
> Explosive whips across the sky,
> And chubby little puffs of white
> And pink, and massive piles of gold—
> So many patterns of delight,
> So various, the sky can hold,
> Our eyes would have enough to do
> Without this earth to notice too!
>   "Patterns of Delight"

To brood over what she couldn't do was not the Merchant way, and Jane set out to do her best with what she had. Aunt Laura, her father's sister, had taught her to knit and crochet, and Jane worked at it every morning, making baby clothes for sale. With her earnings she bought books. A fifteen cent copy of *Alice in Wonderland* was the first volume on her shelf. Next came several Louisa May Alcott books and Dickens' *David Copperfield*.

Nearly everything she read was fiction or poetry—the stuff romantic dreams are made of. The lives of the heroines became her own. She was Jo March in *Little Women,* Emily in *Emily of New Moon,* and Anne in *Anne of Green Gables.* Like them, Jane kept a secret journal and dreamed of becoming the author of "rows upon rows of bestsellers."[12] And like her heroines, she kept her writing ambitions concealed from her family, "for fear of being pitied if I failed, or laughed at."[13]

An author of best-selling novels could do what she wanted most: assist her parents in their struggle to make a go of the new farm. They worked from before daylight until after dark, and Jane was achingly aware that caring for her added much to their burden.

She was fifteen when her oldest sister, Elizabeth, began nurse's training at Fort Sanders Presbyterian Hospital in Knoxville. When the hospital superintendent heard of Jane's puzzling ailment, he arranged for her to be examined by a bone specialist. With soaring hopes, Jane was taken to Knoxville in an ambulance, but the doctor found no clue to a cure. There would be no easing of the physical restrictions on her living, it seemed.

It was a downcast Jane who returned to Dandridge, but a few days later came a wondrous gift from the hospital: a bed on wheels with an adjustable back. Now she could be raised into a near sitting position without straining her bones. "Life suddenly took on a different look!" she exulted.[14]

Clarence widened a doorway to the porch so that the new bed could go through, and Jane spent most summer days outside.

"It was there, I think, I first became aware of loving trees and the mountains. . . . Perhaps one only needs to have to stay inside most of the time to realize how wonderful is outside!"[15]

Her eyes could seek out the distant mountains shrouded in blue mist, and her imagination soared to their lofty heights. As long as she could remember, she had lived on a hill with a view of the mountains.

> That hilltop spoiled me for a smaller view.
> I measure with uncompromising eye
> All later landscapes by the one I knew
> Before I knew that landscapes could deny
> The ampleness of meadowland and wood
> Sweeping to distant mountains with rhythmic grace
> So that within a single glance I could
> Encompass all varieties of space.
> Oh, I was greatly fortunate in living
> There halfway up the sky, with large extent
> Of mountain heights and valleys always giving
> Enrichment to my eyes; but young days spent
> Immediate neighbor of immensity
> Make any other view look small to me.
>
> "Halfway Up the Sky"

Life looked vastly more promising than it had seemed just a few months before. Jane had been given the *Lincoln Library of Essential Information* for her sixteenth birthday, and she began to study it methodically. She had read Ralph Waldo Emerson's essay on "Self Reliance" with mixed feelings of exhilaration and skepticism. "I knew I wasn't wise enough to abandon all I had been taught."[16] Besides, Emerson had shown little appreciation for anyone with a handicap. "He hurt my feelings by saying that 'invalids and the insane pay a high board.' "[17]

At sixteen, Jane saw herself as a participant in the world, not as a shut-in. "I had such vast ideas about life's possibilities for excellence, triumph and delight . . . when I wasn't scared to death by life's possibilities for humiliation and defeat and emptiness. . . . What a queer little bundle of inhibitions and unadmitted terrors I was."[18]

The world—*her* world—was waiting out there, and as yet she had done nothing for it. The world would not come begging for her contributions; she must take the first step. But how? Only one way seemed remotely within her grasp. Grandmother Swann had given her a subscription to *The Portal,* a Methodist magazine for girls between the ages of twelve and eighteen. For years Jane had avidly read the "Inkpot and Pencil" page of contributions from readers—"junior editors"—and yearned to submit her own. At last, in the spring of 1936, she did, in the form of introducing a "letter" from her dog, Friendly. "I've read and loved *The Portal* for ages and eons, but . . . never before found courage to try. . . . I don't know whether it was the new pen . . . or the fact that I'm getting along in years and will soon be too old to contribute. I rather think it was neither, but Friendly's determination to write. . . . I am her slave and always do just as she bids me. I am bursting with suggestions, criticisms and advice." She signed herself: "A hoping-to-be new editor, Jane Merchant, age 16, Tennessee."[19]

In May, *The Portal* arrived with her own words in print, and Jane gazed at them in heart-pounding awe. Would anyone notice? The next issue held a response "to Jane" from Carolyn Ruth Kiddoo, a sixteen-year-old frequent contributor. But not in her happiest daydreams had Jane imagined the contents of the bulky envelope with the unfamiliar Creston, Iowa, postmark that came to her that unforgettable day in June. "That . . . letter . . . had a warmth and zest for life and people and books . . . that won an instant response from the introverted, uncertain, but enormously eager small person to whom it was delivered," she wrote to Carolyn Ruth nearly a lifetime later.

The two girls shared a passion for words and a lively imagination. They immediately launched a voluminous correspondence, mostly about books they were reading. Their letters were often twenty or thirty pages long, and Carolyn Ruth later admitted: "We took a healthy kind of pride in showing off our writing to each other."[20]

The editor of *The Portal* forwarded letters to Jane from three other girls that summer. Jane wrote to one of them, Corrine Martin of Paola, Kansas: "I was completely flabbergasted at receiving your letter . . . the fourth I'd received since my first piece of nonsense appeared in *The Portal*. I'm still slightly dazed. . . . I never imagined that anyone would notice my scratchings, or like them if they noticed them, or write to me if they liked them."[21]

The tone of her letters was light, perhaps especially so when she touched briefly on the painful reality of her circumstances, as she did in the letter to Corrine. "I can't swim, and never could, and never can, owing to an unfortunate habit of breaking my bones every time I try to do anything. . . . I don't go to school, or do any of the things most girls do; but I can probably talk, or rather write—even more nonsense than most."

The devastating drought lasted for eighty-two days—a record for the region. When the rains came in July, it was too late to save the farm. Once again they moved, this time fifteen miles west to Strawberry Plains, where Clarence became the manager of two dairy farms, ten miles apart. The family no longer owned their own place, but Jane's letters made light of the loss. She told of "the extra merry Christmas . . . to celebrate our new home" and of the "white wooly little dog" who replaced Friendly, who had died, "and left me lonesome enough to die myself."[22]

Jane was virtually tongue-tied around strangers, but she was gloriously unfettered in her writing. Words on paper were a magic passport to a world of wonderful encounters, only limited by the number of books she could obtain and correspondents she could find. And that, to her way of thinking, was largely a matter of economics. In *The Portal* she wrote: "If I had a million dollars . . . I would buy a publishing house . . . and sell millions of books just as cheaply as possible to people who love books but can't afford to buy them at the usual prices. . . . Then I'd settle down in a . . . little house with five or six dogs and a thousand dollars worth of stamps and write letters till my pen pals begged for mercy."

Much of what she wrote showed a fervent idealism. "I practically worship Charles Lindbergh . . . and detest prize fights and Adolf Hitler. . . . I'm quite a passionate Republican," she confided to her new friends. Her contributions to *The Portal* were no less ardent. On patriotism she wrote: "Isn't it sometimes more patriotic to oppose one's country if one is certain that her course is wrong? . . . We would not uphold our country in a wrong against our state, or our state in a wrong against our country. And we have no more right to uphold our country in a wrong against the world. . . . We can and should love our country, right or wrong, and do our best to make her always right."

31

Her thinking had been profoundly affected by Henry Drummond's *The Greatest Thing in the World.* She read it at seventeen and followed his advice to memorize the thirteenth chapter of Paul's Letter to the Corinthians in the New Testament. Drummond wrote: "You have life before you. Only once can you live it. What is the noblest object of desire, the supremest gift to covet? It is love. . . . Let it be the first great object of our lives to achieve the character of love, the character of Christ. . . . Get these ingredients into your life. Then everything you do is eternal. It is worth doing."

Many years later, Jane acknowledged the decisive influence of Drummond's book. "My efforts to live up to the concept of love and life presented there . . . and the conviction of the unfailing love of God that the book gave me, have been among the things that have done most to keep me alive."[23]

Most of the books she read at seventeen had happy endings, and Jane believed in a God who promised to overrule the evil in the world and reward the earnest efforts of good people—like her parents. Paul had assured the Corinthians that faith, hope, and love would abide forever, while all else would end. Could it not mean that all suffering would soon be over? In her lifetime? She could envision a bright and wonderful future for her generation.

In a utopian fantasy for *The Portal,* entitled *In a Hundred Years,* she described a monument unveiled in the year 2037, "dedicated to the youth of 1937 who freed the world of the horrors of wars, strikes, prize fights and gangsters, and made it the peaceful, happy world of today."

Jane felt the exhilarating sense of destiny, of being a part of the generation who would fulfill the hopes of humankind. In such a perspective her own hardships were insignificant.

In the fall of 1937, just before her eighteenth birthday, Jane sent her last letter to *The Portal,* and the editor wrote: "It is with very great regret we say goodbye to Jane. . . . Good luck to you . . . and may you give everyone as much pleasure as you have given us who have read your writings."

Several pen pals were going to college: Corrine in Kansas, Carolyn Ruth to the University of California at Berkeley, and Ruth Anne McCrillis in Boston. In comparison, Jane's future looked bleak. She had dreamed of writing novels that would touch lives and teach great truths, but her attempts at fiction were disappointing. It now seemed a "rather preposterous" ambition for someone with such limited experience of living.

Friends had urged her to submit poems to paying markets—*The Portal* had printed several—but Jane held back. Poetry was an intimate part of her, and the thought of the rejection of her poems by an editor—or exposure to a wider public—was terrifying.

Then came a direct offer from Ruth Anne in Boston to type the poems and submit them to any magazine of Jane's choosing. The timing was crucial. "I wanted intensely to earn money and do something for Mother and Dad instead of their always doing things for me" *("Two Scrapbooks")*.

The next letter to Ruth Anne contained several handwritten poems, with marketing instructions. The family had no inkling of what she was doing, and not until years later did Jane mention the outcome: "I submitted a few verses to the large, popular magazines, but I couldn't take rejection slips then." One editor had written, "Sorry, we aren't in the market for poetry now."

"Had I had any idea then how signal an achievement it is even to elicit any comment from an editor, I might not have been completely crushed. . . . I immediately destroyed the verses, resolved never to write another, and felt inwardly demolished for days . . . my frail self-confidence completely shattered."[24]

Later she wrote, in "Each Generation":

> They come, young, ardent, daring, in their season,
> To a novel world of challenge and delight
> And break their hearts for no unusual reason
> And find their fiercest tragedy is trite.

3
DIMENSIONS
1938–1944

The size of silence alternates
Between the shape of star and clod,
Constricted, like despair, with self,
Or vast and eloquent with God.

A small radio by Jane's bedside was her listening post on the world. Few programs or events escaped her. Hit songs, hymns, concerts and recitals, lectures, sermons, political speeches and rallies, quiz shows, radio plays and poetry readings, news and sports—all sparked a lively response. History was taking place within earshot, and it all concerned her: Roosevelt's fireside chats, the abdication speech of King Edward VIII of England and the coronation of his brother, King George VI. Knowledge of events made her a participant; she could never be an indifferent bystander to the hopes and aspirations, struggles and challenges of people and nations. Their destinies were linked with her own.

Her latest pen pal was Betty Washer in England, who was as eager to learn more about the United States as Jane was for a closer acquaintance with the country of her grandfather's birth. Their letters were bulky with carefully researched facts and lively opinions on the differences and similarities of their respective homelands. Jane was continuing her education as she had first started it; by asking questions.

Her sister Ruth, and most of her U.S. correspondents, were in college, and willingly shared lesson plans and reading lists. Their letters brimmed with tales of campus activities, romantic adventures, and new challenges. In contrast, Jane's own existence seemed to be narrowing down. Her hopes for the future considerably diminished.

I was a thousand people
When I was barely seven,
Fairy, leprechaun and elf
And all the saints in heaven.

I was a hundred people
When I was seventeen,
Pioneer and martyr
And shepherdess and queen.

I wish I hadn't dwindled
To this maturity
Of being daily, hourly,
Monotonously, me.
"Individual"

Her friends were moving away from home to discover themselves in a wider world. At nineteen, Jane knew her own need to seek a personal destiny, discover her true self. To challenge, sift and weigh the "truths" she had been taught. To find her own. Make her choices. For her, that inward journey through unknown territory, must be made while her outward self was bound to a bed, but make it she must. And it would perhaps be as difficult for those nearest her—as for herself.

Donia had never probed her daughter's secrets, but now there was a greater need for separateness. A withholding of confidences once shared. A private questioning of things commonly believed. A secret grieving over broken childhood dreams.

Ask of your teen-aged daughter,
Ask of your teen-aged son
No sharing of the glories
And grieving just begun;

Nor think that, having been young,
You can teach them how.
Their guarded eyes will tell you
You are not young now.

Youth's a separate country
Each explores alone.
They will share their thought with you
When their youth's outgrown.
"Song For Parents"

Donia had done much to give Jane the greatest possible degree of self-sufficiency. Morning and evening she placed a large oilcloth on Jane's bed, and made certain that a wash bowl, cloth, and soap were within easy reach so that Jane could bathe and dress herself in private. Books, writing supplies, and handwork were all close by, so Jane could keep her own daily routine with minimum assistance.

Years later she wrote of her mother:

She has a warm and generous heart
And she has mastered, as her own,
The delicate, essential art
Of letting those she loves alone.
"The Generous Heart"

Her father had designed a narrow, five-foot long day bed with an adjustable back, on wheels. In it Jane could be moved from room to room in the house and outside. For travel, Clarence constructed what they called her "go-buggy," a frame and mattress that fit, with some difficulty, in place of the back seat in their car. In 1938 they made two trips over the Smoky Mountains to visit family in Asheville, North Carolina, but the excitement and the curvy road were too much for Jane's sensitive stomach. She was carsick for most of the journey and "felt like a rag" for a week.

That ended her excursions beyond the front porch for a long time.

One personal event, perhaps more than any other, had marked her passing from the sheltered land of youthful dreams to a region of harsher realities: the editorial rejection of her poetry. She must bear the grief of it alone, and no parent or peer could chart her inward journey through disillusionment. Life, as it now appeared to her wakening senses, seemed vastly different from the romantic ideal spun by aspirations and imagination and nurtured by volumes of fiction.

She had believed in the books she read. She trusted them and identified with them. Fitting herself "into life as it actually is" would cause many a painful struggle.[1]

The child was the only early-rising one,
And, slipping out alone before the sun,
She saw a rabbit in the violet border
And held herself as still as dew in order
To see, to see, to see it where it sat.
It was a rabbit, she was sure of that;
It had the lengthy enviable ears
That a rabbit has whenever it appears
On wall or Easter card or handmade quilt.
But this one had an ear that seemed to wilt,
And when it moved to take a larger bite
Of violet leaves, its left leg hung light
And didn't move. This rabbit lacked the air
Of perky rabbits pictured everywhere.
Something about it made her want to try
To hold it close and tell it not to cry.
The grownups came. The real one limped away.

> She didn't tell on it. But from that day
> She viewed with a reproachful, puzzled look
> The beaming rabbits in her storybook.
>
> "The Real One"

The uncertainties and questionings were frightening. If only she could have shared them with a companion, a nearby friend. But even as she longed for it, her heart knew the terrifying truth: the process of "becoming" was a solitary one. In her diary she wrote in October 1940: "I suppose that not even the most fortunately companioned can ever really share or make another feel the love he feels for a crooked, graceless valiant apple tree, or for a prim, small cherry tree in April, with pale frivolity of blossom."

No friend on earth could ease the loneliness of her quest. She must find solace elsewhere.

> Oh, there is beauty singing
> Wherever love may search,
> In birds' wild onward winging.
> And in a slender birch.
> This is the secret that can dress
> Sorrow itself in loveliness.
>
> "The Secret"

Jane had broken her resolve never to write another poem. It was impossible not to. Her survival as a person depended on it, as if, in forming words on a page, she could discover and encounter herself—if there was a self to find. She was aware of a darkening within, a gathering storm, a churning restlessness driving her into a pathless gloom, an abyss of nothingness waiting to swallow her.

Not even to her best friend, Carolyn Ruth, now a student at the University of California at Berkeley, could Jane confide her deepening despair. They had once shared the security of absolute belief in the tenets of Methodism, but Carolyn Ruth had abandoned such "childish and easy absolutes" for the "intellectually honest" uncertainties of modern philosophy. She urged Jane to follow suit.

To Carolyn Ruth, least of all, did she dare confess the crumbling of her faith. For so long it had been her strongest shield against the terror of abandonment and meaninglessness. Could she live without it?

Her first serious questioning of God had begun with the suffering of others, innocent ones who did not deserve the misfortunes that befell them. Her parents were worn with work and worry, though they never let on. How could a loving God—if he existed—let them struggle on with no hope in sight? Jane was no longer fooled by their outward cheer. Their

37

faith did not seem to waver. Her mother's smile was bright, her father's humor always quick to trigger laughter. Were they hiding their pain to shield her, just as she had learned from them to hide her own?

The world beyond their farm echoed her inward anguish. The years 1939 and 1940 brought the ominous sounds of war through the radio into her quiet room. First came reports from the Far East, where Japan and China were fighting, then from Europe. Newspapers were filled with pictures of civilian casualties: women and children dead, cities and villages devastated. Jane felt the pain of it tearing her soul, darkening her mind. What now of God's love? The "greatest thing in the world," the ideal of love she had memorized at seventeen and tried to live by? How could it be true alongside the horrors of war?

Already in the spring of 1939 it was clear that "peace in our time" was another illusion. In March, Hitler took Czechoslovakia, and the following month Mussolini seized Albania. In "Song for April" Jane wrote:

> If hearts could break in April,
>   I think that mine would now;
> But no hearts break in April,
>   When bloom is on the bough.
>
> The whole world laughs in April,
>   And any hearts that break,
> May only break for loveliness'
>   And apple blossoms' sake.
>
> No hearts may break for sorrow
>   When April's on the hill.
> Oh, sing for joy in April,
>   And breaking heart, be still.

In September, Hitler launched his blitzkrieg in Poland. World War II was officially declared, and on Armistice Day in November, Jane wrote "Memorandum to Youth."

> It is not in gay banners
> That flaunt a crimson sky,
> Nor in a drum's quick throbbing
> Nor bugle's keen swift cry;
> Nor in the pride of marching men
> That war's essential lie;
> But in red fields where horror screams
> And youth lies rotting with its dreams.

The radio had become an instrument of torture. Jane listened with mounting horror as Prime Minister Chamberlain, President Roosevelt, and later Winston Churchill advised their nations of war. Reports of battles were broadcast directly from the capitals of Europe, accompanied by terrifying sounds of air raid sirens and bombs exploding. Jane's creative mind recoiled at the assault. In her imagination, she experienced vividly the devastations, the mutilations, and the suffering, as if her own body were being ravaged and torn apart. When hospitals were bombed in Britain and a ship carrying child evacuees was torpedoed and sunk on its way to Canada, Jane's anguish of soul was unbearable. "How could human beings do such outrageous things?" she lamented to Betty in England. "What a terrible way to learn history," she noted in her diary.

How could there be meaning or purpose behind the sorrowful things that happened to those she loved—and "the horrible things that happened to all mankind"? Reluctantly and fearfully she questioned her basic assumptions about God, and found no answers.[2]

Her days seemed long and empty, her own life without significance beyond mere existence and endurance. "Why? What? Who am I? And God? And Life?"[3] She tumbled with the questions. No one seemed to hear—and certainly, no one answered.

Her battle and her inward dying were carefully hidden, while her fingers were busy with needles and yarn, knitting children's sweaters for the Red Cross to ship to young victims of war. And she made booties for the newly expected Merchant. Nelson was married, and his wife, Elberta, gave birth to twins on December 3, 1941. Four days later, the Japanese bombed Pearl Harbor. America was at war.

Outside Jane's window, winter trees stood bare against leaden clouds, "lifting their mitred fingers of faith to that sky from which hope has fled. When we see them, we know it is not really the end" she noted in her diary. But in her heart she was less certain.

> Long I wandered, lost and lonely,
> Down a labyrinth of fears,
> But one thread to guide me, only,
> Frailer than the thread of tears.
>
> Oh, my thread of hope was fragile,
> Spun on spindles of despair,
> And the imps of ills were agile
> All my footsteps to ensnare.
> "Deliverance"

It was more truth than poetry, she admitted later. That year she came close to "losing the thread."[4]

"Queer things" in her ears had started to jam other sounds. At first she was unable to hear speech, then she couldn't hear the radio. Finally, she became deaf to all but loud thunder. Mercilessly the cocoon of silence wrapped itself around her. The soundless isolation was harder to bear than her immobility.

Now the visits from relatives—once treasured events—were painful and embarrassing, wrought with frustration and misunderstandings, leaving her exhausted and dejected, shut out from family conversation and laughter. In "Distances" she wrote:

> The moving lip, the changing face—
> What continents to reach
> Across, what deserts to compass
> With tense, uncertain eye,
> What leagues from sound to silence,
> From question to reply!

For brief, taunting periods her hearing returned, and with the small battery radio perched on her shoulder Jane could again hear the news. Then the sound disappeared, and she was cloistered in silence, the terror of abandonment stalking her soul. The "slow corrosion of doubt" had sapped her inner reserves.[5] In her diary she confessed more than twenty years later: "I had scant faith left with which to face my discovery that there is but one letter's difference between deaf and dead. And in wakeful, uncomforted nights I felt that 'd' was preferable to 'f', although I tried to seem cheerful by day" *(Diary, July 1, 1964)*.

Poetry was her lifeline. From the deep silence of the dark void within came words to poems, giving shape and substance to her "fragile thread of hope." Somehow the words her hand penned slowly and agonizingly gave flesh to the mystery of being her heart yearned to know, declaring certainties she longed to believe, hinting at an incomprehensible joy.

She wrote "Oh, I Have Music" in December 1941, when deafness first assailed her. As yet the words were more poetry than truth for Jane herself, only a faint hope to live on.

> You think me deaf? I heard a snowflake fall.
> I heard a rainbow singing; and the faint,
> Blue shadowed melody that twilight plays
> On spinet trees; and I heard the quaint
> Elf music made by moon-beams on still waters,
> And heaven's anthems as the stars appear;
> And once I heard a star . . . Oh, I have music
> Sweeter than songs that reach the outer ear!

There was another blow to come. In June 1942, the family was forced to move again, to a smaller house on the New Market farm. Her father did not have the strength to keep up the work on two places. With heavy hearts, they left the roomy Strawberry Plains home where they had lived for seven years.

Worse yet, the new place had no electricity, and it stood half a mile from the main road and the mailbox. Jane could no longer see cars go by or watch for the mailman. Her new room was dark and cramped, with little space for books. With gloomy foreboding, she sorted out the ones she would miss the least.

Their first night there, she slept on the open porch, reluctant to "shrink herself to fit the narrow room." There was solace in a beautiful view: a sunset and a moon rising over hills and fields and distant mountains. But she felt uprooted, "like a pulled tooth," permanently severed from a part of herself left behind in a place she would never see again *(Diary, June 1942)*.

The involuntary move had devastated her. With it had come an overwhelming realization of her own complete helplessness in determining her circumstances. Her earlier adjustment to her physical handicap—her peculiar circumstances—now seemed utterly naïve. For the first time she saw herself as the prisoner she truly was, and her dungeon walls were thick and unyielding.

Outwardly she had struggled to maintain her façade of faith, but this was the last straw. Not only were her own circumstances cruelly narrowing—she could, perhaps, have borne suffering for herself—but also her parents were slowly losing their battle against poor soil, fickle weather, crop failures, and mounting debts. And the world beyond was relentlessly ravaged by the atrocities of war.

Helplessly, Jane felt the last shred of determination to believe in a loving God who cared what happened to his creation give way to utter desolation. She could do nothing. Darkness was everywhere . . . except.

Except in her mother's smile, her father's laughter against all odds—their never ceasing prayers, seemed now a foolishly valiant bastion against an all powerful enemy. She determined not to quench their hope, however unfounded it might be. Her unbelief must not darken their faith.

She felt herself in mortal danger and turned inward in her desolation. No one could help her now. In moments of utter dejection she wondered if anyone would care. The friend she longed most to reveal herself to was Carolyn Ruth. Until now Jane had kept up a charade of cheer in her letters, boasting of faith to hide her terror of the atheism Carolyn Ruth so confidently claimed. Her own hypocrisy taunted her. She was a phony, a nothing, but she dared not confess the truth and expose herself to rejection and ridicule. That could be fatal now. Neither could she continue the deceit. There was nothing left to do but slam the door of her heart shut against her friend. In desperation, Jane wrote a terse farewell note to Carolyn Ruth, ending their relationship.

"For Growing," written years later, explains the urgency of her action.

> Today I close my door
> And hope no one will come
> Because I am too small
> For anyone to see.
>
> Sometimes flowers clench their petals,
> Snails curve within sealed pearl,
> Moles nudge deep into darkness.
> I close my door.
>
> Hiding precedes revealing
> And smallness is for growing.
> Tomorrow I will open
> Many doors.

The months that followed were shrouded in darkness. Doubts and guilt tormented her. But to the final point of icy isolation—denying the existence of God—she could not bring herself to go. Deep within her flickered a tiny hope: the possibility of being mistaken, of having turned her back on a Presence, of being guilty of betrayal. It was a twisted hope, but better than the destitution of there being no One to betray. In her darkest hours, she feared for her sanity, that her mind "must be as crooked" as her misshapen body.[6]

Even in the dungeon of despair, shut tight against any intruder, words once committed to memory winged through her thoughts: "The Lord is my shepherd; I shall not want. . . . Yea, though I walk through the valley of the shadow of death, I will fear no evil; for thou art with me. . . . Neither death, nor life . . . nor things present, nor things to come, Nor height, nor depth . . . shall be able to separate us from the love of God, which is in Christ Jesus, our Lord" (Ps. 23:1, 4; Rom. 8:38-39).

Somehow, as the darkness deepened, she perceived a light. In "Cause" she wrote:

> Without the night
> We could not dream
> How beautifully
> A star may gleam.
>
> Without the dark
> We could not know
> How tenderly
> A moon may glow.
>
> And without death
> We could not guess
> How immortality
> May bless.

Looking back, years later, Jane acknowledged that it was "the dull, aching ordeal" of life at New Market that made the beauty of the fields and mountains viewed from their hill seem "a God given exception to disaster."[7]

There is a mountain far beyond my window,
Oh, infinitely far and far away,
And yet as close against my heart as love is,
As liberal love, enlarging day by day.

To love a mountain is to learn of tallness,
Of quiet strength, forever unsubdued.
To love a mountain is to grow a little
Each time one sees its shining altitude.

It may be, if I love it well enough,
That some day I may journey up the far
Aspiring summit, the attaining height,
And lean my heart at last against a star.
"To Love a Mountain"

During Christmas 1942 Jane opened her heart's door again to Carolyn Ruth, with a letter asking forgiveness and reconciliation. Confessing "the sorry truth" about herself had required "rigorous honesty," but the rejection she steeled herself for did not come. Instead, Carolyn Ruth's response was immediate and joyous: "How glad I am to have you back! . . . and sorry I caused you so much grief unwittingly."[8]

Jane had dared take off her mask of self-assurance, and she received unconditional love in return—what deep, deep joy. Beyond that acceptance, she glimpsed something more. In the dark months her eyes had been caught by the beauty of mountains, the light of a star . . . and now?

I looked at a star
Deeply, and long,
Till suddenly I looked beyond the star
For one transcendent instant, and caught a glimpse
Of God.

And now I go with astonishment in my heart
And sorrow,
Knowing that the earth is too narrow,
And the sky too low,
And the souls of men too small
To contain so much vastness
Of love.

43

God,
Help us grow.

"Beyond the Star"

The unyielding walls of her "peculiar circumstances" made any illusions of self-sufficiency short-lived. Perhaps that was something to be grateful for. Human solutions and assistance were plainly inadequate. In her helplessness, she could only turn to something greater—and found what she had always sought, "blindly and unaware . . . in strange and devious ways," she confessed later to Carolyn Ruth *(Reynolds, Dec. 6, 1947)*.

Today I've grown beyond the scope
Of any stifling sky.
Pile all the stars up, world on world,
They would not reach so high.

I never spoke to Him before,
Too weak I was, and wild.
Today I said, "My Father,"
And He replied, "My child."

"Access"

White blooms filled Jane's small chamber that Easter. "An old black woman . . . went up on the hill and broke enough sprays of dogwood blossoms to change my room into a bower. Conservationists would have been shocked at the waste of blossoms; but I thought of Mary and the box of ointment very precious."[9]

She rejoiced in spring, in the "apparently effortless miracle" of bloom, knowing now something more of the usefulness of winter *(Diary, March 1943)*.

I am at home with winter.
I understand the thin
Determined trees, and all the calm,
Bare fields and I are kin.

I am at home with winter,
And I am glad to share
The dull gray days of waiting,
The cold, unfruitful air.

All hearts must master silence
Before they learn to sing.
Must be at home with winter
To be at home with spring.

"To Be at Home"

Jane's sense of at-homeness with the winter of her soul had only just begun. But spring 1943 marked a breakthrough. It was then that she read a newly published book by Harry Emerson Fosdick, whose radio sermons she had often listened to in her hearing days.

The message she received from Fosdick's *On Being a Real Person* was that circumstances do not determine the life of a person as much as his or her *response* to the circumstances. To illustrate his point, Fosdick listed several people of great achievement, among them the blind and deaf Helen Keller, the deaf composer Beethoven, and the blind poet John Milton.

The first step toward real personhood, Fosdick wrote, is self-acceptance, not of an ideal, but of the actual self with all its inherited endowments and handicaps and with the circumstances of living that cannot be altered or controlled. It is as if to say, "This is what I have been given. I will now see what I can do with *this*."

The men and women Fosdick wrote of did not succeed without struggles and conflicts. Jane found it deeply reassuring to read that real persons were not above inner tensions and were often tormented by doubts, fears, and depressions. "I rely on Fosdick saying, 'We all have cellars in our houses, but we don't have to live in them'" she wrote.[10]

No matter how crippled or circumscribed, *any* life can be of value, can find help and meaning in response to God's love. The darkness of her dungeon, her affliction, her uncertainties, and her terrors and rejections, were not the sign of weakness or abnormality, but were common to the experience of living. The outcome of it all would be determined by her response to her circumstances. She was not the helpless victim, a prisoner without a choice. She was a real person with the responsibility for choosing what to make of the life she had been given.

Jane's sojourn in the valley of despair had been long, and her first steps toward acceptance and positive response were timid and uncertain. But she was helped by the discipline of work and outward cheerfulness she had never allowed herself to abandon. The structure of well-ordered days had been the guardrail along the path, keeping her from tumbling into the abyss. Now it led onward.

She had kept regular hours for reading and writing. Now she determined to study more than reading for pleasure. Since poetry was the realm of writing in which she felt at home, she would now make a deliberate effort to write more and better.

It was not an easy resolution, since much of her days must be spent at handwork—knitting and crocheting baby clothes to be sold through a department store in Knoxville. This was Jane's small contribution to the lean family budget. It was also work she enjoyed. She had found it a soothing remedy for a troubled spirit, an aid to quietness and reflection.

45

Often while she was knitting or crocheting, an idea for a poem sprang into her mind. She was tempted to put handwork aside for paper and pencil while the inspiration was fresh, but Jane never liked to leave any task unfinished. Often she pushed herself to a point of exhaustion to finish what she had begun. Perseverance—or was it stubbornness?—was a Merchant trait. Her father was like that, "and you're just like grandmother," her mother had explained.[11]

Jane was grateful for a heritage and childhood training that had given her what she termed "a healthy scorn for haphazard, slovenly ways of doing and thinking."[12]

"I can plan better things," said Sue,
"Much better things than I can do."
And laughing, so as not to cry,
She ripped out seams that went awry
And sewed them neatly back again
As one can do when one is ten,
And wore the apron with a pride
Considerably dissatisfied,
Saying, "I did the best I could,
But it doesn't look the way it should."

I think that since Susanna's one
Who finishes what she's begun,
Who makes her fair and hopeful plan
And does the very best she can,
She'll surely some day find her seams
Entirely equal to her dreams.
                    "Susanna's Apron"

Not yet did Jane dare to think of writing as a vocational goal. The rejection of her early poetry was still a haunting spectre. It was not likely that she could earn a living with her pen. But in her diary she admitted to herself that writing poems was "a thing above all others that makes me feel complete and at peace, even when I know two minutes later that they aren't any good."[13]

Because it was a thing she must do to go on living, she was committed to doing it to the very best of her ability. She would practice the craft of writing as she had once practiced her seams, and perhaps someday her poems, as well, would be more nearly "equal to her dreams"—not for the sake of any possible readers, but because Jane knew "the insidious effect" on her self-respect and her soul of doing anything less than her best.

Other circumstances were looking more hopeful as well. The family was planning another move, this time by choice, to a place of their own. Ruth had married Ed Lee Stone and lived in West Tennessee, but Nelson and Elberta had settled in Fountain City, near Knoxville, where Elizabeth worked as a nurse. The three older children had persuaded their parents to move to a seven-acre property with house, barn, and orchard on Sunset Trail near Nelson's place. Elizabeth had secured a loan to buy the farm and would live at home with her parents and Jane.

They moved in October 1944 to the roomy, two-story house on a hill only five miles from Inskip, where Jane was born. She felt as if she had come home again. The two sisters shared the downstairs bedroom by the kitchen, and Jane's window looked over the sideyard with the driveway shaded by four maple trees; "my cathedral of trees," she called them. The large kitchen had a double set of windows with a view of the birdbath, flower beds, and wide fields beyond the trees. There was a welcoming fireplace in the living room, and Jane's small day bed could be wheeled from room to spacious room without difficulty.

One day not long after their move, Jane wrote in her diary: "I saw a very superior sunrise. The sky was that soft, infinitely tender blue that seems to me the very substance of 'the tender mercies of God, by whom the dayspring from on high has visited us.'"

Her long dark night had given birth to dawn.

> I have seen the dawn begin
> With a thread of lavender
> Hinting, to my leafless sight,
> There is something more than night.
>
> I have seen the dawn begin
> With a sky of scarlet fire
> Declaring, high above each tall
> Leafy tree, that day is all.
>
> Whether that reviving ray
> Shines with great or little power
> On barren tree or grassy lawn
> Matters little—it is dawn.
>
> "Dawn"

4

MY PLACE
ON EARTH
1944–1947

Because of one acre possessed and known
All the earth is mine. . . .

The new place required much work, but it was their own, and they spoke enthusiastically of improvements: a new furnace, new screens and a coat of paint on the porch, a bigger garden come spring. Clarence had found employment in a feed store and would ply his carpenter trade as well. And home wouldn't be home without a cow, pigs, and chickens in the barnyard.

Jane's day began with Bible reading and devotions. Elizabeth brought toast and coffee with the newspaper at 6:30 A.M., before leaving for the city. Daylight slowly colored her garden view while Jane prepared for a busy day. Now that she had determined to renew her writing efforts—without shirking her daily quota of handwork for sale—she tried to do writing exercises every morning.

A recent book on loan from the public library had helped firm her commitment. Never had Jane identified so completely with an author. *The Little Locksmith* was the autobiography of Katharine Butler Hathaway, a frail woman with a hunched back who wrote of her longings and dreams and of finding faith and meaning in her life through the medium of writing. Her tools had been "only a pencil and a block of paper and solitude." Jane had an ample supply of all three.

Katharine's struggle to accept life with a physical predicament akin to Jane's was told in beautifully crafted phrases, the product of hours and hours of toiling over words on paper. The book was a literary gem, a triumphant response to a physical handicap, and it inspired several poems in Jane's notebook. One was "Supplication."

> God, be kind to crooked things:
> To wrenched old trees, misshapen and awry . . .
> Let small birds nestle in their leaves, let rain
> And sunlight, and blue mercies of the sky

Fall, in tender recompense for pain
Upon them softly. Let their gnarled boughs know
The bliss of blossoms sheltered in their shade . . .
And bless all tortured, lonely roads that go
Upon lost journeys, aimless and afraid;
Let shy flowers follow all their grieving maze
Of wandering . . . And bless, oh more than these,
The hunchback child who walks the crooked ways
And draws dark comfort from the crooked trees.
Dear God, be very kind to crooked things.

Like Katharine, Jane resolved to train herself by spending longer and longer periods every day at her writing. By studying the masters, practicing what they taught, she hoped to improve her word-skills, expand her vocabulary.

Her reading and thinking needed some disciplining, too. In the past she had been too easily swayed by what she read; her opinions and judgments were "almost as fluid and unstable as custard," she complained in her journal. Her own timid conclusions were apt to be rejected on the assumption that "almost anyone else was far wiser and better" than she, especially anyone who's words were hallowed by print.

She thought it might help her thinking process to write her comments about what she read. That would force her to clarify and formulate her opinions. And, since she tended to believe almost everything she read, she might even come to believe her own writings! (Notebook, 1940s).

Solitude for practicing was perhaps the hardest to come by. She was still trying to keep her efforts secret, disguised as letter or journal writing. Katharine Butler Hathaway had known the same problem and commented: "There is no greater obstacle to a person who is just beginning to be a writer" than to be living "in the midst of an affectionate, charming family."

Elberta and the three-year-old twins came almost daily to Sunset Trail, and Jane loved to have Joan and Reese snuggle up on either side of her in bed while she read aloud the favorite jingles and stories of her own childhood. Yet, inwardly she struggled with her priorities. She longed to immerse herself in books and writing, but how could she justify such doings when children were in need of loving—and warm knitted sweaters and mittens and baby saques that she needed to make to sell?

I really don't suppose
That God was interrupted
While He designed a rose,
That anybody said,

49

> "You'd best be making grass,"
> Or, "Hurry up and finish!
> You've let a century pass."
> I almost envy God.
>
> "Interruptions"

Serious writing required time for uninterrupted concentration. Perfection could not be attained without personal cost and sacrifice. Over and over Jane read and memorized the poetry of the old masters, scrutinizing their disciplined forms and trying to shape her thoughts to their patterns. She searched the dictionary, page by page, for words to clothe her elusive images, hoping:

> To fit words carefully, like cherished gems
> Into a perfect, patterned loveliness. . . .
>
> "Consecration"

Always the ideal seemed just beyond her reach. For a perfectionist it was often torture. Jane could not abide untidiness, even on paper, and she wrote each sentence again and again, trying to eliminate each blot, even while admitting in her diary that such fastidiousness was "fatal to creation, which usually presupposes chaos as a beginning."[1]

Still, the need to write was compelling.

> It knows no appeasing
> It knows no greed.
> Its seed is hunger,
> Its soil is need.
>
> You will sow and tend
> And at last there will rise
> A harvest that almost
> Satisfies.
>
> "Creativity"

In her diary Jane confessed her frustration: "I tried to write a sonnet. And if there is anything more nerveracking, except possibly having a baby, I don't know what it could be. The anxiety of finding the right words, and the certainty of not doing so. The awful hesitancy in writing down the words that come, knowing that they aren't right, and that written words destroy the unformed thought by its mediocre plausibility. And yet the dread that if it isn't written down it may be lost. All that for the sake of fourteen prosaic lines. Why then do I do it, knowing its unworth? Because one must do what one can, not what one would."[2]

She must do what she could—and keep doing it—until at last, perhaps, she could do what she would. She prayed not to be satisfied with anything "below her ability."

> O Father, this I ask:
> In every test
> Help him to give each task
> His very best.
>
> I ask not that a host
> Of gifts be his,
> But that he make the most
> Of all he is,
>
> And that he never know
> The sad futility
> Of living far below
> His own ability.
>   "Prayer for a Son"

One day in February 1945, Jane's diary records, a "long time lovely dream came true." She had been able to borrow a library volume of Emily Dickinson's poems. No poet had ever struck such sparks of recognition in Jane's soul. After reading, Jane "broke out in a rash of versifying; six in one day."

Not many poems were dated in February of that year, but among them are two sonnets written "almost" to her own satisfaction. One was "No Other Acres."

> No other acres of the earth I know
> Save through one constant window day by day
> And season after season. I have seen the slow
> Bare beauty of fields, like folded hands that pray
> God's blessing on the seed they shall receive
> When all the young insistencies of spring
> Stir men once more to hope and to believe,
> Stir men once more to struggle and to sing,
> And seed is sown and nourished in these lands
> As a dark mother cherishes a child,
> And yielded graciously to men's demands
> With quiet acquiescence. And these mild
> Strong hands of earth have freed my soul of fear
> And made me theirs. My place on earth is here.

Spring that year was the coldest in memory. Four hundred baby chicks ordered in March spent their first weeks beside the kitchen stove. Not until the last days of the month did the weather turn balmy and beautiful, and Jane's window was opened. Her soul "went out under trees." Through glass, spring was only a beautiful picture. Face-to-face, she could breathe in the pungent scents of earth and air and partake in their rebirth.

But even as she rejoiced in the wonders of new leaf and bloom, Jane fought the reawakening of painful longings in her heart. Oh, to be able to walk on new grass under greening trees! To bend and pick a tulip or a daffodil. To hear the jubilant song of birds. It was always like that in spring—joy and anguish mixed, sly whisperings of self-pity from her dark cellar. Her battle was well concealed, but there were hints of it in her diary entry after a day on the porch: "It truly seemed a resurrection to find myself . . . with grass and trees near me again, after the long winters in the narrow, cramped bedroom at New Market, which with its dead white walls and ceiling remains in my mind as a whited sepulchre; though fortunately the comparison didn't suggest itself at the time."[3]

In April, Ruth came to visit with two-month-old Patricia Ann. In a letter to Corrine Martin, Jane described her first meeting with the lively and adorable baby who seldom cried. "If she had, of course I couldn't hear her."

Being deaf made it easier for her to concentrate on reading and writing, but it was a price Jane would rather not pay. When the family relaxed with easy talk and shared laughter, she felt shunted aside in their midst. Lip-reading was guess work at best, usually leaving her bewildered and frustrated, impatient with her own slowness of understanding. The only reliable communication was writing, and that was tedious and time-consuming, even if it was greatly improved by a gift of "Magic Slates" from Carolyn Ruth in California. The slates were actually children's toys, and the writing was done with wooden sticks on a surface covered with transparent film. The message vanished when the film was lifted, and the slate was ready to be used again. Most people enjoyed the new tools for writing, Jane noted in her diary, and seemed to find it easier to "commit their thoughts on slates that could be instantly wiped clean."

But the "no sound" barrier remained impenetrable, causing more pain than privacy. Yet, she tried to count as blessing the ability to concentrate in silence even when the house was full of noise.

Jane had the bedroom to herself now, which gave her more opportunities to write poems without interruption. Elizabeth had responded to a call for nurses to join the armed forces and enlisted in the Navy. She was at Portsmouth Naval Hospital, near Norfolk, where Nelson was stationed. The war had ended in Europe, but wounded soldiers were returning to hospitals in the United States, and fighting continued in the Pacific.

Her sister's courage had spurred Jane to take a bold step of her own. Ruth Anne in Boston had met an editor with David C. Cook Publishing

Company, who published poetry in a number of small magazines and Sunday school papers. Ruth Anne thought this would be a ready market for Jane's work, and she repeated her offer to type and submit the poems. Jane was tempted, but the memory of rejection still hurt. It seemed much too hazardous to send in unsolicited work. Instead, she decided to enter the annual spring poetry contest in *The Progressive Farmer* with one of her February sonnets. Ruth Anne was happy to type and forward it.

The family had, of course, not been told. It would be too dreadful to raise their expectations—and then disappoint them. If she succeeded, it would be a wonderful surprise for all.

With carefully concealed suspense, Jane watched for the issue of *The Progressive Farmer* that announced the winners. She felt better prepared for defeat now. Her ambitions were more moderate. Failure would not stop her writing. If her poetry was not meant for others, it was the language of liberation for her soul. She would always be grateful for that much.

> Not till the Word
> Was said by God
> Did light exist
> Or sky or sod.
>
> Not till the one
> Describing word
> Is said by man
> Does any bird,
>
> Or any leaf
> Or any dim
> Star perfectly
> Exist for him.
> "Until the Word"

On May 28, the magazine came. With pounding heart Jane scanned the list of winners. Her name was not first, second, or even third, but there it was: "Honorable mention; Jane Merchant, Knox County, Tennessee." And five lines of her sonnet "Plowing Song":

> . . . I am not alone
> In any field where the furrows run,
> Ordered and eager to seek the sun
> And carry the blessings of earth and air
> To the need of the nations. My place is there.

The payment was one dollar per line. "The first and probably the last money I'll earn by writing," Jane noted in her diary. "I would have been thrilled once, but now it seems too little, too late."

Actually, she was more elated than she dared admit. Pessimism was one of her deliberate devices to keep her hopes from soaring. But in "Lazarus" she wrote:

> Whoever has descended
> To ultimate despair
> And risen, knows conviction
> No undefeated dare.
> Never again will he accept
> Final finality.
> He understands the uses now,
> Of immortality.

The next poetry contest in *The Progressive Farmer* was held in August, and Jane instructed Ruth Anne to submit "No Other Acres." This time her name was at the top of the list, and the entire sonnet was printed. Again the prize was a dollar per line.

That month Jane wrote "Sunset in December."

> God sifted sunset through a tree
> And so His love came down to me
> In colors I could understand.
> I never saw an April land
> Transfigured so with loveliness
> Beneath spring's tenderest caress,
> As shone on cold December air
> That instant God was standing there.

The bare trunks and branches of trees in winter receive the full benison of sunshine and filter it generously to the frozen ground below. So it seemed to Jane that God's blessings shone brightest in life's barren seasons. Her poetry had been accepted when she was despairing over "the queer unreality of a soundless world."[4] Now she found courage for a bolder move: sending a batch of poems written on scraps of paper to Ruth Anne, with permission to type and submit them to the editor at David C. Cook Publishing Company.

On October 2, Jane's diary records: "2 poems accepted . . . "Lazarus" and "Sunset In December." In her private notebook she penned "Grace."

> "Ask and ye shall receive,"
> So is the promise given.
> But I, past any asking,
> Have received Heaven.

In her Christmas letter to Corrine, Jane could boast that for the first time in her life she had enough money to give her mother "an honest to goodness thrill"—a mail-order dress—under the tree because she had been lucky to sell "a couple of would-be poems to a minor magazine."

Downplaying her accomplishments was a typical defense against high expectations—her friends' and her own. High expectations had a way of leading to terrible disappointments. But in her January diary Jane dared admit that the year just ended had been the best since the family had been forced to leave Strawberry Plains. "Please God, His blessings may continue!"

In the first month of 1946 she sold two poems to *The Progressive Farmer*. So far, no rejections! But she feared the worst and called her "brief songs" a "curt contradiction to despair."

Her depression, as often before, had been triggered by the suffering of the innocent. Once again it seemed that an ominous shadow had been cast over the entire world, this time in the shape of a mushroom cloud over Hiroshima and Nagasaki. The news of atom bombs having been dropped on two Japanese cities to end the war came as a devastating shock to Jane. She was horrified to learn that the bombs had been developed at Oak Ridge, Tennessee, not far, in fact, from where she lived and where their neighbors worked! How *could* a "reputedly Christian and humanitarian" nation commit such atrocities against a civilian population? The implications seemed utterly unthinkable.[5]

What now of her conviction that the war her generation had been forced to fight would put an end to all wars? That illusion had died at Hiroshima. In its place was the terrifying certainty that humanity was capable of destroying all life on earth, and was inclined to do it. The problem, as Jane saw it, was less the bomb itself than the human heart with its disposition toward evil. In "Reactor" she wrote:

> From the split atom
> New energies start
> For good or for evil—
> So with the split heart.
>
> No atom determines
> The way men will use
> Explosions of power—
> The split heart must choose.

The choice was hers as well. She was a part of the nation that had chosen to use the bomb, and she suffered the grief and pain of victim and violator alike. Their anguish was her own, and she mourned for a world trapped in hatred and violence, a world needing love and reconciliation as never before.

The post-war months had exploded another illusion closer to home. Jane had expected black American war veterans to be treated just like their white comrades in arms when they returned home. Had they not fought for peace side by side? Instead, the newspapers carried reports of black veterans protesting unequal opportunities for housing, jobs, and education. Some states even continued to deny them their citizen's right to vote. It was all "utterly depressing" to think about, particularly when she could do nothing to help, Jane lamented in her letters. What good were the convictions of someone bound to a bed? She longed to *do* something, to take a stand publicly—particularly in the matter of prejudice and bigotry. She was convinced that much of it was rooted in ignorance, a learned response, thoughtlessly perpetuated. Perhaps she could put her convictions in writing, help her reader understand what she knew to be true.

Her heart knew the pain of being treated as "different," of being set apart, looked at with repulsion, shunned as "inferior," "less than human." She, too, belonged to a minority and could identify with all of them, with their suffering, their anger, and their humanity. In "Darkness" she wrote:

> The sun rose in the sky again this morning.
> Sometimes I wonder why it wants to rise
> And look at all the wrongs it has to see.
> Perhaps it doesn't want to, and can't help it,
> The way white people don't want—I suppose—
> To be unkind, and yet can't seem to help it.
>   No, nothing happened, more than usual.
> I hunted for a decent place to live
> And found a shanty—fit for us, they said.
> White people went by in a shiny car.
> I heard one say, "They're almost animals
> To live like this. Oh, well, I guess they like it."
> I wonder if he really thinks we like it.
>   We'll move next week. We'll move into the shanty
> And leave the willow tree where mockingbirds
> Sing songs for us as if our skin were white.
> The schools are better there, or so they say.
> They can't be worse, at least, and Jimmy's smart.
> Don't know if being smart will help him any,
> But if there's any chance, he's got to have it.
>   Sometimes I think there isn't any chance.
>   Sometimes I press the darkness to my eyes
>   And wonder why the sun would want to rise.

Jane was not pointing an accusing finger at others. She, too, was to blame. In "The Shadow" she wrote of meeting a black woman. The poem ends with the lines:

> There falls between her gentle face and me
> The shadow of an immemorial wrong,
> And at her smile I feel my spirit wilt
> Beneath a withering, suffocating guilt.

The suffering of the innocent could always prompt a resurgence of doubt and helpless anger. Inevitably there followed the familiar suggestions of self-pity and hopelessness, dimming her days and making her feel utterly useless and worthless. Elizabeth, who had a way of dispelling gloom with cheerful energy, was still in Norfolk and would not be discharged until June. The three at Sunset Trail missed her sorely. And Jane was ever conscious that her parents were working too hard, while she was an added burden instead of a help. Outside her window, birds were gleaning in winter-bare fields, and the sight brought balm for her inner wounds.

> Across brown fields
> The sparrows go
> Flying quickly,
> Flying low.
>
> Within brown fields
> The sparrows find
> Refreshment suited
> To each mind.
>
> They cluster happily
> On thistles
> And offer thanks
> With chirps and whistles.
>
> How fortunate
> For their own needs
> That sparrows feel
> No scorn for weeds.
> "Resources"

The dauntless birds paid no heed to cold winds and darkening skies. They went about their duty and were satisfied. And Jane resolved to follow their example. Raging over the injustices and agonies of the world did not heal them. Sulking in self-pity could only end in total misery. She no longer indulged in doubting the existence of God. Could she not trust that he was in charge of his creation and would bring to a good end the difficult things beyond her control?

The sparrows were thriving on thistles. Could she not glean what was given her and be grateful? She could close her cellar door on gloom and give full attention to the tasks she *could* control—at least within limits—handwork, study, and writing poems. Perhaps she could lighten her parents' burden by her cheer. They never let on when they were worn out, and she carefully concealed her depression from them. No use in complaining about what couldn't be helped, they had always held. It was better to share laughter and easy bantering. Her father was a master at it, and Jane had "caught" his gift for comedy, with the turn of a phrase or a pun bringing instant relief from tension or discouragement.

The wise and witty sayings of the mountain people were a part of their heritage and a wonderful tonic for a droopy disposition. Most anything or any circumstance could be seen from a different and lighter side, with a chuckle instead of a frown. Jane's sense of humor flavored her writing as well—and no doubt helped sell poems. Several had been accepted by editors lately, including one she wrote "solely to sell."

But now came a hitch to her career. Ruth Anne no longer had a typewriter at her disposal. She had been typist and buffer against editorial denouncements; now she encouraged Jane to continue on her own. It meant "coming out" with her submissions as well as with her small victories. And worse—the family would know of her rejections. Until now they had been mercifully concealed in Ruth Anne's letters.

The alternative—to give up what she had just begun—was in the end unthinkable. Poetry sales had proven a real boost to the family income, and that was worth risking defeat and pitying glances for. Besides, when the family knew what she was about, they could better understand and respect her need for uninterrupted time to write and would regard it as work, as useful as making baby clothes for sale.

In June sister Ruth brought her typewriter home for Jane to use. Before summer's end she had mastered the art of typing—by the touch system.

The poetry markets she had tried so far paid relatively little. Now she decided to aim for the top. Rejection from a high-paying magazine could not hurt more than rejection from a lesser one. The competition was tougher at the top; she might not feel quite so much a failure if her poems were returned.

For years she had cast a wistful eye at the poetry columns in *The Saturday Evening Post*. The *Post* was known to be a difficult market to crack, but they paid top dollar. *Good Housekeeping* was in the same league. With nothing to lose, Jane decided to try them both at once. As if to steel herself against the response, she sent "Prescription for Pride" in her batch to *Good Housekeeping*.

> Carry defeat
> With a conquering air

Lest passers pity
Lest strangers stare.

Shelter sorrow
In shimmering pride
Lest friends deplore
Lest foes deride.

But weep, weep well
When you're all alone
Lest your heart congeal
To a small stone.

To the *Post,* she sent "Advice to Advisers"

Never tell a soul in sorrow
There are others hurt as he
Never tell him sure tomorrow
Shall supply his remedy.

Say his grief's unprecedented,
Past time's healing to allay.
Let him agonize, contented,
While time steals the sting away.

and "Look Before You Leap, or He Who Hesitates Is Lost."

The world is full of good advice
To spur us on to victory
In sayings pithy and concise
And flatly contradictory.

The mailman seemed exceptionally slow the next two weeks. Jane was cheerfully confident when anyone was looking, but inwardly she seesawed between high hopes and despair over her own presumptions. In early August Donia brought the self-addressed envelope returned from *Good Housekeeping* and waited tactfully while Jane examined its contents. Her poems were back—except one! They were holding it for further consideration!

It was not much to base a hope on, but Donia's eyes shone with pride, and Jane had trouble hiding her own excitement. Her work had at least caught the attention of an editor whose desk must be overflowing with submissions from aspiring and established poets. That was no small accomplishment!

A few days later came the letter from the poetry editor. "Prescription for Pride" was accepted for fifteen dollars!

Slowly the realization dawned that this was the goal she had "aimed at for ten years and lost all hope of reaching," she confided in her diary. "Oh, but God had not let her die!" Her heart was brimming with light and joy.

Now, for the first time, she dared tell Carolyn Ruth of her poetry sales, and she sent her the printed ones. Her friend's response was gratifying: "How can I tell you the joy your poetry gives me? . . . I am proud for their deserving author!"[6]

Good fortune continued. In September came the anxiously awaited letter from *The Saturday Evening Post*. The poetry editor, Peggy Dowst wrote: "Dear Miss Merchant: We would like to have both "Advice to Advisers" and "Look Before You Leap, or He Who Hesitates Is Lost," for the *Post*, I am happy to report."[7] The payment for each poem was fifteen dollars.

Exultantly Jane noted in her diary: "I've just renewed my poetic license."

In November, her birth month, two issues of the *Post* carried her work, and Miss Dowst bought another poem, to be printed in their New Year issue.

> Be prouder prayers ignored
> Be lesser pleas unsaid,
> If in this New Year, Lord,
> No child need weep for bread.
> "Prayer"

During the Christmas month, Jane made more sales, and the first week in January she sent off twenty-four poems in batches to eight editors. The beginning of a year always seemed "fresh and hopeful" to her. Beginnings held promises. "In the beginning God created—in the beginning was the Word. And in the small beginnings of ours we may perhaps create a little goodness," she wrote in her diary on February 1, 1947.

The first two rejection slips of the year came before the end of the month, and they immediately evoked specters of failure. How dreadful it was to disappoint everyone now that she had "officially" declared her intentions! The fear of failure could instantly open a trap door to her dungeon of depression. More rejections followed, and the coming of spring only made matters seem worse.

Through the open window a warm wind blew on her "stale desiccated indoor mind," she lamented in her diary, making her feel "unutterably estranged" behind "warm relentless walls." She felt far removed from the fortunate ones who "breathe fresh air beneath the open sky and never know that it's a miracle" *(Diary, March 11, 1947)*.

It would always seem incredible that those who were free to walk among the miracles of new leaf and bloom could regard it as "casual and commonplace." For her, there would always be the wonder of it and the longing. She poured these feelings into poetry in "Letter Home."

> I never ask you if the sky
> Still marches like a brigadier
> With tattered battle flags afly
> Above our home since I am here.

> I never ask you if the sun
> Commits celestial arson still
> When all its honest work is done
> Upon the sky behind our hill.

> And if the stars perform their task
> Of constancy, if constant blow
> The homeward winds—I never ask
> Because I could not bear to know.

She sent the poem to Miss Dowst at the *Post,* who bought it and asked for more! They were in need of four-line poems and would like to see anything Jane had on hand. The request made her feel "almost professional" and came just in time. Jane had almost decided to quit trying. The devastating impact of rejection slips could still nearly paralyze her ambitions, but now she sent four of her latest efforts to Peggy Dowst and steeled herself against their return.

Spring had come in earnest, and Donia took her time going to and from the mailbox.

> When it was cold it didn't take
> Grandmother more than half a minute
> To walk down to the big mailbox
> And back with all that might be in it.

> But when the first warm days of spring
> Began it took her half the day—
> She stopped to speak to every leaf
> And blade of grass along the way.
>> "Grandmother's Postal Rate"

Miss Dowst responded in less than two weeks. She bought two of the four rhymes—for twenty dollars apiece—a generous increase in payment. Jane's Easter letter to Carolyn Ruth was exhuberant: "I have had some amazingly, almost shockingly good fortune . . . which I know will please you, however justly indignant you may be over the fantastic prices the *Post* has seen fit to pay for the four line nonsense enclosed. . . . I reflect rather grimly on the necessity which pays twenty dollars for fourteen words, while a baby sacque, which is certainly more useful, and takes ten times as long to make, is worth four dollars. . . . "

Such a distortion of values and blindness to the true nature of things both astonished and saddened her. "Never has it been clearer than in this Atomic Age, that the things which are seen are temporal, and the things which are unseen are eternal. And never has the world needed the Easter message more."[8]

Easter tulips bloomed outside her window.

> This chalice, richly glowing
> Through April's misted veil
> To some appears a tulip;
> To some, a holy grail.
> "Aspects"

5
INTRINSIC
1947–1949

Stripped to the final, clear
Integrity, winter trees
Stand leaflessly austere,
Glad for release
Of the essential bough
From summer's long excess.
They are the richer now,
For having less.

There was a side effect to success Jane had not anticipated. She was suddenly something of a celebrity around Fountain City. It was difficult enough selling "portions of oneself" to magazines, but it was worse that "perfect strangers" should suddenly take an interest in her personal and private life.[1]

Bert Vincent, popular columnist for the *Knoxville News-Sentinel*, called to ask for an interview, and Jane was simply too taken aback to say no. It seemed too incredible that he should be interested in her! But she had read his column for ages and was curious to see what he was like. Too late did it occur to her that *he* would also see *her!* Meeting strangers was always difficult and especially embarrassing—with a gaping hole in her mouth where a front tooth had been missing for eight years. Mr. Vincent was an added risk; he would write about their meeting, and she had hoped to keep her physical handicap from her readers.

She was terribly nervous when he arrived. He was a nice man, wearing a yellow tie, writing his questions, and seeming pleased enough with the answers and the two rhymes she typed for him. Always she felt horribly tongue-tied with strangers, and for once she was glad they weren't *talking!* But the exertion and her own self-consciousness wore her out. She was limp when he left and wished he would decide to drop the story.

He didn't, but wrote glowingly of their visit, praising Jane's wit, her talent, her courage, and her success. She cringed in reading his exaggerated account of her sales. It confirmed what she had always suspected: newspaper stories tended to be careless of facts.

The column occasioned her first fan letter from a reader, a young librarian at the University of Tennessee who wanted to meet her. She likened Jane's poetry to Emily Dickinson's —a flattering comparison, even if Jane knew better.

A friendship with someone nearby who shared her love of poetry was tempting, but face-to-face encounters were just too risky. Besides, who would want to take the time to become really acquainted on magic slates? Friendship by letter was both easier and safer. Jane wrote back, offering friendship through correspondence, but didn't encourage a meeting.

The physical restrictions on her life were painful, but more and more Jane was coming to understand the truth of winter trees:

> They are the richer now,
> For having less.

She had discovered the same apparent paradox in art. On her bedside table was a large illustrated *History of World Art,* a gift from Carolyn Ruth. There, in reproductions of Chinese paintings, was pure simplicity and integrity. "A quiet satisfaction and a feeling of tranquility and peace such as I've found nowhere else save in bare trees against a winter sky, and empty, barren fields receiving rain," she noted in her diary. "Chinese painting, I think, has the same feeling of reduction to essentials, of unadorned verities, that these things give me. . . . It is the purest essence of reality, undreamed of by the 'realists' who, as Robert Frost put it, offer vast quantities of dirt with every potato to prove that it is a real potato. Of course, Frost was talking about poetry, not painting, but since Chinese poetry and painting are so nearly related, the comparison isn't too far fetched."[2]

For Christmas, Carolyn Ruth sent a portfolio of original Chinese paintings, and Jane rejoiced "to own the actual sheets over which the artist dreamed, to see with my own eyes the brush strokes which the artist's hand placed there, and the unbelievable soft tints of flower and birdwing. The amazing communion between artist and observer . . . even when far removed in time, place, religion and culture. . . . I feel so complete a comprehension of the artist's feelings" she wrote in her thank you letter.[3]

The maple trees stood bare against the January sky outside her window, and Jane noted in her diary: "Each season in its own way is the loveliest of all, but in winter there isn't the almost painfully keen enjoyment, but the quiet, contemplative peaceful joy of a chinese painting."

> The trees in summer speak fluent prose
> Their central theme of greenness flows

64

In leisurely reiterations
With rich details and illustrations.

In winter they turn to poetry
And with exact economy
Are clearly unelaborate,
Suggesting far more than they state.
                              "Versatile"

Like the Chinese artist she identified with so completely, Jane sought the "unadorned verities," the "purest essence of reality," in poetry as well as in living. Poetry, by suggesting rather than attempting to explain, could create a communion between poet and reader—and between the words and the reality behind them—closer to the truth than any prose. Poetry linked heart to heart; prose was the medium of the mind. Only poetry could come close to communicating the hidden essence, the mystery of living eluding the understanding.

So many things could not be said, could not be explained or shared with others. So many questions must remain unanswered. That was the reason Jane found publicity so frightening and offensive. Those who probed without mercy for the secrets of others were blind to the sanctity and mystery of all human beings. They boasted of exposing the "real" person, and missed the truth that could only be glimpsed through revelation: heart offering itself to heart.

Jane had dared to reveal something of herself in poetry, but she had fully intended to keep the details of her private life hidden. Instead the widening circles of publicity spread like rings in the water from a single stone throw. Bert Vincent had made much of her handicap, and his column traveled far. *The Saturday Evening Post* printed some of the particulars about Jane on their "Inside Information" page, and the result was a flood of mail from readers, many suggesting home remedies for deafness and brittle bones!

The facts Jane had considered least noteworthy about herself now belonged to the public, who would make of it what they chose, not what she wished! It was small consolation that her poetry had sold on its merit, not because an editor had taken pity, but even *that* she could not be certain of in the future.

Those who noted her handicap seemed to think that her literary accomplishments had required more courage and effort than had she had been physically fit, Jane lamented to Carolyn Ruth. It was an embarassing implication for two reasons: Jane suspected that she was a coward at heart, and she firmly believed that no human being was without some kind of handicap—mental, emotional, or physical. The less visible handicaps could be more disabling, requiring more courage to cope with, than the obvious physical ones.[4]

> People are kind—or try to be—
> To those with hurts that they can see,
> Are always glad and proud to find
> New ways to help the maimed and blind,
> And, seeing the effort of their days,
> Are quick with sympathy and praise.
>
> But one with body sound and whole,
> However deeply maimed in soul,
> Finds there is seldom one who makes
> Excuse for failures and mistakes,
> And, struggling valiantly, may hear
> Folk say of him, "He's just plain queer!"
>
> "Limitations"

Jane had a special reason for questioning her courage just then. Sharing her room—in her old hospital bed, playing with her old doll and attended by the bone specialist who had once examined her—was five-year-old Joan, who had a broken leg. Once again Donia had the all too familiar task of caring for a bone-mending child.

But there the similarities stopped. The wiggly impatient Joan, straining to get out of bed, bore little resemblance to Jane as she remembered herself, placidly bearing her confinement.

Had her "unquestioning acceptance" as a child been a "merciful provision of nature," keeping her from wanting what she couldn't have? Or was it some "stealthy cowardice within," a shrinking from making any effort to gain physical independence?

It seemed in retrospect that she had chosen the contemptible role of passively adapting to her circumstances rather than trying to adapt her circumstances to her needs, she confided to Carolyn Ruth. It was especially painful to acknowledge her cowardice now when people often bragged about her courage, to her face and in print. She wished they would stop doing it. "But I don't wish it enough, of course, to make this admission to them!"[5]

> I have loved courage; I have loved the word,
> Its look on any printed page, its shape
> On any lips, its meaning, clear, unblurred,
> In weathered faces, seeking no escape
>
> In bitterness from bitter circumstances,
> And I have loved it in the candid mind

That, scorning easy falsities, advances
Toward truth, however, seemingly unkind.

I have loved well each winter-blooming flower
And each gaunt, stubborn, twisted tree, that brought
New courage to me in a desperate hour;
For, loving courage, I have always sought

For it in everything that I have known,
Because I have scant courage of my own

"Of Courage"

Courage sought "no escape in bitterness from bitter circumstances," she had written. Bitterness was the fruit of self-pity, grown in the seedbed of hopeless resignation. It was the very opposite of responding creatively through accepting circumstances she could not change. It was capitulating without a battle, being a whining victim instead of a *real* person. There was a problem in discerning the difference; resignation and acceptance looked much the same on the surface. Jane had no desire to deceive others—and even less herself. How to know the truth? The real from the counterfeit? Were feelings of cowardice proof that she lacked courage? Later she would write in "On a Biography":

I thought to read of one
Less faint of heart than I,
Whose steadfast courage might
Replenish my supply.

I learned instead that he
Whom I revered as strong
And wise above all men
Often despaired, was wrong,

Irresolute—and yet,
Wrought worthily for man.
I am courageous now,
For if he could, I can.

There was nothing passive or resigned about the feelings she admitted openly to Carolyn Ruth after a particularly frustrating incident concerning a misplaced crochet hook. The realization of her own helplessness and complete dependency on others for everything she needed erupted in a "wild desire" to "scream or weep or break something!"[6]

She didn't do it, of course. It wouldn't have changed things, and others would have been hurt. But she acknowledged her feelings of anger and didn't bury them. Her circumstances could not be changed, but her response to them could—and there was poetry to be gleaned from it. "Dispensable" sold to the *Post*.

> Whoever has resigned
> Himself to fate, will find
> Fate without hesitation,
> Accepts his resignation.

Miss Dowst next bought "Even a Hen," a parable of the dubious rewards of rebellion. For Jane the sale represented "A triumph over Postal preferences for the short and sharp," she reported gleefully to Carolyn Ruth.[7] The poem was a sonnet—Jane's favorite poetic form.

> With eagle intrepidity, she eyes
> The pole that slants from gatepost to the ground,
> Stretches a wing in arrogant surmise,
> And then, defiantly, as if she frowned
> At danger, ventures up the pole, with most
> Precarious balancings with claw and feather
> Till she attains the summit of the post,
> A vaster altitude, a loftier weather.
> She pauses there an instant, plump with pride,
> Then flaps to outer earth where no grass grows.
> Shelter and corn are on the other side,
> But she, demurely clucking, only knows,
> With chicken-headed pertinacity,
> Fences are for escaping and she is free.

Here was a serious lesson taught with a disarming chuckle. Humor took the sting out of a difficult truth. It punctured pomposity and exposed self-pity without being rude, and it carefully concealed private pain and inward darkness.

In "Apology" Jane wrote:

> Almost it seems discourteous, dear Lord,
> This turning of my darker side to thee
> And showing thee perplexities and griefs
> That I permit no human eye to see;
> And offering my brighter side to others
> Who seem so much in need of any cheer
> That I can give, I hesitate to add
> To all their burdens by a single tear.
> But I am sure it is not rudeness, Lord,
> I long indeed to offer thee my best;

> But only thou canst light my spirit's darkness
> That there may be a bright side for the rest.
> In giving my best to those with whom I dwell
> I think I give it, Lord, to thee as well.

No deceit was intended in hiding her darker side from people. After all, light and dark, joy and pain were so closely interwoven in daily living that she rarely experienced one without the other. It was like the summer storm outside her window—her favorite kind of weather—with its drama of simultaneous sun and rain, shining and shade, more varied and delightful than anything seen on "placid, perfect days," she noted in her diary.

Clouds were piling upon clouds, chased by the wind, ever shifting the pattern of light and shadow on the ground. It was difficult to understand how clouds had come to represent gloom, when they provided such delight for the eye and the essential blessings of rain. Towering clouds resembled castles in the sky, fit "dwelling places for the spirit." Their glory filled her heart with awe, banishing her fears.[8]

Could she not trust the Creator of such orchestrated beauty to order her days with equal skill? Why then, did she sometimes feel so much like the small brown thrush, huddled on the edge of the hammock near her window, as if afraid to fly—or even sing?

Two white butterflies hovered over the white roses, like a poem in flight, and Jane felt an almost physical pain at her own inability to articulate such loveliness. Lately she had come to fear the silencing of her own songs, the loss of her ability to write poems. The cause of her dread was a change in her relationship to words. They had always been her intimate friends. Now there was a difference. She had first noticed it while reading, during the spring and summer of 1947.

Carolyn Ruth had discovered the books of John Muir and sent her favorite, *My First Summer in the Sierras;* to Jane. No book, not even Emily Dickinson's or *The Little Locksmith,* had given Jane such a sense of "pure affection for the writer." She found "Muir's self shining through his love of mountains, stars and trees, and loved not only them, but him," she confessed to Carolyn Ruth.[9]

In "John Muir's Water Ouzel" she wrote:

> The psalmist of the waterfalls,
> It nests beside the mountain streams
> And in my musings often calls
> And often flashes through my dreams. . . .
>
> I have not seen, I have not heard,
> The bird, nor shall I hear or see,
> But Muir with many a reverent word
> Has loved it into life for me.

It sings, inviolate, apart,
Though he who loved it best is gone.
In many an awed and thankful heart
His love for it lives on and on.

A treasure of books had come her way all at once: Mark Van Doren's *The Country Year,* Walt Whitman's *Leaves of Grass,* and volumes of Keats, Swinburne, James Whitcomb Riley, and Robert Frost. As long as she could remember, Jane had rejoiced in reading beautiful or striking word combinations, noting how their shape on page and tongue—their sound in her inner ear—were a part of their message.

Now, to her horror, she found that "even the most magical and illuminating words had lost some of their meaning," leaving her "comparatively unstirred." Five years had passed since she had lost her hearing. The cocoon of silence had wrapped even her memory of sound in its shroud.

Only Carolyn Ruth was told of her painful discovery: "I am tired, and something within me which once responded to all loveliness of words seems mute and unalive, deadened by silence. I suppose it was inevitable . . . but this is my first admission that it is true. . . . So many things won't bear admitting, even for the relief of sharing with a friend the depression one is feeling; so many things in my life cannot be shared at all. . . . But I feel better for writing this" *(Reynolds, Oct. 1947).*

Now only phonetic symbols or a rhyming dictionary could verify the pronunciation of a word or syllable. What effect would that have on her ability to compose poems? Bert Vincent had asked about her goal in life and he quoted the answer in his column. She would like "to be able to write good poetry," but she wanted "most of all to be useful."[10]

In her heart the two ambitions were one. She had hoped to be useful in writing poetry, but now her labored productions seemed largely unsatisfactory. Her poetic license, she feared, had expired, she confessed to Carolyn Ruth.

What if she could no longer write? If her songs were stillborn, how could she be useful then?

Two brown-flecked eggs blown from a hidden nest;
Two mockingbirds whose songs will not attest
That it is good to live, with ardent zest.

In the bright prodigality of spring
It will not matter that some never sing.
That myriad seeds come to no flowering.

And yet with song and blossom everywhere
I breathe upon the shining April air
One wistfully believing April prayer,

That, since the Father marks the sparrow's fall,
No stillborn song, or flower, or thought at all
Be ever wholly lost, beyond recall.

"April Prayer"

Comparing herself to other poets, she inevitably fell short. The wind had blown a hollyhock against her window—"a large pink blossom" looking at her through the screen, with "a fat gold and black bumble bee lying upside down on the central stem, like a picture of sloth hanging from a tree limb." It ought to make a poem, she noted in her diary, but Emily Dickinson had already said it. And Mark Van Doren had described a summer shower followed by sunshine much better than she could.[11]

Measuring herself against others was bound to strangle all ambition and result in self-deprecation. She could wallow in self-pity, letting mournful gloom pile up like blue-gray thunderclouds, pregnant with rain. But rain was useful—a blessing to leaf and bloom. Could her sadness be of some use as well, even without song?

What shall I do, O Father, with this sadness?
Is there a use that I can put it to?
Has it a necessary work to do?

O God, the heavy weight of hopeless yearning,
The drooping heart, the spent and strengthless nerve—
Teach me, O teach me, Lord, how these can serve.

If they serve but to make my heart more tender,
More quick in sympathy with those who weep,
Or have no tears, grief being still and deep;

If they serve but to make my spirit stronger
For bearing the dark burden, as I must,
With patience and humility and trust—

Then it is well. But let this sadness not
Be wasted in self-pity. Let it be
Somehow, O Lord, of service unto thee.

"In Sadness"

Carolyn Ruth had repeatedly asked to see some of Jane's unpublished work. Jane's notebook held nearly two hundred poems, dating back as far as 1937, but she thought they revealed too much sadness and private struggles. Carolyn Ruth was bound to be disappointed, to find them "prosaic, commonplace and trivial," Jane wrote apologetically. Most had been "scribbled" for her own relief, long before any of her "small interior satisfactions had been paraded forth with price tags on them" *(Reynolds, July 12, 1947).*

With some trepidation, Jane had agreed to type and send them. Carolyn Ruth's response to her earlier confessions had been acceptance. This would be a further revealing, made on one condition: Carolyn Ruth must promise not to show the unpublished poems to anyone else. They must remain private.

Writing was depressingly difficult while Jane battled inward despair and a sense of futility, but it was a discipline she did not intend to give up. Sales were slow, and the rejection slips seemed to confirm her gloomiest forebodings of failure.

Outside her November window, the maples made a cathedral of shining gold, "reason enough to remain alive from one autumn to the next," she noted in her diary. Her father had taken the screen from her window and had made a flowerbox—her very own. She could crumble the soil between her fingers and scatter grass seed with her own hand. It was balm for her weary spirit and made poetry.

> A human being needs some pride in knowing
> Some things that he himself can verify,
> If it's no more than the proper time for hoeing
> And planting beans, or how to still the cry
>
> Of newborn things; he needs decisive acts
> That keep his knowledge clear-cut and unblurred,
> To hold him steady in the midst of facts
> For which he has to take another's word.
>
> Although it's fine to know the sun consists
> Of hot atomic gases, anyone
> Who crumbles sun-warm earth in his own fists
> To make it right for seedlings, works with sun,
>
> And, doing what he knows and understands,
> Is proud of having knowledge in his hands.
> "Working Knowledge"

Carolyn Ruth's interest in the early unpublished poems encouraged Jane to send some of them, along with newer work, to editors. The *Post* promptly bought "Easter Absolution," written during the tragic spring of 1942. What a difference "a small sense of accomplishment would have made back then," Jane noted to her friend.[12]

The earth has long done penance
In ashen garb of woe
For the great sin the sons of men
Committed long ago.

But now the winter's sorrow wins
Peace for the ancient pain,
And spring's forgiving grass returns,
And spring's absolving rain.

Even now, six years later, the sale made a difference, breaking the depressing monotony of recent rejections slips from Miss Dowst. In her diary, Jane confided: "Oh, it's true, commit thy way unto the Lord, and He shall bring it to pass. And I am humbly, gladly, thankful" *(Diary, Jan. 22, 1948)*.

For Christmas she had received a paperback volume of Emily Dickinson's poems. "Nothing strikes fire from me as she does, and makes me understand the worth of words . . . to read her is like hearing once again. She makes me write, weak echoes of herself."[13]

The long siege of depression was showing signs of lifting. In her diary, Jane took herself to task for her self-deprecation: "To believe what happens to oneself is important, that one's thoughts and feelings and one's own acts, relationships and daily words are as significant as anything thought and felt and said by all past philosophers, all present poets; That is the normal, healthy way of living. . . . It is good and satisfying and enriching to read books, but to refuse to write a poem because John Keats could do it better, to look at a painting by Turner instead of at a sunset, is to impoverish oneself. It is servile, and contemptuous of one's inherent dignity."

Could that be the true significance of the widow's mite? Jane wondered. The rich Pharisee brought a larger sum to the Temple treasury, but the poor widow believed that her tiny contribution was worth giving. With it she declared the unique value of the individual soul.

"Oh, to do what one can, no matter how much has already been done. No matter how much more, or better, others can do it. That is the thing that can make glorious the most seemingly insignificant life."

Christ pointed to the sparrow and said, "You are of more value than many sparrows" (Matt. 10:31 RSV). "Yet," Jane concluded, "how slow of heart we are to believe in the infinite worth of ourselves. In the inestimable value of our own individual souls. And yet, did a snowflake ever refuse to fall because millions of snowflakes have fallen before?" *(Diary, Jan. 21, 1948)*.

Jane knew the truth of what she had written; yet, how difficult it was to live it when her poetry returned with impersonal rejection slips. How easy it was to be convinced of their worthlessness. How futile it seemed to polish and retype them, offering them again—and again—and again, believing in their worth. . . .

She was reading *The Great Divorce* by C.S. Lewis, and copied into her notebook his warning that "every road after a few miles fork into two, and each of these into two again, and at each you must make your decision." Here was a reminder of her responsibility for choosing—and how vitally important even the little choices were. She couldn't chose her circumstances or how an editor would receive her work. But she chose her response to it: acceptance or rebellion, gratitude or grumbling. Lewis wrote of the danger of indulging in grumbling, gradually *becoming* that hellish grumble and nothing more.

Jane had been far enough down the slope of self-pity to know its treachery. Once the slide had begun she was helpless to stop. Only in confessing her rebellion and casting herself on the mercy of God was there hope. In "Some Better Thing" she wrote:

> Lord, I would be obedient to thy will,
> Not longing for what is not given me,
> Assured some better thing awaits—and still,
> The tears flow, Father, till I cannot see.
> Forgive me, Lord, forgive me that I yearn
> For anything thy pure love can deny.
> Armor my heart against the swift return
> Of the insinuating, stealthy "Why?"
>
> Grant me to triumph, Father, over days
> And weeks when all my world seems wholly wrong.
> Grant me abiding patience and deep praise,
> Grant me to turn my longing into song;
> So shall I be more strengthened and consoled
> Than by the blessing, Lord, thou dost withhold.

She must choose to believe in the answer to her prayer for obedience, patience, and praise. She must believe that she could turn her longing into song. Even when deafness had silenced the memory of sound, making new words more difficult to master, she must choose to write. She must choose not to believe the dark suggestions from her cellar that her best efforts were not nearly good enough.

No matter how hard she tried, satisfaction would always be elusive.

> It always seemed to her, her whole life through,
> There was a song that only she could sing
> Waiting a little way beyond the blue
> Clear air of evening gentled by the wing

Of one white bird, a little way beyond
The haze that lay forever on her hills;
A song to which men's spirits must respond,
Forgetting, for a little, all their ills.

The song was always there, but when she tried
To voice its words and melody, it fell
Dull on her ears, and all the wonder died.
If it was bane or bliss, she could not tell,
To hear not far away, her whole life long,
Faint whispers of an uncreated song.

"The Song Beyond"

As long as an uncreated song called to her spirit, she would try to obey, seeking to enflesh it in words. Her own survival depended on it, and there were indications that others found some meaning and solace in her work as well. Life—even for her physically fit friends and readers—held personal struggles and suffering. They responded to her writing with gratitude.

Carolyn Ruth had received several batches of unpublished poems and wrote: "Your poems have given me a new feeling about all poetry; where have I been that I did not realize what a heady, potent comment on living poetry is?"[14]

Rejection slips would always come, and they served as "lacerations" to her vanity. Jane prayed for strength to "fail successfully, without complaints, excuses, or resentments." It was, after all, true that what looked like failure to people could be success in the eyes of God. He knew the limitations of his children—and what courage it took in some circumstances to make any effort at all. Only if she stopped trying would she be a failure. "Trying was a form of victory."[15] In "After Failure," she wrote:

The careful, unremitting work
I did has not availed.
I gave my best to one large task,
And now I know I failed.

Today I'll do the little things,
The things I can do best.
I'll do the little, easy things
And give my heart a rest.

A dozen little things, well done,
Will lighten failure's sorrow
And give me strength to try, once more,
The larger task, tomorrow.

Doubts of her own ability would stay with her, as well, but Jane had made a conscious commitment now to her vocation as a writer. To shirk for fear of failure was inexcusable. Even a tiny talent—a poor widow's mite—must be used. And it would increase with use, as in the parable in which Jesus told of the servants who put their talents to use and were trusted with an increase in responsibility. But the man with the one talent buried it in the ground for safekeeping and lost even that when their master returned. In "The One-Talent Man," Jane wrote:

> A trusting eager child, he was derided,
> Made shrinkingly aware of lack of worth
> When one he loved rejected work he prided
> Himself on, and he hid it in the earth.
>
> So later, entrusted with one precious thing,
> He hid it lest he lose it, for he feared.
> He bears his punishment; and time will bring
> And equal recompense to one who jeered.

Writing was "the one precious thing" she had been entrusted with. And she, who had never been jeered at but lovingly encouraged by family and friends, had an obligation to use it. For Christmas 1948, she received a book of synonyms and a rhyming dictionary—tools of her craft. Her diary records that in January she spent much time using them in practicing patterns of poetry. She even bought a scrapbook for her printed poems, and she pasted in her "scraps" while wondering if she would ever be able to fill it.

In April 1949, she confided to Carolyn Ruth that an editor had written to *ask* for Christmas poems! "It flattered me beyond imagining, actually having an editor ask. . . . This is a terrifically unpoetic way of going about writing rhyme; I used to share the general impression that poems were written solely from uncontrollable inspiration and not from practical pre-meditation. . . . In the case of magazine verse I can wholeheartedly testify that inspiration never happens unless one has first been thinking and feeling and waiting for it. Of course, it is the rare, unexpected, unpremeditated verse that sometimes appear fully panoplied within one's mind that makes the plodding drudgery of the other sort worthwhile. But they never happen—I've discovered—unless the plodding drudgery is a daily exercise. So I've spent three days considering Christmas and writing stuff I knew was junk, until today, quite suddenly and unexpectedly and easily, I wrote one that I almost like a little. I'll hate it by tomorrow, I suppose, but meanwhile I'm making the most of that all too fleeting sense of satisfaction."

Poetry sales had earned her enough to buy a mule for the farm. Her father had long wanted one, and it was like old times "having a mule in the family again.'' Jane suggested they name it Pegasus, since her "ornery, flop-eared mule Pegasus'' had made the new acquisition possible. But the name was already Kate, and it flapped long ears outside Jane's window with the "stubbornly unreconstructed and indomitable air of independence, the most appealing quality of mules.''

Kate and the memory of their neighbor's mulebarn at New Market, built from the lumber of an old country church, inspired a sonnet.

> The new mule barn was once a country church
> The congregation, prospering, sold for lumber
> And built a fine one. Now the red mules lurch
> And sway from side to side in rhythmic slumber
> In stalls constructed of converted pews
> With all the drowsy rectitude of deacons
> Who half awaken, now and then, to muse
> On places where the pastor's sermon weakens.
> A portly pigeon occupies the rafter
> Exhorting with admonitory mien
> And mules emerge immediately after
> He ends with faces unctuously serene
> To testify that they have seen the light—
> Though still inclined at times to kick and bite.
>
> "Mule Barn"

Jane was writing steadily now, her average output increasing each month, though she lamented her "inability to write a worthwhile poem.'' She had spent considerable time in reading and thinking through her basic beliefs. C. S. Lewis' *The Case for Christianity* had done much to help "sort out, re-arrange and scrutinize'' her ideas, she noted in her diary.

The problem of good and evil existing side by side in a world created by an all-loving God had taunted her since first she had seen the "ideal of Love'' mocked by the suffering of innocent victims of war. Lewis saw the answer in the individual's freedom to choose: "Free will . . . has made evil possible. . . . It is also the only thing that makes possible any love or goodness worth having.''

Humanity's rebellion against God, man's attempt to "invent some sort of happiness for himself on his own,'' wrote Lewis, had resulted in "nearly all we call human history . . . the long terrible story.''

The omnipotence of God was not made invalid by the presence of evil. The final outcome was God's, whatever must come between. Reading the book had not answered all her whys, but she was better prepared to live with them.

> There is no certain shelter
> Against uncertainty
> That can withstand disaster
> Impregnably;
>
> Except that spirits armored
> With fortitude have won
> Security from knowing
> There is none.
>
> "Forfended"

So much was beyond her knowing, and she was coming to accept that it was best left there. All her probing beyond the veil of the future could only give a false sense of security. And her self-analysis of motives or worthiness was just as treacherous. She had learned of her own insufficiency through dark experience. To be stripped of illusions was painful, but the essential truth could be glimpsed more clearly now. God alone could give meaning to her life. He had carried her this far, and without him she could not go on.

To Carolyn Ruth she had confessed openly that she believed, "because I must." Faith was as necessary as breathing. She could no more conceive of living without the Spirit of God than "without air."[16]

> Full half a hundred times I've sobbed
> I can't go on, I can't go on.
> And yet, full half a hundred times
> I've hushed my sobs and gone.
>
> My answer, if you ask me how,
> May seem presumptuously odd,
> But I think that what kept going on
> When I could not, was God.
>
> "Answer"

6

AUTUMN OF
NO RETURN

1949–1950

I remember a day
High-colored and warm,
An innocent day
That did me no harm,
With a bicker of bluejays
Quick in the elms,
With harvest fragrance
From apple realms
And grape dominions
Rich on its breath;
And nothing to mark it
The day before death.

By Jane's bed stood a small table made from walnut cut on their own land. She loved to touch it, tracing with her fingers the rich pattern of polished wood. Her father had made the table in wood-working class, and they called it "Daddy's report card." Jane could imagine his hands cutting, shaping, and finally rubbing the surface smooth, highlighting the grain. The table was a testimonial to the life of the tree—and the man who had put loving skill into making it. Jane treasured it for both.

She had always felt a special kinship with her father. He shared many of her ideas and deep convictions, but their short, treasured moments together rarely allowed time for more than a few words.

Clarence was sixty-six, and Jane ached to see him "nearly always too worn out to have much to say to anyone."[1] She fervently hoped he could someday rest, and there would be time to "really get acquainted."[2]

It was their fifth year at Sunset Trail. Much had been done to improve the house and land, and Clarence worked at it evenings and weekends, often with help from Nelson. During the week they both had full-time jobs in construction.

Fatigue could not dim the pleasure and gratitude they felt in owning their own place. No words were needed to convey the love they shared for the land. In "Family View," Jane wrote:

> [Four] of us view this land we know,
> Severly contoured, winter bare,
> In atmosphere of afterglow
> Without a shadow anywhere.
>
> [Four] of us pleasuring our eyes
> In clarity, our glances meet
> And almost shyly recognize
> A moment perfect and complete.
>
> Not something that we need discuss,
> Joy is, without a why or how,
> If not for others, yet for us,
> If not for always, yet for now.

They were farmers at heart, and they loved working with the soil—Clarence in the fields, Donia in the garden. Their lives followed the rhythm of the seasons, from seed time to harvest, and Jane made poetry of it. "First Plowing in the Hills" was written in 1949.

> When it's too soon for spring, and even too soon
> To think of it, you'd think—some afternoon
> You're sure to raise your eyes and see them there
> Cresting the topmost ridge that tries to pare
> Whole sections from the sky; a man and team
> Of horses plowing. Cloud and clod would seem
> To feel the plowshare equally. You wonder
> If the sun itself isn't apt to be plowed under
> In that steep enterprise. It makes you proud
> Of men who'll start out halfway up a cloud
> To sketch designs for summer on a land
> That isn't sure of spring. You understand,
> Of course, it's hard work plowing on a hill,
> And bottom lands grow better crops, but still
> There's something useful to the heart and eye
> In men who plow the earth against the sky.

The poem sold to the *Post,* and Jane admitted that it was "one of the few" she was "fairly well pleased with."

The fourth of July marked the annual family gathering to celebrate the nation's—and Nelson's—birthday. Ruth and Ed Lee came from Union

City with four-year-old Patricia and three-year-old Edwin. Aunt Laura was there from Asheville.

This time Jane had a surprise for the family: her scrapbook of printed poems (more than forty by now). Aunt Laura, who had always encouraged Jane to write, suggested that she "ought to have a book published." The rest of the family enthusiastically agreed, but Jane voiced a firm protest. She noted the incident in her diary with the comment, "Most of mine [poems] are hardly worth the permanence of a book, however small."

The dream of a book could not be admitted openly, not even to herself. It was tucked safely away in her heart. Perhaps, if she kept working and selling, it would some day come true.

Their family celebration that year was tinged with sadness. Nelson had announced his decision to move to Maryland in August to find more permanent employment. The lively twins would be sorely missed at Sunset Trail. Clarence, in particular, gloried in his small helpers.[3]

> Nothing could ever please my father more
> Than having all his grandfolk tag along
> To help him in the doing of each chore.
> His work was done much better with a throng
> Of little people dashing here and there
> And everywhere, each clamoring for a turn
> At everything from riding Kate, the mare,
> To turning the handle of the frothing churn.
> When he had sent my mother to rest from noise
> One rainy day, and, with his broadest smile,
> Had settled down knee-deep in girls and boys
> To turn the sausage grinder for a while,
> The least one made his happiness complete.
> "Granddaddy," she observed, "is churning meat."
>
> "Helpers"

On August fourth, Jane pasted her fiftieth printed poem in the scrapbook and noted the occasion in her diary. It had taken four years to come that far, four years since her sonnet won the poetry contest in *The Progressive Farmer*. No one could guess how much that "small sense of fulfillment" meant, or on what "rocky, hopeless, submarginal level of existence" she had been living, how "frozen" she had felt in mind, heart, and soul, "as if they could never be warm again," and on what "ragged edge of nothing" she still existed—and perhaps must always remain.

Her self-pity had its origin in her cellar of gloom, and she admitted in her diary that the despair was much her own fault, due more to her failure to respond positively to her special circumstances than to the circumstances themselves. But now she was determined "not to waste more energy in regret and self-reproach." Even if her literary accomplishments were small, she hoped to do more and was "passionately grateful for this much."

Two days, later, Nelson left alone for Maryland. The following day was Sunday, and Clarence and Donia had supper with Elberta and the twins. They came home early to do evening chores and get some rest. The new work day would begin at dawn. Such had been their familiar pattern as long as Jane could remember.

But there was nothing familiar about the strange hour, near midnight, when she awoke and saw Elizabeth by the telephone—a stricken-faced, unnaturally calm Elizabeth, who formed words with her mouth, spelling doom.

Numbly Jane recorded it: "I will write this and put the diary away as I will not want to keep a diary any more: Elizabeth said Daddy had a heart-attack. Within minutes he was dead" *(Diary, Aug. 12, 1949).*

Such grief could not be told in prose, but Jane wrote "Severance" the morning after.

> How long a single night can be
> We learned with anguished care.
> Eternity was every hour
> The night you entered there.
>
> And even when the throbbing gold
> Of day thrilled down the lawn,
> We gazed with unfamiliar eyes,
> Having no use for dawn.

They were stunned by the sudden loss. It seemed "utterly preposterous to have a funeral for Daddy," Jane wrote later.[4] Everything seemed unreal, as if she were watching someone else in her bed, going through the motions of eating, reading, knitting, writing mechanically, unfeeling. How could the sky still be blue over her window view? How could she still be alive when he was dead?

By putting words on paper—in poetry—Jane sought to familiarize herself with the strange reality of death and with the dreadful truth that her father had "worked so very hard, and for such small reward, materially speaking, and that he did, quite literally, work himself to death"[5]

> My father plowed.
> So we were fed.
> But meager soil
> Earns meager bread.

He plowed with zest,
   He plowed with wonder,
But soon we saw
   His youth plowed under.

With hope drought-stricken,
   With heart unbowing,
He bent his back
   And kept on plowing.

With stubborn love
   And a gaunt pride
My father plowed
   Till the day he died.
                    "Plowman"

The first morning after Clarence's death, the birdbath and feeder outside Jane's window were empty of winged visitors.

And trees hung desolately solitary
As if, with you, all life and song were dead.
                    "Return"

There seemed nothing left now but endurance. There was nothing to stir her heart from chill estrangement or to make her feel at home with life again. Then one morning her eye was caught by a quick movement outside the window. She wrote of it in "Glimpsed."

I had not thought of being glad again.
I can endure the opening of each day,
Do small tasks in an ordinary way,
And bear the nights, each night as long as ten.
And I can read the words that people pen
In sympathy, see visitors, and say
The right words, even asking them to stay,
And smile a little, every now and then.

This seemed as much as I could ever do.
To see beyond the doing of these things
Required a vision that I never had.
But when I glimpsed a bird just now, there flew
Across my heart, like fugitive wild wings,
The possibility of being glad.

Once again, writing was her lifeline, the fragile thread that knit her heart anew to living while the necessary anguish of grief worked its way through her soul. Much of the writing was an outpouring of raw emotion—too intimate and personal to be shared. But some poems transcended her private pain, expressing the desolation of loss all hearts must bear.

Several poems were composed in tribute to her father, meant for those who knew him, not for publication. But in the "strange hectic weeks" following Clarence Merchant's death, necessity could not be postponed. The family was in dire financial straits. Jane sent the poem "For My Father" to *The Saturday Evening Post* and was grateful when they bought it.

> The silent strength of hills was his, the constant,
> The necessary, changeless presence, grown
> So usual in unobtrusive giving
> Of strength, that we believed his strength our own.
>
> And the enduring certitudes of earth
> Were his, the richness time could not despoil.
> Our lives were rooted in his deep assurance
> As trees are rooted in essential soil.
>
> Without him, though we trust that his eternal
> Faith is fulfilled and his long task approved,
> We bear within our hearts the desolation
> Of mountains fallen and of earth removed.

Even with a rash of poetry sales, the inevitable could not be postponed; the home at Sunset Trail must be sold. Donia, Elizabeth, and Jane hoped, come spring, to have a small house built on Nelson's property nearby. They would live with Elberta and the twins until then.

The forced move made everything seem worse. To lose the land her father had planted, the rooms where his presence was still felt, would make it final. This was no nightmare. His death was real.

It seemed a strange coincidence that her poem "Home Place," written about leaving Dandridge and sold before her father's death, would be published by Ted Malone in Radio Mirror in December as "best poem of the month." The payment was fifty dollars, the largest sum Jane had ever received for a single poem. It was sadly fitting that the money would help pay for their move.

> "You say you went back there? How did it look?
> They've planted peach trees, as we wanted to,
> Outside the kitchen windows, dammed the brook,
> And screened the porch? I wonder how they knew
> To do all that! We talked about it so
> And planned just how to fix things when we could
> I guess they almost couldn't help but know

From living in the house. Well, well, that's good.
It's nice to know they've realized all our wishes.
I know that woman does her housework well
Looking at peach blooms while she dries the dishes.
I only hope they never have to sell.
Go look at it myself? Well, no. Somehow
I couldn't say good-bye again—not now.''

They left in mid-October, with the maples forming a canopy of bright red and yellow over the driveway. Jane had often sung of their glory in poetry. Now, before packing paper and pencil, she wrote "Change," her last poem at Sunset Trail.

I never feared before
To see the bright leaves fall
And the relentless rain
Erasing all
Their brightness. Now I tremble
For when my heart was brave
I had not seen them falling
On your grave.

She did not turn her head to look as they drove out the gate. Not at the tulip bed—she wouldn't see it bloom again in spring. Not at the dogwood trees he had planted in view of her window. Not at the basement steps next to the driveway—she had watched him mix and pour the concrete.

Not even at the flower box beneath her window where a few late petunias waved in the chill wind. No need to look at it again or say goodbye. She would carry it with her; his love had "Established it eternally in her heart."[6]

On the day of their moving, *The Saturday Evening Post* printed her poem "Afterward."

After the worst has happened
With nothing more to fear,
The sun continues rising
With undiminished cheer,

And winds continue blowing
And skies continue fair,
As hearts continue bearing
The thing they could not bear.

They had planned to spend the winter with Elberta and the children, but six weeks later, at Ruth's urging, Jane and Donia traveled by ambulance four hundred miles west to Union City, while Elizabeth remained behind. They hoped the change would do some good, but Jane felt worse away from the hills. Even with Edwin and Patricia snuggled in her bed for story time, the inward ache was ever there.

Outside the window, the land was flat as far as the eye could see, and she was plainly homesick. In "High-Minded" she wrote:

> A level land may satisfy and fill
> Eyes that are born to it, for all I know,
> But everywhere I look I want a hill,
> Far off, or near. Sight has somewhere to go
> And something worth while, every hour, to do,
> Climbing a dozen ridges to the top
> Or searching for them through the misty blue.
> I like a land where looking doesn't stop
> With flat horizons, where my gaze can roam
> Up hill and down, and always be at home.

Their hope was in returning to East Tennessee, and Jane mustered all her strength to write and submit poetry, hastening the longed for day.

Elizabeth joined them for Christmas—a strange and different Christmas, but somehow the joyous message of the Savior's birth meant more than ever before. "Love came down at Christmas," Jane wrote later, a "lovely echo" of eternal song.[7]

She was beginning to feel "more normal," enjoying some things again, but had caught a nasty cold before Christmas that lasted into January. And then, without warning, Ed Lee's father died suddenly, "just as Daddy had," and their grief was laid bare again. Jane began seeing spots in her right eye. The eye got worse until she could see very little with it *(Diary, Feb. 1950)*.

Elizabeth was notified and thought it best for Jane and Donia to leave the grief stricken atmosphere in Union City. She suggested that they buy a home in Knoxville instead of waiting to build. Reluctantly they gave up their dream of living in the country. Elizabeth found a brand new house on Emoriland Boulevard, and two weeks later Jane and her mother were brought home.

It was high time. Dr. Leach, the eye specialist who was called to examine Jane, diagnosed advanced glaucoma. He took Elizabeth aside to tell her that the sight in Jane's right eye was seriously impaired and that the left eye was threatened. He was almost certain that the condition had been brought on by shock and stress, and he prescribed rest under hot compresses several times daily.

The possibility of becoming blind as well as deaf was more than Jane could bear to think of.

It is too huge a doom
Too vast for me to fear it.
The hazard set so high
The racing heart must clear it
With one great surge of faith. . . .
                    "Blindness"

It could not happen—it must not happen. Darkness as well as silence—not to see the faces of those she loved—the sky and trees beyond her window—the shape of words on a page—the implications were too terrifying to dwell on. And yet, should it come, that, too, must be borne.

Say not that any sorrow
Is past your strength to bear.
To learn the disavowal,
Implicit, of despair,
Rise in the earliest dawning
And see the sun take flight.
Whoever knows the morning
Need never fear the night.
                    "And See the Sun"

Jane had seen light arise in darkness before, and now she must put aside her fear and follow her doctor's orders: an hour's rest behind hot compresses five times daily. This gave her plenty of time to familiarize herself with darkness—and to consider poetry to write in her alotted hours of sight. She must learn to use those precious hours carefully, reading selectively, writing with the "exact economy" of words she always strove for. Here was a further "stripping to the final clear integrity." And she must hold to the faith that she was "richer for having less."

The small gray house with the bright red front door seemed liked a doll house to Donia and Jane. It had no basement, little storage space, and a kitchen tiny enough to fit comfortably in one corner of the farm kitchens they had known. But the house had electric heat, and it would save Donia "worlds of trouble," Jane wrote to her friends. All in all it was "lovely beyond our fondest expectations."

Jane shared the largest bedroom with her mother, but it measured less than ten-by-twelve feet. Treasures must be parted with once again, a reduction to essentials that hurt each time—even if the things she *could* keep were twice treasured now.

We who love little objects rendered dear
By long association, have this much
That we can keep with us through the severe
Sharp hurt of leaving our own place. The touch

Of a little Dutch girl pitcher that has held
Tulips of many springs and the smile upon
A tiny china gentleman's face, that quelled
Quick tears, remain when larger things are gone.
If we must leave the sunny generous rooms,
The window with its wide familiar view,
And the garden's sweet processional of blooms
And go where all is cramped and strangely new,
No change, at least, is great enough to sweep
Away small treasures—small enough to keep.

"Of Loving Little Objects"

The walnut table stood by Jane's bed in the new room, a familiar source of comfort. With her fingers she traced the pattern of grain in the polished surface. The tree's growth through the seasons—its response to frost and heat, drought and rain—had slowly formed the rings in the wood, creating a thing of beauty—the truth of the tree—the soul of it. And so might it be that her own response to the seasons of her living was creating a pattern: the grain of her being, the truth and soul of her. But it was not for her to see with her own eyes anymore than the tree could know its own grain.

Her hand rested on the table top, touched where her father's hand had touched, and she wrote:

My father hewed the walnut tree
That grew upon the land he tilled,
And of its wood he made for me
This table. Now his hand is stilled
And others plow the uphill land
And reap its crops; but warm and good
I feel the strong touch of his hand
Upon this richly gleaming wood.

"The Table"

On the table was her father's watch in a holder and always a small vase of fresh flowers to touch and smell. Donia had arranged Jane's favorite books on the nearby shelf, and above it were pictures of the nieces and nephews. Writing supplies and handwork were within reach, and so were her portfolio of Chinese paintings and the book of art masterpieces. Donia knew well to provide the essentials of home.

Content is sunlight in an ordered room,
Beauty is lilacs in a crystal vase,
Peace is a maple's rhythmic blowing plume.
Love is your face.

"Tangibles"

88

The bedroom window looked out on the backyard. It was only a stretch of frozen red earth now, but in the spring Donia would start planting. For now, Jane's small bed could be maneuvered through the kitchen and dining room to the picture window in front, which had a view of the boulevard. There was little traffic, but school children walked past on their way to the elementary school nearby, and down the center of the boulevard paraded a row of young dogwood trees. Small front lawns bordered the sidewalk, and the well-kept houses were shaded by maples.

It was a pleasant view, but Jane would gladly have traded it for "one large unpremeditated field," She could sympathize with a bewildered cow who wandered down their boulevard one day.

> She paces our astonished boulevard
> With grave, sedately pitying disdain.
> The smooth concrete she walks upon is hard
> As she had never known a country lane
> Or any luscious pasture lot to be.
> Our small attempts at grass hold no temptation,
> Nor is there space, beneath a single tree,
> For munching cuds in cosmic contemplation.
> Our neat, trim houses, elbows well tucked in,
> Quite obviously afford no ample store
> Of hay or ensilage that might serve to win
> Approval, and persuade her to deplore
> Conditions less. She gazes, mellow-eyed,
> About her with a kind, solicitous
> Concern; then hastens homeward to her wide
> Uninterrupted meadows, leaving us
> Considerably unnerved at seeing how
> Profoundly we are pitied by a cow.
>
> "Cow on the Boulevard"

Self-pity was best conquered with laughter. That had been her father's way of defying despair. He would have chuckled approval at her "boulevard guest," as he had done so often in the past when she wrote in hopes of making him smile.

> I hope there may be laughter where he is
> Since it was by his laughter we were saved
> From many griefs, and it is by the power
> Of his remembered laughter we have braved
> The terror of his absence, and have found
> Within our hearts something of the strong
> Courageousness and faith from which his laughter
> Rose like a lifting challenge and a song.

Perhaps he has no need of laughter now,
Having all joy. But through the lonely years
We shall recall his laughter and shall pray
That we may find him when our vision clears
Laughing at all the little jokes we loved
Without the earthly undertones of tears.

"We Shall Recall"

So much in her life just now could be braved only with laughter. So many things were uncertain. So many frustrations triggered helpless anger, fear, and despair. Jane found vicarious relief in watching—and writing about—"Boy Kicking Box."

Just what he had against it I can't say.
It was a harmless-looking box enough
That he was treating in a shameful way,
Kicking it ahead of him with rough
Enthusiastic kicks, with such a fierce
Impetuous joy, it seemed as if his toe
Was surely bound, with each kick, to pierce
Right through the cardboard side. It didn't,
    though,
And he kept kicking at it out of sight
And getting happier with every kick
Like all of us who watched him with delight.
We'd been hurt, too. We'd been hurt to the
    quick,
And we were eased of angers and of shocks
By every kick he gave that empty box.

The main burden of maintaining their small household was now on Elizabeth, and Jane could not indulge in idleness, however justified it might seem. Neither could she cheat on resting her eyes. If she did, lights would flicker in her right eye as "in a pinball machine," signaling the need for hot compresses again.[8]

With all the strain—and the loss of five hours seeing time daily—it was a wonder she was able to write at all, Jane confessed in her diary. It seemed incredible that she was writing and selling as much as ever. She was profoundly grateful. Without writing she would "indeed be desolate, with nothing to justify" her life.

Behind the dark compresses her mind was flooded with ideas for poems and exactly how to write them. The short verses could be worked out entirely in her head and jotted down as soon as the compresses were off. Humorous four-liners were her forte. Besides helping to see her

90

circumstances from the lighter side, they also brought the most income for the least eye strain.

Two quick sales to the *Post* were born of her frustration over unread magazines and books piling up while she rested her eyes.

> Culturally estimated
> All my mental range has narrowed.
> Other's minds are cultivated;
> Mine is merely harrowed.
> "Parent's Report Card"

and "Bookworm's Turning":

> A luxury I revel in with gay
> Abandonment, is this:
> Ignoring all the books reviewers say
> I can't afford to miss.

The shocks and changes of the past months had been devastating, but life for the three in the "doll house" continued on. With what Jane called typical Merchant mulishness, they were restructuring their lives. Donia held up with amazing fortitude. In "Unvanquished," another *Post* sale, Jane wrote:

> When ultimate disaster's
> Destructive work is done,
> The stubborn heart repairs the sky
> And reconstructs the sun.

As soon as the red soil in their small backyard was free of frost, Donia started digging. From her command-post at the window, Jane watched another miracle begin. Their "strange flowerless interlude" would soon be over.

> The winter after he died
> She ordered far more
> Brilliant seed catalogs
> Than ever before.
>
> She had no garden then;
> The farm had gone
> When he did. The catalogs
> Were for hoping on.

Turning the pages of pictures
Of huge, indomitable flowers
She could believe in spring
Through dark, frozen hours.

Their children would find a way,
Understanding her basic need
For putting down roots again.
They were grown of good seed.

She had a house and garden
The summer after he died,
And a bundle of seed catalogs
Verified.
"Grandmother's Garden"

Elizabeth slept in the smaller bedroom down the hall, but the sisters continued the cherished ritual of having coffee together before dawn. Few words need pass between them. Like her mother, Elizabeth showed love in action. She rose at 5:30 A.M. and brought Jane her cup of steaming brew, along with toast and the morning paper.

My sister knows there is no ill
So dire a cup of coffee will
Not help to soothe its pain.
A cup of coffee, hot and black,
Is balm for any loss or lack,
Is ease for any strain.

My sister knows that life must be
Still lived with grace and gaiety
Whatever may befall.
She sips her coffee, and she goes
Undaunted by life's harshest blows;
And she has borne them all.

So when to lighten my distress
And comfort me in loneliness,
She brings her favorite brew,
I lift the steaming cup, and think,
Of strength and courage, and I drink,
To you, my dear, to you.
"Ritual"

When Elizabeth left for work, Jane sipped the last of her coffee in the still dark room, waiting for dawn to break outside her window. The house was snug; her mother slept peacefully across the room. Once more their little world was secure—for a season. They had survived another dark night of terrors and uncertainties, but morning was at hand.

> There winds across the dimness
> Of earliest Eastern gray
> A path of pebbled crimson clouds
> Like stepping stones to day.
>
> "Dawn"

Slowly, light illumined the small garden, sparkling in dewdrops on tender new leaves. The sight of it never failed to thrill her. She had read in the Old Testament book of Hosea: "I will be as the dew unto Israel; he shall blossom as the lily, he shall strike root as the poplar" (Hos. 14:5 RSV).

> God is as dew upon the desert places
> Where rain falls seldom, where the dew alone
> Sustains and nourishes the tender graces
> Of grass and herb; dew comes when light has flown
>
> And all is darkness, as, in times of grief,
> We feel God's cleansing presence close to us
> And find, when light returns with sweet relief,
> All things refreshed and gently luminous.
>
> Dew comes when all the world is calm and still,
> As God comes when our hearts are hushed and holy,
> And richest on the valley, not the hill,
> As God dwells with the humble and the lowly.
>
> Oh, let us claim the promise, and renew
> Our lives, for he will be to us as dew.
>
> "I Will Be as the Dew"

7
MEETINGS
1950–1951

There is a silent question
Whenever strangers meet;
All hearts, except the largest,
Persistently repeat:

Are you the good companion
I've always sought, to be
A wisely understanding
And loyal friend to me?

Our hearts are eager, seeking;
But selfless hearts transcend
The question, saying clearly:
I am your friend.

Never had Jane needed a close-at-hand friend more, and never had friendship seemed more hazardous. Even by letter there were risks of hurts and misunderstandings, and she had little strength to bear them just now.

There was an open wound deep within, a secret place where she dared not trust another human being—not yet. No relationship was safe from sudden severance. Instinctively Jane was poised for retreat behind protective walls of self-sufficiency, keeping out of harm's way. But she knew that to say "I don't need anybody" was dangerous self-deception building walls of bitterness, self-pity, and despair, shutting others out.

She had written "For Many Maimed" a sonnet inspired by the life of Helen Keller, including the lines:

The lone equipment of will's naked knife
Constructs strong habitations that protect
Or tall cathedrals soaring to the stars.

Self-defense was a natural response to hurt, and her wounds were still raw. When the threat of blindness assailed her, she had turned for comfort to her closest pen-friends, and she anxiously awaited their response. Weeks had gone without a reply, and behind dark compresses Jane wrestled with gloomy thoughts: *Why* hadn't they written? Had she imposed on them? Asked for sympathy when they had troubles enough of their own? Were the letters lost in the mail? Were her friends just too busy to write? Or could it be that they didn't care? Her imagination teemed with miserable possibilities until the letters finally came. They were sympathetic, of course, but were filled with details of active, busy lives, triggering waves of self-pity—a bitter balm for hurt feelings. The trap door to the cellar of depression was wide open, and Jane clung to its edge, resisting the lure of darkness.

The sane and sensible part of her knew better than to suspect her friends of indifference. She was wrong to reproach them, and she loathed herself for doing it. In the book of Psalms she read: "O Lord. . . . Who shall dwell on thy holy hill? He . . . who does not slander with his tongue . . . nor takes up a reproach against his neighbor" (Ps. 15:1-3 RSV).

> To live a life above reproach must mean,
> I sometimes think, not merely living so
> Upright and virtuous a life that no
> Critic can harm us with censorious spleen.
> I think it is to keep our minds serene
> Above reproachful thoughts of what friends owe
> Of thoughtfulness, and fail in; to forego
> Nursing our little hurts, however keen.
>
> For much tranquility and much delight
> Are lost by counting, time and time again,
> The small neglect, the unintended slight.
> Grievances rust our spirits; let this, then,
> Become our constant effort, to live quite
> Above reproach both from, and to, all men.
>   "Interpretation"

She knew herself to be far too "quick to resent small neglects and to suspect slights."[1] The cause was likely to be her own self-love, pride, and strong will. The remedy was to admit the truth and ask for help in keeping her heart open. She could voice the prayer, but to live it was another matter. She dared not let go of her defenses. Not quite yet could she believe in friendship—at least not for herself.

Eight months had passed since her father's death, and she was functioning again. Her days were ordered with dependable regularity around meals, rest, and work. The house and her room with blue walls and view of the garden were slowly becoming familiar possessions.

City living brought a new challenge to Donia and Jane, who were both shy of strangers. Donia stayed either indoors or so close to the house that she could hear when Jane called. Elizabeth did all the shopping on her way home from work. Their new neighbors were friendly, but not intrusive. Only eight-year-old George from next door was apt to barge in when Donia was still in her bathrobe and Jane in pajamas. He had instantly become a substitute nephew and grandson and was sure of his welcome at any hour—especially on an urgent mission to introduce his new pet rabbit or puppy. When he brought his pets to her. Jane held the soft warmth against the aching loneliness of her heart, remembering all the young furry things brought to her bedside in springtime on the farm.

Her "Plea for All Children" had just been printed in the *Post*.

> Let them have little living things to clasp
> Against their hearts; give them the gentleness
> Of throbbing, purring kitten warmth to grasp
> In loving arms, and puppies to caress
> With shy discovering delight, as they
> Find how the tender feel of magic lingers,
> And let them learn the delicate soft way
> White rabbit fluff clings to enchanted fingers.
> They who are new to living need the warm
> Quick reassuring touch of things that live,
> And every little breathing furry form
> Has necessary certainty to give.
> They who are new to living need, so much,
> The warmth of life, responsive to their touch.

Directly across the boulevard lived Dr. John Wesley Hoffmann, head of the history department at the University of Tennessee. He was a pleasant grandfatherly figure, but Jane was overawed at living near "so much erudition, entirely out of my element. Cows are nearer my intellectual equals."[2]

She was astonished to hear from Donia, who had met Mrs. Hoffmann, that the professor read and admired her poetry. Apparently a number of people in town did. Some even kept her poems in scrapbooks. Elizabeth often brought home reports of the nice things said about them. Not that Jane believed much of it, she noted to Corrine, but it certainly helped her morale.

Lucille Hart, one of Elizabeth's friends, showed her scrapbook to Eva Venable, the librarian at Central High School in Knoxville, and mentioned her acquaintance with the Merchant family. Eva was also a collector of Jane's poetry and had long wanted to meet the poet. She lost no time in asking for an introduction.

The day before Easter, Eva and her sister, Annie, paid a brief call at Emoriland Boulevard. Jane was shy and much impressed by what she had learned about her visitor. Eva held Master's degrees in library science and English, with minors in psychology and philosophy. She even had a pilot's license!

Nothing betrayed that Eva was shy, as well, and equally impressed with Jane's accomplishments. She had hoped that they might get better acquainted, but it was time for Jane to rest her eyes behind dark compresses, and the Venable sisters left, afraid they had already stayed too long.

The summer passed, and another crisis threatened the Merchant household before Eva found courage to contact Jane again. Elizabeth had been called back on active duty in the Navy Nurse Corps, with orders to go to Oakland, California—possibly Korea. Without her, Donia and Jane could not manage life in the Doll House, and the prospect of breaking up the family again was unbearable. Elizabeth's pastor, two doctors, and the Red Cross put in a plea to the Navy for deferment, and it was granted—but not until Elizabeth was in Memphis, on her way to Oakland. They had survived again—just barely—and they rejoiced in the miracle.

Eva heard of the emergency through a mutual friend, and she wrote to express her sympathy. It was a long letter, the kind Jane most enjoyed, telling in vivid detail of summer excursions to the Smokies. And she apologized for having "outstayed" their welcome in April.

"Not by any means," Jane assured her by return mail. The Venables would always be welcome. Not that she *expected* a visit from someone as busy as Eva, but the tales from the Smokies had thrilled her. She responded with a summer adventure of her own: a visit from a hummingbird among blue petunias in her flower box. "Hummingbirds are something I could never have thought up! This was my first close-up view of one."[3]

> When I
> See hummingbirds,
> This thought never varies:
> Why do people disbelieve in
> Fairies?
>
> "Why?"

The day before Thanksgiving, Eva and her mother came to call. Afterwards, Jane wrote "The Rare Fulfillment."

> Whenever two hearts have understood each other
> With deep affection, even for an hour,
> They cannot be entirely strange again.

Though silence and differences may devour
Long years between them, if they meet a moment
They will experience, silent and surprised,
The always sought and always rare fulfillment
Of the heart's need of being recognized.

The morning after Thanksgiving, Jane woke to the surprise of snow flurries
and bright leaves coming down in glorious accord outside her window. But
she would remember the day for an even more astonishing gift. Through the
snow came the mailman bearing a sixteen-page letter from Eva, continuing
their visit. She expanded on thoughts they had condensed on magic slates and
more. Here was a heart trusting itself to another.

There was pure poetry in her telling of an autumn trip to the mountains,
of a waterfall tumbling down sheer cliffs to form a small pool below. At
the water's edge stood a maple "with one slender branch full of brilliant
red leaves reflected in the black surface like a scarlet saber. . . . I wish
you could have seen it . . . because you could have put it into words clear
enough for others to see it . . . in a few short lines, while I write on for
pages and pages without ever getting anything said."

Abruptly the letter turned to confession: "I ask your forgiveness if this
seems too personal. . . . Since I first [read your poems] . . . there have
been things I wanted to discuss with you because you seem to see things
so clearly. . . . I suppose that we all have days of despondency when we
wonder what life is for and what are the things that make living worth
while, but it's the sort of thing one would feel free to discuss with most
people only when *not* feeling deeply about and, of course, most people
would have only a superficial and repetitious answer anyway, but it seems
to me that you must have reached some valid conclusions of your own
which I would very much appreciate you sharing with me if you could. If
this seems too personal, just ignore it or postpone an answer until some
later time when we know each other better, as I hope we shall."[4]

Never had Jane received a letter that expressed such trust. It required a
confession of her own. "It seems rather wonderful that you could feel
about me as you say you do. I hadn't dared believe you could feel so. I had
only thought that you would be a fine person to know well, 'if only'—that
large 'if only' that has separated me from people all these years—if only I
could hear. Since I can't, and am far too shy and reserved myself (I'm so
shy it hadn't occurred to me other people are too!) to show anything but
my protective surface to anyone without some assurance of their
understanding, which it is impossible to acquire just by *seeing* people, I
had long since accepted that the only way I could really become
acquainted with anyone was by letter. That is why I must have seemed
rather unresponsive to your efforts to become more personally acquainted

98

with me; I was so convinced that people wouldn't want to take the trouble to 'get through' to me (and I didn't see why they should) that I didn't realize it was happening.''

As for any original conclusions about the meaning of life, she dared not claim to have reached any. "I think I might have to reword St. Paul's 'We believe and therefore speak,' to 'I believe and therefore think it unnecessary to speak,' taking it for granted that if I, ignorant as I am, know anything, then everyone else, being much wiser and more experienced in living than I, must of course know any aspect of truth far better than I do. And I sometimes wonder whether it is possible for any person really to tell another anything worth knowing, whether anyone can learn anything except by actually experiencing it in his own life. The *Ladies Home Journal* recently bought, but hasn't printed, a little verse I wrote about wisdom. (With apology for poets who recite their own poetry)"

> Those who have suffered and grown strong,
> May have a right to say
> To those who suffer, "There is strength
> And wisdom from dismay."
>
> Those who have suffered and grown strong
> Are silent, having learned
> Man's wisdom, like his suffering,
> Is separately discerned.
>
> "Wisdom"

Jane concluded her letter: "If I were to put into a few words, though, what it is that makes life worth living to me, even when there seems nothing else worth living for, I'd have to quote St. Paul again: 'For me to live is Christ.' Without Christ, without the assurance he gives that life has meaning and purpose and dignity for even the humblest, lowest, and unworthiest of us, none of the other lovely things like friendship and family love and children and trees and birds—none of them have any special meaning. But with Him, everything has meaning and significance, even the things that seem completely cruel and senseless. And that, I know, is a rather repetitious conclusion, having been repeated by millions of people down through the years. And I know that to many, if not most, of the philosophers and wise men it seems a very simple minded and superficial conclusion, besides. But it isn't superficial with me."

She wanted to tear it all up and rewrite it, as she so often did with letters to Carolyn Ruth. But that was a luxury her eyes no longer allowed. "I'll send it, and am afraid it will profoundly disillusion you concerning me! I'm sending the maple sonnet too, which should complete the work of disillusionment. Without undue modesty, I think it's one of the worst I've ever written."[5]

There was a gentle falling all this day
of single leaves from the maple tree; the vast
Lone tree that waited till the rest were gray
And gaunt before reluctantly, at last,
It left off being green and turned, instead,
Its hoarded wealth of leaves into a store
As vividly, as absolutely red
As they were resolutely green before.
But now the leaves were falling, never two
By two, but slowly, slowly, one by one,
As if, as well as we, the maple knew
That there would be no more when this was done.
A curious privilege, devoid of grief,
To watch an autumn ending, leaf by leaf.

"Autumn Ending"

Eva's reply covered thirty-two pages, written during late night and early morning hours. She immediately took Jane to task for her modesty concerning the maple sonnet. " 'To watch an autumn ending, leaf by leaf,' seems to me to be a line so near perfection that I believe anyone who reads it will think of it each time . . . he or she sees leaves falling. Are you really not satisfied with it yourself, as you implied? I can't imagine why?"

The letter had a more urgent purpose, and Jane's heart pounded as she read on: "Do you know whether there is any possibility that your eyesight could be improved by 'transplanting' . . . another eye in place of your own? . . . If it has never been considered, would you ask Dr. Leach about it? If he feels that it might help, you are truly welcome to one of my eyes. . . . This isn't a casual or unconsidered offer, because I've thought it through from every angle, including the possibility of injury to the other eye. . . . However, my general health has always been practically perfect . . . a specialist once declared my eyesight 'most extraordinarily excellent.' I am pretty sure that if anyone's eye could be swapped for yours, it would be difficult to find a better one than mine."[6]

Jane was overwhelmed, and she wrote back that evening. "I've been holding the thought of that offer, the most beautiful and generous act I've ever known, reverently in my heart all day, unable even to begin to comprehend the absolute selflessness of it. I wish I could tell you what it means to me.

"It is out of the question, of course. I could not even mention it to Mother or Dr. Leach or anyone, though I would like them to know there is generosity like yours in the world, simply because such a knowledge makes everything in the world so much more beautiful. But even to speak of it would seem like sacrilege to me. . . . My slight glaucoma is much better now, requiring only three daily rest periods with hot compresses. Soon I hope to be able to use my eyes fairly normally again. . . .

"But even if I were totally blind, Eva, I wouldn't consider for a moment depriving you of one of those eyes which can see the Smokies and red maple leaves in black water, and all the wonderful beautiful things there are to see in this world. The very thought is so appalling that I'm sure I wouldn't be able to sleep tonight before writing this note begging you not to think of such a thing again. . . . And trying to tell you how unutterably grateful I am to you for thinking of it, and how deeply I shall cherish the memory of it all my life.

"If I did have your perfect eyes, and were able to travel all over the world and see everything beautiful in it, and in Heaven itself, I couldn't see anything more beautiful than your letter. The rest of that letter I'll look forward to answering soon, but this much I have to send you now, to say, inadequately, thank you. With gratitude and affection."[7]

Eva had written again of her compelling need to discuss religious beliefs with "someone who's advice and opinion, beliefs and example would have true validity." She had taken note of the last lines of Jane's poem on wisdom: "Man's wisdom, like his suffering, / Is separately discerned." "But . . . will you . . . be patient with me while, for the first time ever, I try to express my beliefs and doubts and fumbling attempt to arrive at such religion or philosophy of life that I can attain to a state of adjustment as you have?" *(Letter to Jane, Nov. 30, 1950).*

Jane flinched. Eva had not yet discovered the distance between the ideal of the poetry and the real living poet. The adjustment she admired was too often a precarious teetering on the edge of darkness. But that wasn't something Jane was ready to reveal yet. She dared not risk the friendship—or become a stumbling block on the pilgrim road Eva had embarked upon, that private road leading to an encounter with the Friend no human companion could equal. She wanted to be encouraging, but Eva must find her own answers.

"It seems just too enormous a subject to approach without great care . . . along with my very real shyness about discussing something that means very much to me," she wrote. "Yet I do want to help you in any way I can . . . how very sincerely and earnestly I hope and pray that you may find the faith you seek."[8]

Eva was satisfied: "Just knowing you is a long step towards helping establish my faith and answer my questions anyway."[9]

Their friendship had deepened quickly. Eva came regularly on Tuesdays and Fridays after school. Between visits, they wrote voluminous letters to cover all they had not had time to "talk" about on magic slates. Eva thought letters offered the "best of all possibilities" for developing friendships, transcending the narrow limits of time, and giving uninterrupted opportunities to share ideas in depth.

They marvelled at the things they had in common, their likes and dislikes.

High on the latter list were racial bigotry and hypocrisy. Jane had written "Dislike-Minded" the year before.

> Nothing serves to put a pair
> Of new acquaintances at ease
> Like discovering they share
> Common animosities.

But even as they reveled in mutual discovery, there were perils of misunderstanding. Eva was as much a sensitive perfectionist as Jane, and their letters brimmed with apologies and reassurances—fears of disappointing, offending, presuming, or imposing.

When Eva climbed a frosty hill to pick pine branches before Christmas, she thought to bring one to Jane. But on her way to Emoriland Boulevard, she suddenly remembered that her arrival would be unexpected and possibly inconvenient. She took her pine branches home and wrote a note instead.

Jane's reply was dispatched to the nearest mailbox by Elizabeth the next afternoon: "I think I have to scold you for being so incredibly modest as to think we could possibly find any visit from you unwelcome. . . . We would have been delighted to see you, and would have loved the pine—this is our first Christmas without a real Christmas tree" *(Venable, Dec. 16, 1950).*

Eva brought the bough the next day. She told so vividly of her walk in the pine forest that Jane could nearly imagine being there. In "Pine Bough at My Bedside," Jane wrote:

> What happens when you breathe the sky?
> What happens when you go
> To gather pine? I touch a spray
> And almost—almost know.

It was difficult to fathom that Eva was as greatly in need of reassurance as Jane was herself. "It had never penetrated very far into my consciousness that seemingly self-assured, self-confident people of whom I felt so shy might possibly be feeling equally shy of me. Although I did discover that there is no use in worrying about what people think of you, since in most cases they are too busy thinking about themselves to think of you at all. That discovery was a help in overcoming my very intense embarrassment over what I might be revealing about myself in my verses. If you could know how I used to writhe inside, and still do sometimes, at thought of people reading some of the more personal verses, you'd know why I sometimes feel that writing for publication is just indecent exposure and not worth any of the satisfaction it brings" *(Venable, Dec. 16, 1950).*

For Christmas, Eva carved a pair of bookends for Jane. "One of the most special gifts I ever have received, [from] one of the most special people I've ever been privileged to know. I still can't quite believe my good fortune . . . at a time in my life . . . when I've been tempted to feel that nothing very wonderful or reviving is ever likely to happen to me again. But something wonderful always does happen, after all, and this year the something wonderful is knowing you. And in the optimism engendered by Christmas, I'm even hoping that just possibly I may be able to deserve you."[10]

In "Design for Friendship," Jane wrote:

Let there be wonder always, and a shared
Delight in constant growing toward the best,
In books and thoughts examined and compared
With eager curiosity and zest.
Let there be laughter, and the interchange
Of glad experience enriching each
With double joy, as there must be the range
Of understanding only tears can teach.

And let there be continuous deepening
Of love in fruitful silences, whereby
Each heart communicates the urgent thing
That each heart must communicate, or die.
And you shall learn in this way, and no other,
Friendship is hearts refreshing one another.

After Christmas, Jane felt that the time had come for a confession. "I, far from being the 'definitely superior person' you think me, I have been for a long time now so sore and frightened and bewildered inside, that I haven't dared respond to your friendship as warmly as I otherwise would, because I feel sure you'll be disappointed in me, and I just don't want to be hurt anymore. . . . That doesn't sound like the poised, well-adjusted person you've been calling me, does it Eva? But that person is only the one I try to be—and am sometimes almost too tired to try any more to be. And I really haven't evolved any rare philosophy of my own, as you thought I must have done. . . . I can only try to appropriate and apply in my own living the wisdom of others, which is 'to the Greeks foolishness,' and keep on trusting . . . and trying, even when I can't, on my own power keep on any longer.

"You can see, Eva, why I'm so ashamed to have you take me, as you said once you were doing, as an example of Christianity. I wonder if there is any Christian living who wouldn't be dismayed and humbled by a responsibility such as that. . . . Don't look at Christians, Eva, look at Christ."

She had made the same confession in "Midnight Prayer":

Words I said in sunlight
Kindled many a spark
Of hope in others. Help me, Lord,
To mean them, in this dark.

and in "Unexampled."

What deep amazement they evoke,
What awe I feel for each
Of the few, rare, superior folk
Who practice what I preach.

The admission was risky. Would Eva judge her? Reject her? In self-defense she added: "I have long felt that one of the most basic teachings of Jesus . . . is 'Judge not.' Our business is to follow Christ as far and as fast as we are able, each in his particular area of living, and if we do that honestly and sincerely, we aren't apt to be blaming others for their inconsistencies and failures, seeing our own."[11]

"Lesson" was published that month.

That I should love my neighbor as myself
Was pure impossibility, I said.
Why, look at him! illiterate, unwashed,
And steeped in sin, and thoroughly ill-bred.

But then God showed me how I look to Him,
And now I go about my little labor
Of love, in overwhelmed astonishment
That God should love me as He loves my neighbor.

Eva's response was not rejection, but gratitude for Jane's confidence. They were both freer now in letting down their defenses, even if misunderstandings and hurts were apt to occur. The habit of hiding was well entrenched, and there would always be differences that could never quite be understood or revealed. In any relationship it was difficult not to probe the mystery of the other, but rather to simply rejoice in the glimpses given. "I am very much an amateur at personal relations," Jane explained. "You're the first real friend of my own . . . and I often feel I am very awkward at expressing my thoughts and feelings with you."[12]

To be given the confidence and trust of another person was an awesome responsibility. Just a few months earlier, Jane had not dared to believe in friendship. Now she had a friend, and she must be one. She must be someone to depend on and dare to depend, admit her need, be vulnerable, knowing the risk. There was no guarantee against hurt, rejection, betrayal, or loss. In "Forever Vulnerable," she wrote:

Pray to be loving always—
But only if you dare

The yearning and the sorrow
That all who love must bear.

Pray to be loving always—
Pray always to be strong
To love past ridicule, neglect,
Small anger, and great wrong.

Who loves can wear no armor
Of carelessness or pride
Against misunderstanding.
Who loves can never hide.

The ache of small betrayals,
Love's daily, hourly test,
Is felt with special poignance
By those who love the best.

But he who loves the best loves on
With the pure love that gave
Itself to scourging and the cross.
Himself he cannot save.

Laughter was a staple in the Merchant household. Puns and lighthearted teasing often punctuated conversations. Once, when Jane thought to poke playful fun at her friend, Eva was hurt, but she tried to hide it. Jane's apology was in the mail that evening: "It is a foolish and dangerous way of expressing affection, as I should know, having often been painfully hurt in the past by teasing words, even when I knew certainly that there was not the slightest hurt intended. But I think my teasing of you has hurt more than others' teasing of me ever did" *(Venable, undated)*.

In "Prayer for Our Laughter" she wrote:

Master of mercies, who hast given
The gift of laughter for our need,
Lest any heart be hurt, and driven
To loneliness, help us to heed

Most carefully, how we use thy gift.
O let our laughter, Lord, be kind
And gentle, having power to lift
The tired, discouraged heart and mind

Into the wider realms of being
As wings lift birds into the sky—
Let it not be stones flung, unseeing,
That stun a bird about to fly.

Lord, save us from regrets hereafter;
Keep us aware, through all our years,
That thou hast given the gift of laughter
For ending, not for causing, tears.

The incident was an eye-opener. It taught Jane that accomplished people like Eva could be as thin-skinned as she was herself, the bedridden cripple. Eva was straightforward and open, her laughter honest and true. Early in their relationship, she had asked Jane what quality in a friend she appreciated most—and what quality she disliked most. The answer to the first was "the keeping of promises," and to the second, "the breaking of promises" *(Venable, Dec. 31, 1950)*.

Eva was a promise keeper, and gradually her faithfulness brought healing to Jane's battered soul. Broken dreams and expectations and the shock of her father's death had driven Jane into hiding. Now a new realization was dawning: it was possible after all to have a really satisfying relationship in person. Deafness had not prevented it. The miracle had come just when grief had left her broken and bewildered— when she needed a friend the most.

In a thank you note to Eva, she wrote: "How much it does help to have someone to count on, and what a steadfast anchor it is to know there's someone nearby on whom one can absolutely, unreservedly and undeservedly depend, not just in the big crises and troubles, but in the everyday joys and satisfactions too. I can always, always count on you Eva, but I don't suppose you or anyone can imagine how like a little lost dog I was feeling before I had you to count on. . . . Thank you for being my best friend."[13]

I think I must have met you long ago,
For when I think of all the years gone by,
There seems no moment when I did not know
You well, and love you deeply, and rely
Upon the daily wonder of your love
For rich delight and comfort in distress
As I rely upon the sky above
With perfect knowledge of its power to bless.
I met you, surely, in my youngest dreams
Of friendship, dreams so long relinquished,
    stilled
By all-engulfing loneliness, it seems
A dream that all the dreams have been fulfilled.
I met you long ago, for you are part
Of all the deepest longings of my heart.
                                        "Lately Met"

8
DELIGHT IN DUTY
1951–1952

It is, no doubt, the duty of a lark
To sing, the obligation of a thrush
In leafy sanctuary, to remark
With lyric syllables upon the hush

Of reverence that necessarily
Accompanies a sunset; and a wren,
In May, would surely be remiss if he
Should fail to utter rapture now and then.

It would be censurable indeed if one
With music in him should refuse to sing;
But oh, that men, like meadow lark in sun,
Could do their destined, their appointed thing

Without suspecting duty could be less
Than pure delight and perfect loveliness!

In March 1950, when terror of blindness threatened to overcome her, Jane read *I Will Lift Up Mine Eyes* by Glenn Clark. She dared to pray specifically for her "soul's sincere desire": to have a book published, "but at no cost, by some good publisher."[1]

Aunt Laura had offered to pay for the printing of a poetry collection, but Jane had no intention of accepting money—even from kin. The very principle of self-publishing went against her "stubborn conviction that poets are laborers worthy of their hire," she wrote a friend.[2]

The subject of a book came up from time to time in conversations and letters, but Jane made no commitment. Her soul's sincere desire was a secret and private prayer, given words in "For Loveliness."

Along with all the beauty of thy world
That thou has given me, dear Lord, to see,

Along with dawns, and brilliant clouds unfurled
From mountain peaks, and varied artistry
Of shell and spider web to marvel at,
And myriad excellence in shape and hue
Of flower and leaf and wing, my prayer is that
Thou give, as well, some work that I can do.

Some work to do for thee, that shall express
My thanks, as words cannot; the humblest task
May offer gratitude for loveliness,
And since thy world is lovely, I would ask
To work with heart and hand and mind and will
To make it, if I may, more lovely still.

The greatest obstacle to her dream, as she saw it, was not just in finding a royalty-paying publisher, but the very real possibility that her poetic energies were expended. Outwardly she was her cheerful self, inviting laughter with her quick wit, ready to encourage the downcast in person or by mail. No one knew the great effort it often required. Only in her diary did Jane confess how much the last years had drained her of zest and hope, until there seemed to be "nothing left but endurance."[3]

But now she had Eva, and to her friend Jane dared admit that her mind was no longer as alert as it had once been. Often she was sluggish and forgetful, "less able to create."[4]

Making light of the matter, she quoted "Undone":

My feet feel mired
And my head feels hazy.
I hope I'm tired,
But I fear I'm lazy.

Eva was not alarmed. She was certain that Jane's loss of energy was a normal symptom of grief after the death of her father. Soon it would pass, and her career would gain momentum. Eva could report praise from readers who eagerly hailed each new poem in print and could hardly wait for more.

What was meant as encouragement had the opposite effect on Jane. Praise from readers usually triggered "a panicky feeling," she lamented, a dreadful fear that she would "never be able to write anything again,"[5] causing her to try "too hard, probably," but with little results. The mere thought of readers turning the pages of each new issue of the *Post* looking for "Jane-poems" brought a new wave of weariness to her.

Eva had quickly realized her mistake and made it clear that her love of Jane's poetry was by now far exceeded by her love for Jane herself, with or without poems.

Jane was immensely relieved and confessed that she had felt almost dishonest about enjoying the friendship, since it had begun with Eva's interest in her poetry. Now she could relax.

The fear of never being able to write again is common to writers, but Jane had a habit of playing down her accomplishments and talents. It was an obvious defense against high expectations—and disappointments. But it was also a cultural response, the heritage of mountain farmers who worked a poor soil in fickle weather. They knew better than to count their gain before the harvest was in, and they considered it bad manners to boast of their own accomplishments—or even admit they were pleased with them.

Eva was determined to encourage a more confident attitude and she took Jane to task for every exaggerated display of modesty. Eva was as frank in criticism as she was in praise of a poem, and Jane soon came to trust her. If Eva rated a piece of work as "not one of your better ones," Jane took her advice and put it aside.

When editors returned a batch with rejection slips, Eva provided a reliable second opinion. Editors, it seemed, were not infallible in their judgment. One of them rejected "Tenacious Is the Heart" because it was "unclear to the reader," and Jane was afraid the poem was "too personal and obscure for publication" *(Venable, Dec. 16, 1950)*. Eva disagreed. She thought the writing was clear enough. Any problem with understanding would be the reader's fault. The work sold to the next editor without changes.

> Whatever loveliness the heart has found
> It will remember. Shaken with distress,
> And wild with weeping, it recalls the sound
> Of thrushes' song in twilight loneliness,
>
> And is not desolate. Beset by new
> Dismay, or heavy with familiar woe,
> It finds relief in unforgotten dew
> On little leaves, where little breezes blow.
>
> Tenacious is the heart of every frail
> Least loveliness the stricken must not miss
> Lest faith should perish. Delicate its scale
> Of balance whereon one instant's bliss
>
> Of petals shaken from an April tree
> Outweighs uncounted hours of agony.

The message was beginning to sink in. Jane's "perpetual dissatisfaction" with her writing was perhaps not entirely justified. It seemed to her too good to be true that readers would like best the things she really wanted to write, as Eva kept telling her, but sales were proving it, again and again.

Others were affirming it as well. Eva introduced her to Josephine Breeding, president of the Knoxville branch of the Pen Women of America. Jane was persuaded to join the organization, and she soon had a whole new band of boosters who proudly claimed her as Knoxville's star member.

Reader letters came from afar, but Jane especially cherished one from Dr. Hoffmann across the boulevard: "I have read your 'Growing Days' in the *Saturday Evening Post* with much interest. I like the homey spirit of it. The thought in it is so sound. We, who teach, tend to make assignments and to 'pile it on.' We should remember, I guess, 'No use to give them things . . . unless you give them time to keep them, too.'"[6]

> "You've had as much excitement as you should,"
> Our mother very often used to say.
> "The fun you've had won't do you any good
> Till it has settled down in you to stay.
> Go listen to the creek and nibble cress,
> Go count the grass and catch up to your living."
> So we would revel in green idleness
> And never realize what she was giving;
>
> A chance to savor new experience slowly
> And thoroughly, assimilating all
> Its deep significance, till it was wholly
> Our own past any possible recall.
> "No use to give them things," she always knew,
> "Unless you give them time to keep them, too."

Dr. Hoffmann became the inspiration of several poems. Eva knew his grown children, and she had been told how he taught them about nature with tales, beginning, "When *I* was a toad" or "When *I* was a cornstalk." Inspired by this, Jane wrote "Grandfather's Transmigrations," a quick sale to the *Post*.

> "When I was a cornstalk," Gramp would say.
> Or, "When I was a duck, migrating—"
> There wasn't a thing he had never been,
> And he had a way of relating
> Experiences that made us look
> With vast commiseration
> At children whose grandpas weren't pigs or fish
> In a previous incarnation.
> And even when we became aware,
> Astonished to perceive it,
> That he was never really a frog,
> We didn't quite believe it!

"Dr. Cornstalk," as they fondly called him, continued to take an interest in Jane's writing. He thought she had much to teach about rearing the young. Eva agreed and suggested that Jane write a book on her home schooling, with advice for teachers and parents. Eva felt that Jane had been fortunate to escape the mediocrity taught in public schools.

It was a flattering challenge, but Jane felt poorly equipped to meet it. She remembered few actual details of her early education and didn't have the energy to complete a large project. Besides, a few lines of poetry in the *Post* paid more than a long prose piece in a smaller magazine.

She wasn't mercenary, but it was, after all, what Eva called "a fortunate need"—economic necessity—that spurred her on to write and sell. Jane would have much preferred to do as Emily Dickinson had: write solely for herself and hide the result from the embarrassment of public scrutiny and rejection.

Eva could see her point. Jane's strength was in poetry, and she often taught more in a few lines than many a pedantic text. No more was said about writing prose, but Eva was quick to point out lesson topics for poems. Jane had noted that "treasured small people and treasured small objects are mutually incompatible." Eva responded: "Haven't you a good start for a rhyme in that statement? It seems too good to waste just on me" *(Letter to Jane, Dec. 29, 1950).*

The result may have been "Heirloom."

> The cup my great-grandmother brought
> A thousand miles or more
> To make a home of wilderness
> Lies broken on the floor.
>
> The fragile, gently cherished cup
> From which she drank delight
> Lies broken by a careless girl
> Who looks at me in fright.
>
> My great-grandmother was too kind
> For any heart to shatter
> About her cup; I smile, and say,
> "My dear, it doesn't matter."

"There are more poems in your letters . . . waiting to be written, if I could just get up steam enough to write them," Jane acknowledged. "I think I'll refer to you as my collaborator, and perhaps offer you a sales commission."[7]

Suggestions were not always welcome, she explained in a letter. Deep, spontaneous enjoyment would usually turn itself into a poem eventually. "That sounds as if I believe only in 'inspiration,' doesn't it? Well, in a way I do—not the kind of irresistible, white hot flash that gets a poem down on paper at unpredictable moments without the writer knowing how it is done; such moments come rarely, and if writers waited for them, there would be very little writing done, ever.

"But one can daily, by self-discipline—and it takes a great deal of it—prepare . . . with paper and pen and a quiet, uncluttered mind to seek for, and be available to inspiration; the half-pleasurable, half-painful moment when, out of all the impressions and thoughts and feelings in one's mind, a word or phrase or emotion becomes urgent and one knows that one has, finally, something to say, and settles down to the anxious, demanding task of saying it as well as possible.

"That sounds like quite a bit of effort to expand on the bits of nothing which many of my rhymes are, but it's usually much harder to write a poor verse than a good one, because a good one is more anxious to be written than a poor one, and helps itself more . . . and if one doesn't keep in practice by writing poor ones, if that's all one can do at times, one is pretty certain not to write a good one."

She apologized for writing at such length about her own doings. "It's your own fault. . . . You make me feel you are interested in whatever I'm interested in—thus making me more interested in everything than I would be otherwise."[8]

That was precisely what Eva had hoped for. Jane's energy was returning, her approach to writing more professional. In her notebook, she drafted "Advice to Aspiring Writers," addressed to herself. "I give my whole attention and mind to whatever I'm doing at the moment . . . unhampered by any feeling that it is trivial, unworthy, or profitless. Forget time, forget pay, forget myself, forget everything except the task at hand. And if I spend all morning finding one right word, or even in deciding that no word is right, the time is well spent.

"Don't work for too long on any one verse. Poems need to mellow. Put them away after the first draft for a day or two, or several days, and go to something else. If they don't jell, even after several attempts, don't be discouraged. Above all, *don't tear them up!* Put them away again, without anxiety or frustration, for a week or a month or a year, and when I least expect it, the right idea or phrase will come. . . . Merely have faith and wait. And meanwhile, work.

"Never send in a verse merely because it is time to send one. . . . unless the verses are finished, mellowed, ripe. I've tried the other course with the *Post,* without success. Write first of all for myself and only secondarily for editors. If I'm trying to please everybody, I'm pretty sure to please nobody. If the thing is true, the market will be found.

"Be on the alert for suggestions, illuminating ideas, poems, material, in all I read. Whenever anything strikes an emotional spark, *stop* and consider it. Jot it down. Don't shut it off to think about tomorrow. When I get an idea, if I crochet, put it down. That's the best time for getting ideas. The actual writing time, important as it is, is the least of writing. Writing is a full time job, however much I might wish sometimes that it weren't" *(Notebook, undated).*

Poems often sprang from odd sources. Jane described the origin of "Grandfather's Shock Absorber" to Eva: "You remember last winter all the furor over mercy killings, and all the arguments which professed humanitarians advanced to prove that mercy killing is truly benevolent and ethical, etc., etc. I remarked to Mother that I had too much faith in human cussedness ever to want that much power legalized, and from that remark, much later [the poem] was written. The story used as an illustration as was suggested . . . I think, by an incident . . . in a book I read ages ago. I'm usually astonished when I start trying to figure out where a rhyme comes from, what long forgotten incidents, either read or seen, go into it" *(Venable, Jan. 22, 1951).*

> Grandfather Robbins always treated others
> Exactly as he wanted to be treated.
> He practiced his belief that men are brothers;
> The poorest tramps and vagabonds were seated
> As promptly at his table as deacons were
> And given all his help; yet when a pair
> Of them made off with Grandma's cherished fur
> Neckpiece, Grandfather never turned a hair.
> "Of course I realized they might be bad,"
> He said with perfect equanimity.
> "It's right to deal with men as if you had
> Unbounded faith in human decency;
> But you'll be in for quite a shock, unless
> You keep some faith in human cussedness."
>
> (original version)

Grandfather Robbins was a fictional character, named after the jaunty robins who patrolled the garden. Later—so that no one named Robbins would take offense—Jane changed the first line to: "Grandfather has a way of treating others" *(Venable, Jan. 22, 1951).*

Eva voiced the question many readers asked: how could Jane write with such insight of things she had never seen or done herself? Jane replied: "I seldom write of things I haven't verified for myself and I'm always uncomfortable when I have to say, 'Well so and so says it does,' of something I have written. And yet, writing about things is a form of experiencing them, isn't it? I don't know that I actually saw a bur oak fighting the wind, as in the 'Staying Power' verse, but I had been reading of how trees, especially oaks, seem to enjoy their struggle with storms, and I've often thought the same thing myself, watching winter trees. . . . (Of course, writing only of the way things look to *me* doesn't guarantee accuracy, but at least any errors will be my own.)''⁹

The first lines of the sonnet ''Staying Power'' read:

> The blizzard winds are snarling for a fight
> They'll try again to get the bur oak down.
> But watch it meet them with the huge delight
> It always seems to feel from trunk to crown
> At tangling with its wild antagonists.

Letters from her friends furnished much vicarious living experience, and so did books. Eva brought armloads each week, and when Central High closed for the summer, Jane was able to borrow library reference volumes. She found much delight in the illustrated Audubon book on birds, but she wrote wistfully afterwards: ''There's a special wonder and satisfaction and unmistakeable reality of the actual seeing, and I always prize with particular astonishment the one goldfinch I have actually seen.''¹⁰

In her sonnet ''Sunflower'' are the lines:

> And one who has not seen, in vivid hours,
> A goldfinch gleaming in the great green leaves,
> Glad for the good provision it receives,
> Has never learned, joy-smitten, wonder-stirred,
> Exactly how it feels to be a bird.

Seeing just one bird, or one flower was enough to know something of them all. In ''Jonquil Lore'' Jane wrote:

> I never saw bright beds of jonquils blooming
> In golden hosts beneath new-greening trees,
> A tapestry of springtime's deftest looming
> From all of earth's enchanted gaieties.
> But I have seen one jonquil flouting snow,
> Lonely and frail and blithely unafraid,
> Warming the sun with its exultant glow
> Of concentrated courage on parade;
> And thus I've learned as much of jonquil lore
> As if I'd seen a million blooms or more.

Her ability to identify with her object was born of a strong sense of oneness with all living, growing things. How else could she, who had never walked, know the truth of ''Surefooted''?

> A child must walk barefooted in wet grass
> A child must walk barefooted in hot dust,

Barefooted in cool softness of mud.
A child cannot explain it, but he must
Feel how his arches fit the arch of earth,
Feel how his feet fit all earth's various ways.
A child must walk barefooted through his summers
That he may walk surefooted all his days.

"The 'I' in my rhymes isn't always me, but just as I would feel if I were someone else," she explained to Eva. "I don't think that expressing other people's emotions is . . . insincerity—rather it's a sort of empathy, isn't it?" *(Venable, July 29, 1951).*

Her insight into the human heart made it all too easy to see the failings and flaws of others and to be scornful instead of kind. It was necessary to remind herself that what she saw in others were traits that lurked in her own heart as well. Her poems were meant to enlighten, not to expose, and that was better done with a chuckle than a jeer.

All her early sales to the *Post,* her most reliable high paying market, had been humorous four-liners, and she had long feared that her more serious work was not good enough. "The prospect of doing only 'funny' things was a most appalling one," she wrote to Eva. "The only thing worse than a verse that tries to be funny and isn't, is one that isn't meant to be funny and is, and it seemed for a time that all my things fell into one category or the other. And the harder I tried to write funny things, the more sad, solemn things I wrote!"[11]

The hazard was as much the other way. When she was at her most earnest and solemn in a sonnet her mind could take a sudden turn and produce a "sassy four-liner." It was small consolation that with all her broken bones, her "funny bone, at least, had never been broken."[12]

Eva and Carolyn Ruth met via mail and telephone, and they freely exchanged copies of Jane's poems. Jane found it necessary to remind Carolyn Ruth of her promise to keep unpublished poetry to herself. Eva showed no reticence in lending her scrapbook of printed poems "on the slighest provocation," Jane lamented to Carolyn Ruth. Once she lent it to an exhibit when Jane refused the use of her own.[13]

Modesty was still a strong deterrent, but under Eva's influence, Jane was overcoming some of her shyness. Her letters revealed a new boldness, even if she qualified statements with, "Eva suggests," "Eva insists," "Eva won't take no for an answer," or "When Eva wishes to be contrary, I seldom interfere."

In truth, Jane was not likely to submit to any proposal she didn't fully agree with, and Eva was well aware of it. In 1951 Eva taught summer school at State Teacher's College in Milwaukee, Wisconsin, and didn't tell Jane that she was taking her scrapbook to show other faculty members who were writers or college English teachers, many with doctoral degrees. But she wrote that they were impressed with "the extraordinary consciousness of the exact shadings of word meanings and usage" in the poetry and that they read passages out loud to one another, over and over.

The time had now come, Eva thought, to promote the book idea again. She offered to visit publishers anywhere in the nation on Jane's behalf—or pay expenses of self-publishing. A book would put the poems in wider distribution, she argued, and "more permanent preservation."[14]

The offer was tactfully refused, but Jane had confessed to giving permission for a public poetry reading by Virginia Peace at Bethany Hills, near Nashville, and Eva was delighted. In her opinion, Jane had "hidden her light under a bushel," and had been entirely too modest, instead of allowing others to benefit from the inspiration of her life and poetry. Jane's quick retort was "Measured."

> The charge you make, that
>   I'm unduly modest,
> I must refute, at risk of
>   seeming gruff.
> I never hide my light
>   beneath a bushel;
> I've always found a
>   peck quite large enough.

The Nashville reading was a definite success. Elizabeth attended and came home full of enthusiasm. Several people had asked where they might buy copies of Jane's poems. The idea of a book was suddenly the main topic of conversation. Donia, who was usually reticent, mentioned it to Mrs. Hoffmann, and that evening Dr. Hoffmann sat on the Doll House terrace beneath Jane's open window, eagerly explaining to Elizabeth all he knew about publishing books.

It had all happened too fast for Jane to prevent it. She would, of course, *like* to have a book sometime, she wrote Eva, but she knew the difficulties and wasn't at all ready to attempt it now, "if ever." And she had not expected to have it discussed "outside the family!"[15]

Jane had, in fact, been toying with the idea of making a book proposal to one of the large publishing houses, but she would keep it secret unless she succeeded. Too many people expected too much of her. What would they say if she failed? She'd rather not find out.

For the moment, she discouraged all further talk about a book, but with her next submission to the *Post,* she asked about book rights to printed poems. Peggy Dowst Redman replied that book rights automatically reverted to the writer once the poem was printed, and she sent her best wishes for "the book project."

At least Mrs. Redman had not been discouraging. With a surge of optimism, Jane wrote to Eva: "I had about decided that my poetic license had permanently expired, but . . . I'm hoping that . . . was just the result of being completely tired out, mentally and physically, and . . . now I am feeling so much better and happier—largely because of you—I may be able really to get into writing again" *(Venable, July 29, 1951)*.

Some time later she sent a proposal for a poetry collection to a major publishing house, but when they rejected it, Jane destroyed all tell-tale correspondence and buried her disappointment. She was grateful for the shroud of secrecy and for the brisk magazine sales.

The year had produced 120 poems, and she recorded in her diary: "I have sold or had accepted exactly 100 verses. It seems rather incredible to me that this can be true. . . . At least I know that my eyes can take it far better than I thought last year . . . and with God's help I'll use them more judiciously."

Her income for the year was the best yet. As for the book, she had committed it to God. If it be his will, "He'll open a way for me to have it, without compromising my ideals. And if He doesn't want it, I don't either" *(Diary, Dec. 31, 1951)*.

God knew her soul's sincere desire for a book, but she feared the public attention such an accomplishment would bring. Her greatest desire was to be what God wanted. If she could serve him—and help her family—in a quiet, unobtrusive way, she would be gratified.

Earlier in the year she had sold "The Idle Grass" to the *Washington Evening Star*. Eva thought it one of the best Jane had written.

> The grass has nothing to do but grow,
> Nothing to do all day
> Except to practice being green
> And ripple and surge and sway,
> Giving the fluent contoured grace
> Of sea to stubborn soil.
> Oh, fortunate is the idle grass,
> Exempt from any toil,
> With nothing to do all day but be
> Green in sunny weather,
> Nothing to do but feed mankind
> And hold the earth together.

She had done a meditation in prose on the same subject. "To make our days as deeply rooted in the eternal Source of life as grass is rooted in the steadfast earth, to make our days as merciful and kind, as full of love for all . . . as is the universal grass that gives itself abundantly, scorning no neediest or meanest place, that nourishes and gladdens . . . would not that be an ideal worth attaining?''[16]

The less attention she called to herself the better. But in the spring of 1952, Jane allowed *The Progressive Farmer* to publish a feature article on her life and work, written by Lillian Keller. It immediately rekindled talk about a book, and the Knoxville Pen Women proposed to print a collection of her poems. Jane firmly squelched the notion. If any books were to be printed, an established publisher would have to do it, and that didn't seem likely.

Then in September *The Volta Review,* a national magazine for the deaf, printed her own lengthy autobiographical article with several poems. It was the sort of thing Jane disliked exceedingly, she lamented to Carolyn Ruth. But it meant an opportunity to express appreciation for her mother and to encourage the deaf. If her story need be told, she would rather do it herself—and get paid for it—than suffer the exaggerations of others.[17]

The sudden willingness to endure publicity had much to do with the ''fortunate need'': economic pressure. Poetry markets had taken a drastic plunge. Though Jane was writing more—150 poems in 1952—she had sold less. In October she wrote a note to Eva, who was ill and had missed their Friday visit. ''I needed you this afternoon. I got twenty-eight verses back . . . and no sales.''[18]

In a lighter mood, she called her poems ''applications for rejection slips,'' but receiving them was shattering. An ''overdose'' of them prompted ''Time Out.''

> I have given myself a little while
> In which to remember how to smile.
>
> I will not think, or speak, or act,
> Or weep. I will wait. And the numbing fact
>
> Will grow familiar, and I will face
> It—sooner or later—with smiling grace.
>
> I will not wonder, since hearts grow tough,
> Whether a lifetime is long enough.

In November 1952—after a long look at the dismal magazine market—Jane decided to try for a book again. She sent a handful of the poems Eva and others had praised most highly with a query letter to Abingdon-Cokesbury, the Methodist Publishing House.

Her diary in December noted: ''I expected a plain 'No,' but they want to consider them longer—something to hope for over Christmas anyhow! Haven't mentioned it to anyone!''

Her prayer ''For All People'' had sold that year. The second stanza was her own heart's cry:

> God bless and fortify them,
>   God hear when they entreat,
> The strong, courageous people
>   Too brave to own defeat.
>
> And oh, God bless and help them,
>   God answer when they call,
> The tired, defeated people
>   Who are not brave at all.

9
THE GREATEST
OF THESE
1953–1955

Men send their speech across blue miles of space,
Across great continents their words ring clear,
Yet all their eloquence does not efface
The mountain barriers of hate and fear.
Men chart the heavens' mysteries, have explained
The atom, given their bodies to be burned
In war's fierce hells; and yet have never gained
The good for which their hearts have always yearned.

And I—ah, well indeed, dear Lord, I know
That all that I can say, or think, or do
Is utter nothingness, an idle show,
If I have not deep love, sincere and true;
Love for thy loveliness in star and tree,
Love for my fellow men, pure love for thee.
"If I Have Not Love"

Jane grew more tense each day she waited for word from Abingdon. In January she developed familiar symptoms of stress and fatigue: heart beating abnormaly fast, neck so stiff with neuralgia that she couldn't turn her head. The doctor prescribed medicine and hot towels for her neck and more rest for her heart. But anxious thoughts multiplied with each mail delivery, and the physical troubles evoked old fears that she would become unable even to use the typewriter.

Such doomsday predictions would soon put her in despair. It was an old stratagem; expecting the worst to guard against disappointments. She ought to know by now it didn't work!

In her diary, Jane reminded herself of reasons to be grateful. She was less fearful now than a year ago. She was more experienced at living in "precarious circumstances"—three women alone with only God to help. But he had provided more than she could have thought to ask for. He would preserve them still from sorrow or give strength to bear what must be. Whatever happened, she would keep faith in life and its possibilities.

Her troubles and weaknesses were fit reminders of the line she had marked in Psalm 39: "That I may know how frail I am." Yes, indeed, she was "frail in body and spirit, and utterly dependent on the Lord."

February came without word from Abingdon. Jane caught flu and was "tired to death and edgy," she confided in her diary. She was tired of everything—her room; the house; the bleak winter street where children, bundled against the cold, hurried to school without as much as a glance at her window. She was tired of the monotony of her days, with the "ever present, insoluble problems" *(Diary, Feb. 8, 1953)*.

Outwardly she tried to remain cheerful while feeling "inwardly cross, critical and unloving." If only Abingdon would hurry up with their rejection of her book proposal! At least it would put an end to her uncertainty—and yet, in the next instant she was glad it hadn't arrived. As long as she didn't have a definite no, there was hope for a yes.

Her career in writing seemed to hang in the balance. The poetry market was definitely dwindling, and she had little energy for essays or stories. What could she do? At the moment she didn't feel like writing at all, but that was no excuse. She could not allow uncertainty to stifle her ambition nor let anxiety affect her attitude toward people—those who loved and cared for her and editors who were still buying. She must keep trying, keep doing—and keep smiling!

On the fifteenth of February Jane recorded in her diary that she was "renewing her resolves" and praying for help to remember that "any sincere effort counts, even if it seems outwardly unproductive."

> If for one day
> I can forget
> The nagging care,
> The needless fret;
>
> For one day, keep
> My spirit clear
> From anxious doubt
> And useless fear;
>
> If for one day
> I can believe
> In life, and joyously
> Receive
>
> The blessings that
> Are always mine
> Of earth and air
> And love divine—

Oh, then at last,
At last, I may
Learn how to do it
Every day.
"If for One Day"

The outcome of the book proposal was still pending and Jane asked a more important question of herself: how was she "serving God, living love"? She was "no saint or mystic," but like them she must seek to love God first, with all her heart and mind and strength. She must love Him and serve him in her own way and place. But how could she be certain that her way was his? "So many voices say so many things, and I am fond of doing as I please, of thinking as I choose. Of having people think me good and wise when I am not. Help me, oh, Lord, make known your will for me" *(Diary, Feb. 15, 1953).*

Quite suddenly their small world was shaken with news that made all other concerns seem minor: Annie Venable, who lived at home with Eva and their widowed mother, took ill with flu-like symptoms and within three days was dead.

In her note to Eva and her mother, Jane sent "For Annie."

If there are seasons in eternity,
    A time of flowering in the home of prayer,
Then surely it is spring in heaven now
    Since she is there.

"You must be feeling as I felt about my Dad. However faithfully we believe 'He is not here, He is risen' applies to every follower of Christ, it is easy to lose the 'He is risen' in the lonely sadness of 'He is not here.' Mother is making bread for you. I wish I could send you the odor of it baking."[1]

Whenever any loved familiar friend
Or neighbor learns the lonely ways of grief,
My mother bakes large loaves of bread to send,
Knowing no surer way to give relief.
"There is a time for cookies, pies and cakes,"
She says, "A time for fancy, rich desserts,
But not when trouble's in the house; it takes
A sturdier food to ease the sudden hurts
That come to all. Bread has the quiet power
Of sun and earth to reassure folk's hearts
And give them courage in the saddest hour.
In easier times they relish cakes and tarts,
But when a trouble's new they need, instead,
The good, plain comfort of a loaf of bread."
                                        "Plain Comfort"

After the funeral, Eva gave Jane a book of devotions Annie had been fond of: *Daily Strength for Daily Need.* Jane marked a passage to read regularly against self-pity. The author was the eighteenth-century mystic William Law, and his text was based on the scripture, "Beloved, think it not strange concerning the fiery trial which is to try you, as though some strange thing happened unto you, but rejoice, inasmuch as ye are partakers of Christ's sufferings" (I Pet. 4:12-13).

Law wrote: "Receive every inward and outward trouble . . . with both thy hands, as a true opportunity and blessed occasion of dying to self, and entering into a fuller fellowship with thy self-denying, suffering Saviour . . . and then every kind of trial and distress will become the blessed day of thy prosperity."

Jane would try to greet the rejection of her book proposal as a blessed day of prosperity, and in the meantime her mail brought happier surprises. She was named Pen Woman of the month for March and was profiled in the Pen Women's magazine. Her poems appeared in sixteen different publications, bringing the total in print to over three hundred.

Then, when signs of spring had come in earnest, with swollen buds and crocus blooms, the mailman delivered the letter from Abingdon. It was not the bulky self-addressed manila envelope Jane had been expecting, but a slim white one with the publisher's logo in the upper left corner. With racing heart and trembling hands, she opened it and scanned the lines. Editor Robert Roy Wright wrote matter-of-factly that although Abingdon could not publish poetry alone, they liked her work. If she cared to try a devotional book, they wanted to see a thirty-page sampler.

It was not what she had hoped for, but the door had not slammed shut. It was left slightly ajar, and that was enough of a miracle for now. She would try the sampler, but to be on the safe side, she would tell only her mother and sisters, Eva, and Elaine V. Emans, fellow poet and pen-friend. They would keep her secret.

Eva's indexed scrapbook was in California with Carolyn Ruth, and Jane asked to have it returned, deliberately obscuring the reason. "I had hope of using it in compiling a selection of my stuff for a book publisher who showed a few signs of interest, but I'm afraid nothing is going to come of that, after all, though I was rather excited about it at the time."[2]

To focus the letter on something other than a possible book, Jane enclosed a clipping from the Knoxville *Journal,* a three-column wide front page picture of herself, her mother, and Elizabeth under the headline: "Acclaim as Poet Is Won by Invalid."

The story—with the details of her handicap—distressed her, but the picture was the best she had seen of herself and Donia for years. Perhaps it was because she was smiling, showing her new front tooth! She had finally agreed to spend money on filling the gaping hole. Now she could admit it had embarrassed her as much as the more publicized handicaps and had taken "as much Christian fortitude to bear."[3]

Publicity about her "peculiar circumstances" always evoked fears that her poetry would be accepted for pity's sake—a worse fate than honest rejection.

In "Purchase" she wrote:

> I almost bought a dozen combs today,
> A dozen combs I didn't need at all,
> Because the thin boy offering the array,
> At the back door, of various large and small
> Combs of all kinds and colors, when I said,
> "Good morning," showed me, with a resolute
> White face, a narrow card on which I read
> The neatly lettered words, "I'm deaf and mute."
>
> A thrush was singing then. I would have bought
> His whole supply, but that his look forbade
> My charity; so after careful thought
> I took just one, the finest one he had.
> I could not sleep tonight if I had tried
> To buy his courage of him, and his pride.

It was one of the poems she wanted to use in her book, with the meditation: "O Father of compassionate understanding, give us imaginative sympathy and warmth of heart to enter into the feelings of others. Let us never offer other people the pity that we would not accept ourselves, that would destroy their self-respect. Lord, help us to give, rather, the compassion that helps them to help themselves."[4]

The sampler was ready in June, and when it was off to Abingdon, Jane felt worn out and empty. She admitted to Eva that she was bored with her own writing, "plumb tired of rummaging around in my own thoughts day after day."[5]

In "First Person Singular," she wrote:

> I've spent all day arranging my
> Affairs, and doing just what I
> Desired. It's been a total loss.
> I'm tired, discouraged, bored, and cross,
> And even I myself can see
> I've had an overdose of me.

It was summer and family time, and Jane tried to suspend all anxious thoughts about her sampler in the hands of Abingdon editors. Ruth's fourth baby arrived in July, and Jane was glad to be making tiny baby things with needles and yarn. With all attention focused on wee Margaret Lee, no one was apt to ask more than politely about writing.

In September came the editorial verdict: Mr. Wright wrote that they were pleased and wanted a book! Since this was her first attempt, the editor thought to help by sending two recent devotional books by popular authors. They became instead an immediate hindrance. Jane invariably compared herself to the highly qualified authors and felt woefully inferior. Her first attempts at meditations read like poor imitations of her forerunners. Not until she set them aside and realized that for better or worse she best be herself did her writing begin to take shape.

The theme of her book had suggested itself from the start: Paul's hymn to love from the thirteenth chapter of his letter to the Corinthians—the chapter she had memorized at seventeen and had been comforted and challenged by since. In the preface she voiced her "earnest hope that these poems and prayers may help deepen the reader's responsiveness to the love of God, and to others' need of love in daily living." Before Thanksgiving, the completed draft of *The Greatest of These* was in the mail, dedicated "in loving gratitude, to my mother."

The work had taken much of the year, but Jane had sold 130 poems as well, and her earnings were up from the slow year before. Even if Abingdon rejected the book, she had learned much from doing it, and she felt more hopeful of surviving in a competitive poetry market. That hope grew stronger in January when she won first prize in the first annual contest of the Poetry Society of Tennessee. It was her very *first* first prize, she wrote to Shirley Kerr, a new correspondent and fan in Virginia. The poem that won was "Tennessee."

> There may be fairer country than these valleys
> That look up, each one, at a hazy hill.
> There may be country better made for living.
> I haven't seen it though. I never will.
>
> There may be better people than these people,
> People with less about them to object to,
> People with kinder hearts and braver spirits.
> I haven't met them though. I don't expect to.
>
> This Tennessee hill country and its people
> Are mine, this haze my breath, these hills my bone.
> There may be fairer country, better people,
> But these are what I know. These are my own.

Robert Roy Wright called from Nashville in February. The editorial board was pleased with her draft, but wanted a few changes. He would come by to discuss them, if that was convenient. With considerable trepidation, Jane told Donia to bid him welcome. She might have been less fearful had she known how much he admired her poems—without knowing anything of her physical handicap—and how eager he was to meet her.

When his taxi from the airport stopped outside the Doll House, Jane was watching from the window. Donia greeted him at the door, explaining that Jane was deaf and that they would converse in writing. Then she ushered him into the sunny dining room where Jane was waiting, smiling and self-possessed.

Robert Roy Wright saw a young woman reclining against a cluster of pillows in a small white bed. She wore a soft blue-as-her-eyes day gown with a lace collar. She bid him warmly welcome, and he was instantly captivated by her.

Jane was thirty-four, but looked ten years younger. She measured only forty-eight inches, and her face—with smooth complexion, bright, perceptive eyes, and quick smile—seemed ageless and vibrantly alive. On special occasions, like this one, she powdered her nose and put on lipstick.

The meeting was a happy one. Each recognized a kindred spirit, and communication was easy. He knew her talent, and she trusted him. Their wits matched, and they exchanged jokes and puns while working out the details of the manuscript—"Little matters of editorial quibbling," he called it later, "not very weighty in the balances against a really creative talent."[6]

Already on the first day of March the revised manuscript was back in the mail, and just over two weeks later came the "quite enthusiastic acceptance." Then it was proofreading, grueling for a perfectionist, even with Eva reading the proofs. The exertion and anxiety brought a flare-up of neuralgia.

Finally, in May, the page proofs were in Jane's file and the publishing date was set for September. Now at last she dared to tell her friends. They were, of course, ecstatic, but she herself was worn out. The work had been more taxing and involved than she had anticipated. Had she known as much beforehand, she might not have dared try it at all, she confided in her diary. How "piously presumptuous" it was of her to have written a book of devotions—for "unworthy reasons" and with "no real qualifications" *(Diary, May 10, 1954).*

The "unworthy reasons" were her need to earn money and her desire to please family and friends with her accomplishments. Jane suspected that she shared with other "handicapped people a deeper urge than most to prove themselves worthy." It was, perhaps, not a bad urge, she wrote later to a friend. She would rather have it than the opposite: the inertia of doing less than she could.

Almost worse were the moments of conviction that her writing was not good enough—no matter what Eva and others believed. In the manuscript was "Little Songs." The last stanza read:

> Although our music be subdued,
> Our God is listening
> To little songs of gratitude
> That anyone can sing.

The thought of placing her little songs of gratitude before the public in a book was frightening. The poems and prayers were outpourings from her heart to God alone, and so it ought to remain. And yet, she had prayed in all sincerity for "some work to do for Thee" and couldn't refuse when it was asked of her, even if her motives were impure and she was unworthy.

Now it was done, and she counted it a miracle. It had seemed virtually impossible in March 1950, when she first dared pray for a book, while terror of blindness dimmed all hope.

Rest behind dark compresses was still necessary, but hour-long enforced suspensions of physical activities were fruitful times of thinking or praying and for practicing patience, learning to abide in the One she knew herself utterly dependent on. The past year had brought a stronger sense of inner equilibrium, Jane noted in her diary. Experience, as well as faith, had taught her the use of difficulties as disciplines. Hard, hurtful things were often as much evidence of God's love as the pleasant, easy things. That was a truth to be lived and learned in new ways again and again *(Diary, May 10, 1954)*.

Getting copyright clearances from magazine publishers was an exasperating part of the book making process. Jane did it so quickly and efficiently that her editor commented later, "She was a publisher's dream of a perfect author."[7] But Jane was exhausted afterwards and confided in her diary: "I'm weary of writing verse at all, which having said it on paper to myself, I'm certainly not going to say out loud to anyone!" *(Diary, May 16, 1954)*.

It was hardly the thing to confess just as her first book was about to be launched. She was thankful the day of reckoning was still months away. Summer had arrived with visits and family activities. Jane had little time to think and less to write without interruptions. Their small house was brimful with six grandchildren, and Jane was "an aunt, not a poet" for the duration, she observed to Shirley. "And *ants* are notably practical and unpoetic creatures!"[8]

She wrote only two poems during those four weeks. One was "First Time."

The new house has a most astonished air,
With curtains wrinkled, and with blinds awry,
No longer trimly neat, it seems to stare
With curiously apprehensive eye
At little girls who leave mud pies to scorch
Upon its steps while chasing little boys
All up and down the uprights of its porch
With clamorous, before unheard-of noise.
There's ample reason for its glassy gaze;
It's new and unprepared for manic stunts
And its owner never before in all its days
Had six grandchildren visiting at once!

With only weeks to go before the birthday of her own first "offspring," Jane's anxiety was growing. There was talk of an autograph tea (though she wouldn't be there, of course) and advance publicity. There was much too much excitement, with her the center. If only she could go back "and live among the hills" again, she lamented to Carolyn Ruth. Have time alone without the clamor of people who had read her poetry and wanted to comment on it. She admitted it was a foolish wish. Her poems in print had brought most of what she cherished in life, including her friendships with Carolyn Ruth and Eva and a growing list of rich relationships by correspondence. But a book was like "sending one's baby out into the world, with all it's imperfections," to be stared at and examined—and perhaps found wanting. For a shy person, that was more than she could comfortably contemplate. It was too late now to wish she had written under a pen name and let her poems and prayers be received on their own merit—apart from any connection with their author.[9]

September the seventh was publishing day, and the slim volume bearing Jane's name was available for all to see—a heart-pounding realization. The autograph tea sponsored by the Knoxville Pen Women was held at Miller's Book Department, the largest bookstore in town. An orchid from Abingdon was delivered at Jane's door. More flowers came from well-wishers, along with flowery compliments on her poetry. It was almost like "going to one's own funeral," Jane quipped to her mother *(Diary, March 15, 1956)*.

Eva brought a gift, a dinner bell for use to "summon the vassals who should be at the beck and call of anyone who can delight a whole batch of editors!"[10] She could report that the book was selling well in Knoxville. Jane had read in a writers' magazine that a publisher must sell 800 books to break even. It seemed a great number for poetry those days.

Judging by the reviews, she should have reason for optimism. In the clippings from Abingdon her poetry was described as "perceptive," "inspiring," "arrests attention and kindles the imagination," and as having "appealing freshness," "meaningful simplicity and beauty," and "originality of thought and word."

Jane had hoped the public interest in her person would fade, but it was quite the contrary. *Christian Herald,* who had printed many of her poems, ran a feature article on "The Poetry Merchant," and in December the Pen Women of Tennessee joined the Poetry Society of Tennessee in asking the State Legislature to appoint Jane their state poet laureate. In December 1954, *The Knoxville Journal* endorsed the petition: "We find ourselves in thorough sympathy. . . . Jane Merchant writes with perception, grace and feeling on a wide range of subjects. . . . The state has had no poet laureate since the days of the late John Trotwood Moore. It would be a fitting thing, and we think a deserved honor, for Knoxville's Jane Merchant to be selected for this post of honor."

The *Journal* had not mentioned her handicap. Too many others did. In January 1955, *The War Cry* printed a full page of what they called her "unusual" poems, then praised her "even more unusual" faith and fortitude.

Had Jane wanted to become a celebrity, there was ample opportunity. The combination of her poetry and her handicap caused more stir than either alone. She tried not to take the accolade too seriously and was well aware of its danger. In "Uncamouflaged" she wrote of the safety of anonymity and the hazards of drawing attention to oneself.

> Rooster, strutting in your sheen
> Of iridescent bronze and green
> While your dull-hued hens evade
> Notice in the dusty shade;
> Cardinal, flaunting blazing red
> While your brown mate blends, instead,
> With the brown of earth and trees—
> Lordly creatures, tell me, please,
> Why you parade, with this immense
> Pomposity, the evidence
> Of nature that your gaudy lives
> Are less worth saving than your wives'!

There was more at stake than the perils of exposure. In her book Jane had written: "Let us be anxious only lest we may not be seeking thy righteousness first of all."[11]

The greatest temptation was to think that the source of her talent and the courage to use it was in herself. That was dangerous self-deception, and she could never be quite sure of how much she indulged in it. She could only pray fervently that the One who was the source of her strength and her song—and who knew her heart—would keep her from seeking her own glory instead of glorifying him.

Fame could swell her pride, dull her heart, and still her song. The only antidote she knew was to quiet herself in the presence of God. That was the theme of "That We May Sing," one of her poems in the book. Jane was pleased to learn that it was read on television by a Methodist bishop in Ohio.

> Thou art not far from any one of us,
> However far we are, O Lord, from thee.
> Give us the grace of quietness, to know
> Thy presence and thy holy harmony.
>
> Within our hearts through all the hurried hours,
> Through all the clamourous din of busy days,
> Till in the listening silence of our souls
> There stirs a song of worship and of praise,
>
> A song of praise to thee for all thy love,
> A song of love for every living thing
> That thou, our Father and our God, hast made.
> O teach us to be still, that we may sing.

Publicity was temporal and would fade away—and so, most assuredly, would her small measure of fame. They were like all earthly rewards: to be enjoyed, but not too well.

Jane treasured a letter from Carl Sandburg, who had been given a copy of her book and termed it "a good companion." His favorite poem was "But Not Too Well."

> Love well the sun,
> Love well the earth,
> All miracles
> Of bloom and birth;
>
> All little rains
> On tender grass,
> All seeking winds
> That softly pass;
>
> All glories of
> Gold morning light,
> All dear tranquilities
> Of night;
>
> Love well the earth's
> Enchanted spell,
> But love, oh, love
> It not too well.

For earth will die
And dies the sun.
Keep loves that live
When earth is done.

The book was selling remarkably well—4,800 copies in the first three months, earning a larger royalty check than Jane had dared envision. It was proof, indeed, that she was "a servant worthy of hire." To Abingdon, the signals were clear. On March 10, Jane recorded in her diary: "Letter from Mr. Wright, wants me to do another book."

Now that she knew the long hard pull ahead, she wasn't sure she dared say yes. Once the project was started, her "ornery mind" wouldn't let her rest until it was done, she complained to Eva. Such "perpetual mental motion" could be too much for her eyes and energies.[12]

There was a more serious reason for hesitating. Did she, an isolated invalid, have anything new and relevant to say? The royalty check had provided a television set, and Jane could *see,* if not hear, what went on beyond her pale green walls. The glimpse of the world of her readers only reinforced her sense of being out of touch.

Dwelling on thoughts of her isolation and inadequacy loosed her old foes, self-pity and hopelessness. Jane battled despair and writer's block. Help came from an unexpected source: a note scribbled on the back of a rejection slip from editor James Waldo Fawcett of *The Washington Star:* "Dear Jane, I think we are 'cousins the mind makes.' Let me test your power of collaboration by asking you to write me a poem about Hermann of Reichenau to help the Crippled Children's Fund campaign. He was the author of 'Come Holy Spirit' and many other famous songs. See Britannica."[13]

It was Jane's first introduction to the lame monk and scholar of the eleventh century who, from his isolated cell, made significant contributions to science, philosophy, and theology.

Within the convent walls his spirit shone
One of the darkened age's purest lights.
He who could neither walk nor stand alone
Wrote treatises on measuring the heights

Of stars; translated Aristotle; penned
The world's known history in scrupulous pages;
And he, whose maimed speech none could comprehend,
Composed *Come, Holy Spirit,* for the ages.

In constant suffering gentle, brave, and kind,
In reverent eagerness for truth and learning,

> He kept the records of the questing mind,
> And voiced the heart's deep love and holy yearning,
>
> And all the clouded centuries have not dimmed
> His luminous spirit or the faith he hymned.

Hermann of Reichenau had accepted and responded creatively to his limitations, refusing to become a whimpering victim of harsh circumstances. How did Jane choose to respond to her challenge? The choice was hers anew each day, as it was for everyone else: the choice between brooding over difficulties, unfairness, and evil or lifting sight and thoughts to greater realities, living creatively instead of destructively. It was a challenging topic for a book as well, she thought. The poem about Hermann of Reichenau would be included with a prayer of gratitude for "those through all the ages who . . . preserved . . . the heritage of faith, truth, and knowledge, and added to it their own lives' shining examples of virtue and excellence."[14]

The theme of the book was suddenly clear. She would base it on a favorite passage from the Bible, Paul's message to the Phillippians: "Whatever is true, whatever is honorable . . . *think about these things*" (Phil. 4:8 RSV; italics added).

Reading Paul's words to herself, Jane always had "a sense of mental snarls being untangled, a homecoming recognition that that's what I should be doing, of course, instead of fuming about unlovely things," she wrote in the preface.

"I think Paul's singing text has this effect upon us all. We have an instinctive awareness that 'as he thinketh in his heart so is he,' and that we cannot habitually entertain grudging, deprecatory thoughts and still live constructive, satisfying lives. We have all learned that thinking of the many excellent, pure, praiseworthy things in life makes the unjust, ungracious things seem less tremendous, and helps us deal with them in a better spirit, and more effectively. The difficulty, for most of us, is in remembering what we know, and doing it."

Her first book was far better received than she had anticipated. How could she live up to the expectations it created? One success did not guarantee another. But fear of failure was rooted in pride. She had better ignore it and get on with her writing instead.

In her first book was the poem "Ascent."

> This is the hill I thought so high
> I could not hope to reach its crest
> However long I climbed; yet I
> Have reached it now, and paused to rest
> A moment, and, triumphant, view

The stones and briars I struggled past,
Unable to believe it true
That I have conquered them at last.

I cannot really catch a cloud
As I had half believed I could;
Attained, the height is not so proud
As I supposed, but it is good
Indeed to know that, having done
This, I can climb a taller one.

10
IN GREEN
PASTURES
1955–1957

Upon green grass,
Beneath green leaves,
By gentle streams
My heart receives
Surcease from strain,
Abiding balm,
Deep amplitudes
Of healing calm.
In scanty quarters,
Dark and bare,
My heart sometimes
Has been aware
Of one who makes
The narrowest space
An ample green
And growing place.

Summer roses bloomed by her window, and Jane looked at them with longing. It was five years since she had been outside. Five years since they moved to town. Five years of living within monotonous walls—at times it seemed she had scarcely space to breathe. On such days irritations multiplied, and outward calm was a victory. Bitter experience had taught her that complaints led to sure defeat. In the new manuscript was "Vacation Plans":

I cannot take long, leisurely vacations
In the green peace of some high mountain crest,
But I can give my often-voiced vexations
A long delayed and greatly needed rest.
I cannot take a trip to some far shore,

> But I can give complaints a holiday,
> And little irritations by the score,
> I'm packing up and sending far away.
>
> The habits of being anxious, and of doubting,
> And making tart remarks that need amends,
> I'm going to give a calm and peaceful outing
> All summer long; and when the summer ends
>
> I shall be glad, indeed, if they should shirk
> The woeful task of going back to work.

The cure for weariness and irritability was usually less a change of scenery than a change of self, Jane wrote in her meditation. She need only open her eyes to "loveliness in familiar surroundings."[1]

Outside her window, new beauty was unfolding daily. Donia had planned the small garden to yield a changing display of color and shape from early spring until late fall. Elizabeth had laid the terrace of Tennessee marble scraps. Flowerbeds and shrubs surrounded it and the small lawn where nieces and nephews could play within view. The birdbath and feeder were close enough for Jane's observation. Beyond them were rows of berries and vegetables and as many varieties of trees as space allowed. Each season Donia planted something new, a fresh wonder of sight and touch, fragrance, and often taste.

> A stretch of bare red earth when she arrived,
> It is a place of sweet surprises now.
> A slim young elm and four dogwoods have thrived
> In gratitude for love, and they allow
> Space for a lilac, and a bridal wreath,
> A pussy willow, and a golden bell—
> "No proper garden ever yet beneath
> The sun lacked those," she says; and she will tell
> Us that their blossoms, and the daffodils,
> The irises, the sweet peas, and the deep
> Red roses whose enchanting fragrance fills
> The air, are not, of course, for her to keep.
> "Half of the joy of raising them," she'll say,
> "Is in the joy of giving them away."
>
> > "Mother's Garden"

The small dutch-girl pitcher on Jane's table held fresh flowers daily as long as any bloomed outside. Donia cut them in the early morning, bright with dew. They brought the wonder of all gardens into the room.

Abingdon had accepted her book theme, and Jane determined to live what she learned through the writing. That was the best part of doing a devotional, searching for the source of an idea in the Bible, finding the text to fit a poem or a prayer. With concordance and Bible commentaries at hand, she journeyed through the scriptures, pursuing a thought or a word, meditating on what she read, and occasionally finding new light illuminating a dark and difficult passage.

It was easy to lose herself completely in the work—difficult to accept interruptions with cheerful equanimity. They were especially frequent during the summer, when visitors were apt to come. Now that Jane's fame was spreading, there were more of them.

Eva was the faithful buffer against awkward first meetings with strangers. She brought a wide variety of friends, from foreign exchange students in national costumes to neighborhood kids, and eased the visits with her presence. But Eva was away in Milwaukee teaching summer school again, and Jane found Knoxville empty without her.

A first-time visitor that summer was Shirley Kerr from Virginia, who had become one of Jane's steady correspondents over the past year. Shirley was a busy homemaker with young children, but she found time to write book reviews and letters to editors in praise of Jane's poetry.

She quickly caught on to communicating on magic slates, and she soon confessed that she had a particular request to make. Would Jane consider publishing a straight collection of poetry—and allow Shirley to write to Abingdon with the suggestion?

The thought had occurred to Jane already. A collection of poetry alone, including her lighter things, could be put together with less effort than a devotional. Perhaps Abingdon would be open to the idea now that her first book had proved a good seller and another was underway. Shirley received permission to write—provided she *not* refer to their friendship.

The second royalty check for *The Greatest of These* showed that sales had reached 7,800 copies. Jane celebrated the first birthday of her first book by getting the second one in the mail. In October came word that it was accepted, and when the contract was safely signed, Jane informed Shirley, who promptly wrote to Abingdon to ask for a complete edition of Jane Merchant's poetry. Within a month Jane could report that her editor had indicated they were considering a collection, to include some of her lighter things. Shirley's letter appeared to have done some good.

For their Christmas greeting, Abingdon had printed "I Wish You Christmas" from Jane's new book, *Think About These Things.*

> How strangely, thoughtlessly unnecessary
> It often seems to me that we should say,

"I wish you merry Christmas." How can merry
Or any other adjective, convey

A wish for greater gladness for our friends
More than the one word, Christmas, all alone,
The singing, shining word that comprehends
The utmost grace and glory men have known?

I wish you more, much more, than merriment;
All faith and hope and love and holy peace,
All quietness and radiant content
With blessings that continually increase,

And when I say the simple words and small,
"I wish you Christmas," I have wished you all.

Jane's own Christmas mail included a clutch of fan letters—one from Jesse Stuart, who asked to buy an autographed copy of her book. Jane was flabbergasted, she told Eva. Jesse Stuart was a writer and poet she regarded highly. What would he say about the book?

His reaction was sent to Abingdon: "[Jane Merchant] is the writer of some of the finest religious poems that are being written in America today. Her poems remind me of the early religious poems by Elizabeth Barrett Browning and Christina Rosetti."

Jane was elated by the endorsement, but she was immediately fearful that her next book would be a flop. She was proofreading *Think About These Things,* and her zeal for perfection had once again caused eyestrain and neuralgia in her neck.

Abingdon had asked to see some of her fan mail, and only after sending it did she think of their reaction to letters from convalescents and people with handicaps. What if her next book would be advertized as suitable especially for shut-ins? That would only scare off readers, including shut-ins, she noted in her diary. Books intended for invalids had made embarrassing reading, as if the authors assumed that "physical incapacity induces mental atrophy, and that sentimentality may be substituted for sense *(Diary, Feb. 27, 1956).*

The word *shut-in* made her feel almost subhuman, she confided to Shirley. But she could not deny the accuracy of the term—or its application to herself. "Why should anyone bother to say 'a person who is confined to the house' when there's a short and ugly word like 'shut-in' handy?"[2]

It was not a pleasant subject. She had reluctantly agreed to an interview by Mildred Luton for *The Nashville Tennessean Magazine* (Eva insisted she owed it to her publishers and readers!) on the condition that her physical difficulties be downplayed. The results remained to be seen.

All gloomy thoughts were dispelled by the astounding news that *The*

Greatest of These had won first prize for best book in the National Pen Women's Bicentennial contest. The award would be given at the national convention in Washington D.C. in April, with a cash prize of $150.

Congratulations poured in, and the Doll House was astir with excitement. One of the nicest surprises was a large bouquet of pink snapdragons, irises, and tulips from her eye doctor. The flowers smelled "like Easter and all outdoors" and quite "dumb-founded" her, Jane noted in her diary on March 4, 1956.

On the bare branches of her window dogwood, tiny buds had begun to swell. This was the time of year when Jane was made most aware of the narrow boundaries of her life. But it was also when her heart rejoiced in daily miracles of new life under a spring-blue sky. She would "think about these things" with all her might and banish self-pity.

Her resolve was put to the test a few days later when Robert Roy Wright came to call. They enjoyed Donia's home-baked cake with coffee, and Jane expected him to talk about a collection of poetry. The editor was hedging and seemed unhappy, "like a small boy hoping not to be scolded for mischief," Jane wrote later in her diary.

When he spoke his piece, it was her turn to be unhappy. The editorial board wanted her to compile a book for convalescents, using some of her lighter, as well as serious, poems, with suitable Bible passages and poems by other authors.

This was far indeed from what she had in mind. After a moment's hesitation, Jane decided not to hide her reaction. Tactfully, but firmly, she voiced her disdain for the proposal. Convalescents, she argued, were not a race apart, but enjoyed reading the same things as other people. Would it not be wiser to aim a book at the wider market instead of limiting the appeal?

Robert Roy Wright agreed, but the editorial board had based their decision on a survey among salesmen who saw a need for such a book.

Jane was instantly apologetic for having vented her ire at an innocent messenger. "Sorry I was 'ornery,'" she wrote on her slate.

"Are you *really* sorry?" he penned, smiling.

"If you are disappointed or annoyed!" she responded earnestly.

He assured her that he was in full sympathy with her feelings on the matter, and he apologized for the request from the editorial board—and the pressure from the public. He would do what he could to make it easier on her in the future.

Before the editor left, Jane agreed to think over the proposal. In her diary she recorded her willingness to do what the publisher thought necessary and to trust in their judgment. But she didn't like it and confessed: "I feel I don't ever want to do a book again" *(Diary, March 15 and 17, 1956)*.

Easter was only two weeks away. If only she could have some time alone to herself. The mechanical details of writing and the growing mail from those who wanted help and advice (she answered them all) were sapping her time and strength. Not enough was left for "the slow interior living" she found absolutely essential for poetry writing.

> The dream within the heart,
> The shape within the stone
> Is visualized apart,
> Is realized alone.
>
> No one who would express
> Essentials, can exclude
> The arduous inwardness,
> The searching solitude.
>   "Renewing Fellowship"

Her pressing inward need was to create. The outward need—to sell—was of lesser import. If Abingdon wanted a book for shut-ins, and Jane shuddered at the thought, she would comply. And perhaps some shut-in would gain from it.

The Nashville Tennessean article—with eight of her poems and photographs of spring—was printed on the first day of April. The title was "Unheard Melody," and a picture of Jane bore the caption: "From her bed, Jane Merchant has earned the unofficial title 'Poet Laureate of Tennessee.'"

Miss Luton wrote: "This fragile, dreamy girl, shut in by a wall of complete silence, is turning out some of the most charming poetry of this or any generation."

Her physical condition had made the headlines again! The editors had insisted on it, Miss Luton explained.

Fussing about it deepened her gloom. But dogwood blooms, pressing at her window, contradicted despair. "Because of Spring" was in her new book.

> Because of dogwood's blessing on the hill,
> Because of lilac odor drifting through
> These lonely rooms, because of wings that fill
> The vast sky's infinite extent of blue
>
> With eager, onward joy—because once more
> Earth grows more beautiful than I had dreamed
> It could become again, my praises soar
> To God, and I am stronger than I seemed.
>
> I know I could not find a lovelier way
> Through life's bewildering sorrows, than with the sight
> Of dogwood blossoms, lilac's scented spray,
> And April birds' exhilarating flight.

I find fresh courage for my journeying
Through every troubled year, because of spring.

One hundred autographed copies of *The Greatest of These* had gone to the Pen Women's convention in Washington, and Jean Mergard, who attended the awards banquet, wrote: "It was really *your* night!"[3]

But in Knoxville the day was gloomy, with dark clouds and rain. Jane was prepared for callers, but none came—no flowers, no congratulatory messages. She tried to think about a book for shut-ins, and went to sleep weary and depressed.

Self-pity had won a round and was not easy to get rid of, even if she knew the remedy. In her new book was "The Sacrifice of Praise."

If we would offer praise
To God continually
Our hearts must sacrifice
Some things that seem to be
Peculiarly dear;
The pleasure of complaining
When little things go wrong
And little hurts are paining;
The joy of feeling abused
And envious of our neighbors,
And sorry for ourselves
And our unrequited labors;
The pride of pointing out
The small defects that mar
Our satisfactions, to prove
How skilled in taste we are—
All this the heart intent
On offering praise, foregoes,
And sacrificing, finds
All freedom and repose.
And yet by some perverse
And curious mistake
It seems a sacrifice
Our hearts are loath to make.

No matter how dismal her feelings, self-pity must be sacrificed on the altar of praise. A few days later rejoicing was suddenly much easier. Robert Roy Wright wrote that the editorial board had relented and were willing to consider a general collection of her poetry. They would like to see a plan and sample pages.

With singing heart, Jane selected favorite poems from her store of printed ones. Her book title would be *Halfway Up the Sky,* from the poem "First Home," Her theme was simple: "My hills are Tennessee hills (which are earth's loveliest ones), and my sky is the Tennessee sky (which is earth's fairest). But I hope there may be something in this book for all who love a hill, who take an interest in the sky and what goes on beneath it, and who view their neighbors on this earth with a sympathetic if somewhat quizzical eye."[4]

The book plan and sample pages went to Mr. Wright on April 17, and Jane declared to her mother: "When I've had three books published, I'm going to take a vacation!"

"You won't!" replied Donia, who knew her daughter *(Diary, April 1956).* But with dogwood and azalea at their loveliest, Jane gave in to Eva's promptings and the desire of her own heart. She asked Donia to inquire of McCarty's Mortuary the cost of a three-hour ambulance ride. When they heard who was calling, they insisted on charging nothing. Jane was too embarrassed to back out, and the trip was planned for the following day. Eva and Elizabeth would go along.

Not since before her father's death had Jane known such happiness, she wrote afterwards. To her the ambulance seemed "a near relation to Elijah's chariot."[5] Their destination was Norris Dam on the Clinch river, northwest of Knoxville. They drove through Fountain City, "past the lake, park, willows, up Garden Avenue bursting with dogwood, phlox, tulips, then the Norris Freeway. I told Eva she had forgotten to remind me there is so much space lying around loose in the country! At the dam they took me out of the ambulance into the gift shop where I signed the register, and out on the boat dock, almost into the water. That was the best of all, being under the bare sky" *(Diary, April 21, 1956).*

> It wasn't that I hadn't seen the sky
> And earth for months. I saw it all through glass,
> But hard transparencies can foil the eye
> With sparkle, and when brilliant sunbeams pass
> And dark looks in where sunbeams danced and whirled,
> Then glass shows one himself and not the world.
>
> The hour they wheeled me out beneath the bare
> Astounding distances of blue, I saw
> Colors of things untouched by glassy glare,
> And used light words to them against my awe—
> Against my heart's embarrassing demand
> To tell them things they couldn't understand.
>
> "Recovery"

On the way home they drove down Merchant Road, named for her father, along the boundary of the old Inskip farm and orchard, now a crowded suburb. The day had been pure joy—her first time out from under the roof of the Doll House since they moved there six years ago. And wonder of wonder, Jane noted in her diary, she was not too tired!

A few days later came a gift from McCarty's: an ambulance cot, cut down to her size. Now she could be on the front porch and—when someone strong helped carry the cot down the steps—in the back garden. "The Shining Day" was written on the terrace in May.

> All day the sky's deep blue has shone
> With vivid gentleness. All day
> A little sunlit wind has blown
> Rose-fragrances our way.
>
> There has been no intemperate glare
> Nor any overwhelming heat,
> Only the deep sky, coolly fair,
> And the small wind, coolly sweet.
>
> There is no more than this to tell
> Now that the shining day is done;
> Save that our hearts have loved it well
> From sun to sun.

The manuscript for *Halfway Up the Sky* was put in the mail in June. The following day Eva's brother came with his station wagon and took Jane, Donia, and Elizabeth to Eva's house for a celebration supper. Such adventures had been unthinkable before the ambulance cot. "It seems that no matter how often I die, I don't stay dead, thank God," Jane exulted to Carolyn Ruth *(Reynolds, June 17, 1956)*.

But the next day she was overcome by nausea and chills. Her good eye had a blind spot and flickering lights; her bad eye hurt, requiring longer rest periods behind hot compresses. The troubles soon cleared, but Jane felt again as she had five years before: "Too utterly tired" to write or think or "do anything but sit" *(Diary, July 1956)*.

The lesson was a hard one. There was a penalty for pushing beyond the narrow physical boundaries of her living. Once again she must accept the limits of what she could do and be grateful for that much.

Publishing day for *Think About These Things* was September 10, but this time there was no autograph party to worry over. The reviewers praised her work again, and there were public readings of her poetry and fan letters with requests for autographed copies—all pleasant, and not too exhausting.

In October the manuscript for *Halfway Up the Sky* came back to her for minor changes, and when the work was done Jane allowed herself another vacation in Nelson Venable's station wagon—this time to the Smokies in all their autumn glory. It was a happy party who headed for the mountains. The road went "straight up . . . on and on . . . where every view is the loveliest view you ever saw!"

At Cades Cove they carried her on the cot down to "a happy little creek" under oak and pine trees and rhododendrons. There, by the side of the stream, they ate the picnic lunch Eva had prepared.

Never before had Jane been under open skies in the Smokies, to see and breathe such wonders and to feel the rippling water against her fingers. "All the poems I ever wrote poured into one and running over rocks," she wrote in her diary.

After lunch they drove through the Cove—"surely one of the most beautiful places on earth"—and on up to Newfound Gap, stopping to see a bear near the road—her first. There were golden birches and evergreens and "the incredible loop," where at one glance they could see the road curving where they had been and where they were going. Over the flaming mountains hung a shimmering blue mist. How could she ever be thankful enough, to those who brought her and to God? And especially for sight! *(Diary, Oct. 14, 1956)*.

The next day she wrote to Eva: "I'm still floating in a Mountain haze of happiness. . . . I was floating yesterday . . . my heart lighter than it had been in a long time. . . . If it weren't for you, Cade's Cove still wouldn't be real to me, and till a thing is real, of course, it hasn't been created."[6]

In "Oak Leaf and Acorn" she wrote:

> I've an oak leaf and an acorn
> I picked up off the ground
> Beside the merry water
> Of the little creek you found.
>
> We had come up together
> Through the blue mountain air
> I'd loved afar, not dreaming
> Of ever being there.
>
> The little creek was golden-brown
> Save where it rippled whitely
> Around the rounded pebbles.
> It touched our fingers lightly,
>
> And then we had to leave it;
> But let nobody say
> An oak leaf and an acorn
> Are all I brought away.

Jane half expected the contract for *Halfway Up the Sky* before Christmas. It didn't come, but Abingdon sent an eight blossom poinsettia. Jane was instantly apprehensive. Could they have sent flowers to soften the impact of rejection? She never felt certain of acceptance until the contract was signed.

Finally, in February, it arrived. Jane could breathe easy and tell her friends what she was up to. But the most tiresome aspect of her task was still ahead: proofreading and copyright clearances. It was the time of year when she once wrote rhymes "in appreciation of jonquils and red maple blooms." Now she was too tired to do more about jonquils than be thankful they weren't affected by her fatigue, she lamented to a friend.[7]

The manuscript was back in the mail in early April, and Jane took to the dogwood trail in the Venable station wagon. They followed the route marked by the Garden Club, "where Knoxville puts on the dogwood the most," and "saw all of April's blooms in most satisfying profusion. . . . There was an especially darling bed of pansies in full bloom and a yellow butterfly hovering. And the rural mailboxes on the post . . . had their tongues hanging out panting for mail!" *(Diary, April 14, 1957).*

> We rode for several April hours
> And everywhere we looked were flowers.
> The dogwoods lifted drifts of white
> Behind, before, and left, and right:
> And over us, the flowering quince
> Exclaimed in pink and crimson tints;
> And phlox made steep embankments gay;
> And tulips flaunted rich array
> Of red and gold; and at the end
> Of one wide-sweeping lawn, some friend
> Of gentleness had filled a space
> With many a guileless pancy face
> Like smiles embroidered on the grass
> To greet and gladden all who pass.
> I hope the owner saw us smile
> And linger there a special while.
>
> "Flower Tour"

The self-assertive red banks of clay along the roadside looked especially good, after seeing only city streets and concrete sidewalks. But it was the glimpse of mountains "shining bluely through blossoms, and the incurably ragged up-and-down-ness of this beloved and cranky Tennessee earth that brought the rush of passionate at-homeness to my heart," Jane confessed to Carolyn Ruth.[8]

The price she must pay after any exertion was utter fatigue. But she had shining memories to feed on and write from—if only she could get rested! Compiling the last book had been easier than the first two, but it was still exhausting. Weighing the balance, Jane found devotional books more worth the time and effort. In her diary she wrote out her considerations. She would never feel worthy to do devotionals, but having learned to do them, and readers having found them helpful, she probably ought to ''use her talent lest she lose it.'' But first she must get rested. Even then there was no guarantee that she would write anything good enough for a book or that her eyes would hold up. Two rest periods were still required daily.[9]

The two books in print continued to sell well, 13,000 copies of *The Greatest of These* having sold and 6,000 in just three months of *Think About These Things*. Abingdon had already asked for another volume, but Jane would not commit herself yet. She was resting and reading and struggling with the recurring conviction that people ought to read better books than hers; such as the one she was currently reading: *A Testament of Devotion* by Thomas Kelly. Jane was most impressed by his chapter on ''Holy Obedience,'' and she copied into her notebook the statement: ''Humility and holiness are twins in astonishing birth of obedience in the heart of men.''

In her own heart Jane desired more than anything to do the will of God, and she thought it likely that his will was expressed in the publisher's request for another book. If so, she would do it, even if her weary mind was unable to settle on a theme. She was inclined toward Psalm 121, with ''I Will Lift Up Mine Eyes'' as the title poem.

Let us be always willing, Lord,
To lift our downcast eyes
Above the baffling mysteries
That always must comprise
Much of our living, day by day,
Above the grievous pain
Of wrongs that men commit, to where
The constant hills remain.

From soaring mountaintops of truth,
From great ideals that tower
In majesty, from human lives
Lived in thy spirit's power—
Forever thou art offering, Lord,
Thy help for every ill;
Yet none can ever receive thy help
Unless he says, ''I will.''

Jane knew only too well the pitfalls of looking down. In a meditation on the poem, she wrote: "Keep us aware, Lord, of the danger of being willing to indulge our low moods, lest our will to faithfulness and righteousness become too weak for us to receive thy help in times of urgent need."[10]

Halfway Up the Sky was released in September. Donia instantly named it her favorite, and reviewers tended to agree. Alfred Mynders, columnist for *The Chattanooga Times* wrote: "Miss Merchant . . . should have been given the Pulitzer Prize. . . . *Halfway Up the Sky* is the product of a remarkable talent." Murray Wagner, of the *The Virginia Newsleader*, called the book "a luscious piece of work . . . gems from a pen that sparkles with good humour, profound common sense, and a splendid sense of the worthwhile in life." *The Saturday Evening Post* commented: "her poetry suggests a wide and perceptive range of living. There is love, courage and sympathy in both her serious and her lighter work."

Public praise was pleasant, but the personal notes from readers meant more. One came from Dr. Alwin Thaler, professor of English literature at the University of Tennessee and a renowned Shakespeare scholar. He wrote: "Your book *is* beautiful; true and moving enough to keep old men from the chimney corner, if not children from play. (Who wants to keep children from play?) . . . Not long after your book arrived, serious sickness laid me low . . . your lovely verse about the sweet names of trees kept running through my head while I was struggling through the nights at the hospital."[11] He was referring to "Slumber Song."

> The names of trees are good to say
> Over and over, in the night.
> The names of maple and linden sway
> In drowsy semblances of flight,
> The names of spruce and cedar sing
> Green lullabies; the names of trees
> Have langurous sorcery to bring
> Tranquility and healthful ease.
> Repeat them gently, softly, so;
> The names of aspen, larch, and willow,
> Alder and elm, and cool winds blow
> Deep-shadowed sleep across your pillow.

Jane could well have needed some rest herself, but she was already deep into the new manuscript. Her first idea for a theme had been put aside for Psalm 23. It had "insisted on being used," she explained to a friend, in spite of her serious misgivings over daring to write on such a "best-loved and much quoted passage."[12] The Shepherd's Psalm, singing of rest in green pastures, was a fitting theme for Jane's attempt to put into words her recent "inexpressible joy of rediscovering . . . the ordinary miracles of earth and sky."[13]

She was pushing herself to get the first half of the manuscript in the mail before Christmas, when the family would be there for a festive reunion. The bulky manila envelope got off on time, but Jane was more than usually dissatisfied with the contents. In her diary she confessed that she half regretted sending it and would "feel more relieved than otherwise" if it was rejected—even if it *would* devastate her! *(Diary, Dec. 1957).*

She intended the book to be a song of praise for two good years when the constricting walls of her physical circumstances had yielded a little. In the manuscript was a quotation from Psalm 18:19, "He brought me forth into a broad place," with the poem "After a Country Day."

Now we have satisfied ourselves
That shining mountains keep
Faith with the sky and faith with us;
That fields of wideness sweep
In rich brown furrow, or in rich
Green of exuberant grass
Up to the sunlit mountains' feet;
That myriad wildwoods mass
Their shadowy cool mysteries
Of leaves about the flowing
Of large calm rivers, and little streams
Excited in their going.

Confirming ancient certainties
Is never an idle thing,
And each heart needs to verify
The countryside, in spring.

11
THROUGH THE
VALLEY
1958–1959

I love the brown December earth,
I love the gray December sky,
The calm acceptances of dearth
Without complaint or question why
The bird has left the barren bough,
Or why the bough should be left bare,
Or why the field is empty now
And open to the piercing air.

I love the grave simplicity
Of faith that, acquiescent, still,
Abides the tempest, tranquilly
Obedient to the Father's will.
I love to know that, yielded thus,
The saving Christ may come to us.

The Doll House was decked with greenery and filled with rich smells of cooking and baking for the first family Christmas reunion since the year before Clarence Merchant died. Aunt Laura came from Asheville and Nelson and his family from Maryland. Christmas morning was pure joy, with candlelight shining on the small decorated tree and the circle of happy faces around it.

But the first mail of the New Year brought a dreadful let-down. Along with a bundle of rejection slips, Jane received the first half of her new manuscript in return, with a long letter from Robert Roy Wright explaining that it needed more work. He apologized for having pestered her into writing it so soon, and he allowed plenty of time for a rewrite. The publishing date was set for spring 1959, and they did not need the finished manuscript until fall.

Jane was devastated. She had prayed, before submitting the manuscript, that it not be accepted unless it was good enough. Obviously it was inferior, and she doubted that she could improve it.

Familiar questions tormented her. Had it *not* been God's will that she write the book? Was she no longer able to do devotionals? Had she said all she had to say in poetry? The more she pondered the possibilities, the darker they looked.

Things looked a bit brighter in February after a visit from Abingdon's editor-in-chief, Dr. Emory Bucke. He brought greetings from Robert Roy Wright, who "would just quit if he couldn't be Jane Merchant's editor!" *(Diary, Feb. 5, 1958).* Apparently her publishers did not think it was time to give up what she thought of as "this mediocre writing."

The February rain had turned to snow outside her window—always a fascinating sight and balm for weary thoughts.

> I am of those who cannot let the rain
> Fall without benefit (to me) of my
> Close supervision; work may wait in vain
> While with intent, appreciative eye,
> Watching the silver mystery descend
> With steady undeviating grace,
> I exercise my right to superintend
> Essence of wonder for a little space.
> It is a usual right; but strangely rare
> Is sight of snowflakes, in my southern land,
> And when they briefly animate the air,
> I gaze, and wholly fail to understand
> How any work can be performed at all
> In any place where snowflakes often fall.
>   "Supervision"

Editorial rejections had brought more than their usual share of heartache, but Jane's burgeoning private correspondence kept the mailman from seeming "a figure of doom," she noted to Shirley.[1]

Her printed work brought a steady trickle of fan mail from "lovely strangers" who seldom remained strangers for long. Back in the fall she had heard from two fellow authors: Gurre Noble in Hawaii and Kay Gudnason in California. They wrote to thank her for *The Greatest of These,* and a lively three-way correspondence soon flourished.

> There were two friends; now there are three.
> Hearts recognize their own.
>   "Friends"

Gurre and Jane shared a particular interest in birds, and confessed to being "under the dominance of parakeets." Pretty Boy was Jane's fourth parakeet. He was prone to nibbling holes in manuscripts, pulling at typewriter ribbons and was "a great hindrance to worrying," even if he caused a few.[2] His predecessor, Puck, inspired "Lost and Found."

Of course, the world's not coming to an end
Because one sassy little parakeet
Flew out the door last night. No use to spend
Tears on a bit of feathery conceit
Who'll make a tasty morsel for a cat
And won't be pulling anybody's hair
Or nibbling books they read, again. What's that?
Somebody's found a bird? Where is he? Where?
My word, he's got tar on him! Frowsy-feathered,
And nearly starved, almost too weak to fly,
He's wholly unsubdued by all he's weathered,
With the old puckish glint still in his eye,
Bring him on in, and double latch that door;
The world can wag upon its way once more.

Puck's death only a few months after his return caused such grief that Jane resolved not to risk owning another pet. For a whole year she remained firm, until "a small lost bird" took shelter in the nandina bush below their dining room window. They advertized in the newspaper and were relieved when no one claimed him. Pretty Boy instantly took possession of their house and hearts and was by far the most affectionate of her "babies." Jane fervently hoped he would be with her for a long, long time.[3]

New friends usually provided new adventures in reading. Kay and Gurre thought Jane wrote much like Amy Carmichael, the late British author and missionary to South India, and they were surprised to find that Jane had never heard of her. They sent several books, and Jane was instantly captivated. Amy's phrases evoked "the joy and envy of writers," she confessed to Kay.[4]

There was much gentle wisdom in Amy's words, and Jane copied several sections to read and ponder often. In *From the Forest* she found a particularly apt passage: "How easy it is to mistake the leading and be altogether very trying to one's Guide. . . . And so one learns . . . that where we failed, He comes in and takes the poor, little mangled attempts and perfects them, and the thing we tried to do and could not do, is done."

Perhaps she had mistaken God's leading and mangled her attempt at doing another devotional. Could God take her failure and make something perfect of it in the end? There was hope in the thought.

Amy's description of a jade green pool in the river, where worries were "kissed away," invited a poem. Jane often pretended to float in "cool water under open sky" when she was extra weary, she confided to Kay and Gurre. Even "imaginary water kisses" could be comforting *(Gudnason, March 2, 1958).*

150

Imagine now a deep green pool
Within a mountain wood
Where grasses, leaves, and moss maintain
Harmonious livelihood.

Shake gently out of your heart the stones
And drop them into the deep
Cool silence softly, one by one.
Lie light on green, and sleep.
"For Pleasant Dreams"

The poem went in her next submission to the *Post,* earning their "negotiable approval," and ending a series of rejections—what Amy would call "weary little things."[5]

One book was destined to become a lifelong favorite. *Rose from Brier* was written sometime during the last twenty years of Amy Carmichael's life, while she was in bed with chronic pain. The collection of letters and poems was addressed to "fellow sufferers."

"There couldn't be another book like that in all the world," Jane wrote her friends. She didn't feel deserving of Amy's roses—Jane was, after all, not suffering physical pain. But Amy understood other hurts as well. "Bless [her] consecrated, unregimented heart for admitting that tracts for the ill [written by the well] didn't say anything to her. . . . And bless her for admitting that a bed can be a place of dullness of spirit as well as body; that being in bed isn't necessarily an aid to 'effectual fervent prayer' as people blithely suppose."[6]

Amy Carmichael could not explain *why* suffering must be humanity's lot throughout history, but she wrote in *Rose from Brier:* "God never wastes His children's pain . . . pain nobly borne strengthens the soul, knits hearts together." Even so, there is no explanation why *that* must be the way of strength, "why need hearts be knit together by such sharp knitting needles?" The answer will be given when "we see Him who endured the cross . . . face to face," wrote Carmichael. Until then only one thing is helpful: childlike trust. We must imagine ourselves at the foot of the cross until our souls are steadied and we know that "love that loves like *that,* can be trusted about *this.*"

Amy had trusted when living was full of "weary little things," and from her bed of thorns bloomed roses. She had trusted that nothing need be wasted. The dullest, dreariest days and the smallest, mangled efforts could be used by God for the good of his children. Jane knew the truth of Amy's words and felt a surge of reassurance.

April bloomed at her window, and once more she was persuaded to ride the dogwood trail with Eva and her brother. This time they drove up on Sharp's Ridge for a view of the mountains. In "Quest," written a few days later, are the lines:

151

> The lowland trails held pleasures
> Of April bloom to view,
> But when the heart needs mountains
> Nothing else will do.

The trip wearied her more than she liked to admit, and when her mother, Elizabeth, and Aunt Bess went on their annual picnic to Cade's Cove, Jane was happy to have a quiet day at home with Eva, playing "Scrabble." Confinement was painful in spring, but this year she had the books of Amy Carmichael, she who had "loved so well the pools and forests" and been shut away from them for twenty years without complaint.

"I've always felt with Amy that it's strange people sometimes think the One who died on Calvary is to apologize because we suffer pain" (*Gnudason, March 23, 1958*).

A collection of Amy's poems was entitled *Toward Jerusalem*. Jane thought it should have been named *Window Toward Jerusalem* instead. The book had inspired a poem about "windows open toward April—almost the same as toward Jerusalem!" she wrote to Kay.[7]

"The Wall with a Window"* sold on first submission. The first stanza read:

> In a certain stony wall
> That shuts the spacious world from view
> Chance—or miracle—has made
> A space for looking through;

There are stubborn walls in every life and windows made by chance, or miracle. It seemed to Jane that Amy Carmichael was such "a little blessed window space," showing God's mercy close at hand. For that she would be eternally grateful. And now she was ready to put aside her fear of failure and go back to work on her unfinished manuscript. Her publisher had shown confidence in her by asking for improvements. She would try to meet their expectations—and God's.

Summer visitors were already arriving. Kay Gudnason came just as the Doll House was filled to the brim with grandchildren and their parents. She observed that Donia, at seventy-six, was still cooking, cleaning house, and caring for Jane. When a book manuscript was under preparation, there was the extra work of carrying and fetching boxes of papers and files. Jane worried much about her mother's health and increasing weariness, but could do very little about it.

The completed manuscript was in the mail before the fall deadline. *In*

*poem used to introduce the first chapter.

Green Pastures was meant for those "who strive to follow faithfully wherever our Shepherd leads, whether through green pastures or dark valleys," Jane noted in the preface. In her own life, it seemed that shadows were deepening ahead.

November 1 marked her thirty-ninth birthday with a small avalanche of mail, visits from churchwomen, Pen Women, her minister, and Eva. Aunt Laura and Aunt Bess had come from Asheville to help celebrate. "All this fuss over me," Jane wrote to Kay. "And Mother's the one who had the baby!"[8]

Kay's gift was as much for Donia as it was for Jane: a generous check for "the automatic washer fund." Household chores would be easier now.

But the best birthday gift was a letter from Robert Roy Wright. The editors were pleased with the manuscript. Jane was deeply grateful, and she prayed for strength to complete the first proofs in time for Christmas. Nelson and Elberta, with the twins, were coming again.

The work was done by mid-December, but Jane was limp with fatigue and eyestrain. She had pushed herself too far and had no energy for holiday preparations. A phone call from Maryland cancelled their plans. Nelson was in the hospital and would have one kidney removed on December 29. No sooner had they received news that he was safely out of surgery, when Donia was rushed to the hospital for an emergency removal of her gall bladder. Impending doom darkened the Doll House.

Elizabeth stayed by their mother's bedside while Eva remained with Jane until Ruth arrived from Union City. Donia was doing better than they had dared hope, but was not out of danger. Jane was grateful to have her mind on second proofs, even if she anguished at reading "Each Winter."

> Even while the bright leaves darken on the ground
> And skies grow heavy and the cold wind shrills
> Across the earth, and sullen raindrops pound,
> Our hearts are sure of spring and daffodils.
>
> And yet, our hearts are wistful, now and then.
> Each winter some plants freeze, some great trees fall.
> We know that April always comes again;
> We know that April never comes to all.

"Things have altered for us in a week," Jane wrote to Shirley, "and may alter more. But Mother and Nelson are both doing well, and that is cause for deep gratitude. . . . We hope eventually she will be as well as ever, but it will be a long rough road.'"[9]

Amy Carmichael had written of just such a time of darkness, in her book *Gold By Moonlight,* and Jane had copied into her notebook: "Sooner or later God meets every trusting child who is following Him . . . and says. 'Now prove that you believe this that you have told me you believe, and that you have taught others to believe.' God knows, and you know, that there was always a hope in your heart that a certain way would not be yours. 'Anything but that, Lord,' had been your earnest prayer. And then, perhaps quite suddenly, you found your feet set on that way. . . . Do you hold fast to your faith that He maketh your way perfect? It does not look perfect. . . . And yet, either it is perfect, or all you have believed crumbles. . . . There is no middle choice between faith and despair. . . . Joy is not gush. . . . Joy is simply perfect acquiescence in God's will, because the soul delights itself in God Himself."

Her mother's death was the one circumstance for which Jane had prayed, "Anything but that, Lord!" This was the challenge to her faith: to trust that God would make all things work together for good—even the thing most feared. Otherwise, her faith meant nothing.

Ten days after the surgery, Donia came home. She was weak, but able to prepare lunch and care for Jane. Housework and heavy lifting must wait until the evening or on weekends when Elizabeth was home, which meant that Jane could only use her typewriter on Saturdays. Writing was slow, and sales were slower. Editors seemed most contrary when she needed money most. Donia's surgery had depleted their small reserve.

Another trial was worse. Donia was too weak to lift the backrest on Jane's bed. So it remained in one position all day, causing increasing discomfort. A wedge-shaped pillow only gave temporary relief. Jane hid her pain and suffered more from the frightening implications: what if her mother could no longer care for her? Hiring help was out of the question. Must they break up the household again? Go back to Union City?

In her manuscript was the verse: "For God hath not given us a spirit of fear, but of power, and of love, and of a sound mind" (II Tim. 1:7). In "The Healing Message" Jane had written:

> Our God is very patient with our fears.
> He understands our dread of loss and change,
> And ever to his people, through the years,
> Whenever anything is new and strange,
> "Fear not," the healing message comes again. . . .
>
> Beset with questions no one comprehends,
> Our hearts may hear him saying still, "Fear not,
> O little flock"; and, trusting him, may find
> The spirit of power and love and a sound mind.

She had quoted another biblical promise: "Thou dost keep him in perfect peace, whose mind is stayed on thee, because he trusts in thee" (Isa. 26:3). The poem began;

> God of eternal glory, keep my heart.
> O keep my heart stayed on thee all this day,
> And if my old hurts ache and new tears start,
> Let me remember these will pass away.
> Let me remember pain is not forever
> And grief and loneliness will finally cease,
> But thou abidest, and no power can sever
> Thy people from thy love and joy and peace.
>
> "All This Day"

Outside her window, crocuses and robins promised spring, and a sale to *Good Housekeeping* indicated a thawing of editorial ice as well. The break in winter came in time to greet a long-awaited guest: Betty Washer, Jane's English correspondent of twenty-one years, who was en route home from New Zealand. The Hoffmanns across the boulevard offered their guest bedroom, and Betty stayed for three days. Her visit inspired "Winter-ripened," a quick sale to *The Christian Science Monitor.*

> You came to us in our brown chilly season
> When this huge earth is winter-shabby,
> You with remembered green
> Of many English Aprils in your heart.
>
> And we who have not seen
> But have ancestral memories of the green
> Of England, and the little flowering lanes,
> And small sequestered gardens rich with bloom,
> Showed you the hills we love, the fields we cherish,
>   saying,
> "If you could only see them when clouds of dogwood
>   blossoms float
> Over them, and the rose-purple froth of redbud, and
>   all greens—"
> And then we paused,
> Seeing your deep sincerity respond
> To the unpretense of bare trees and dark hills
> And to the truth of our desire for your delight,
> And feeling affection flowering in the warmth
> Of mutual understanding, and gladly knowing
> This winter-ripened friendship long will be
> As green as April in Kent and Tennessee.

Donia was pronounced cured, but in early March she awoke one night with excruciating stomach pains. The doctor was called at midnight, and diagnosed a kidney infection.

Such things could be expected from now on. Donia had never been ill before, and she was loath to admit her diminishing strength. "Darling Mother, she always dreaded being helpless and causing concern to others, but she is sweet and patient, and makes no complaint at all. And she is up and doing now, thank God," Jane wrote to Kay a few days later. The bed problem had not been mentioned, but Kay had thoughtfully sent a check to Elizabeth, asking her to buy a crank-up hospital bed for Jane as an Easter gift.

"We three are most surprised and excited and relieved, and oh, most grateful . . . who but you would do such a thing in such a way that even we stiff-necked Merchants feel no hesitation in freely accepting what you so freely give!"[10]

A few days later Donia was besieged with pain again and was admitted to the hospital for a week of tests. Margaret Funk, a friend of the family, stayed with Jane during the day, while Elizabeth was at work. The gift bed had not arrived yet. Jane promised to send a "Hallelujah" to Kay when it did.

A regulation-size hospital bed presented a different problem besides being too wide to go through doorways, it would crowd the small bedroom. Elizabeth was trying to find a smaller, child sized, crank-up bed, or a crank-up screw to fit Jane's own custom-built bed. If that proved impossible, Jane would have to "abdicate as supervisor of the boulevard," and be confined to the bedroom—not a happy thought.

Donia was home in time for Easter, and she was baking bread—a good sign. The tests showed a touch of hepatitis, but she was getting visibly stronger daily. Aunt Bess was there to help as long as needed.

"Two backyard dogwoods are shedding white radiance on my window as I type, this green shower-blessed day," Jane wrote to Gurre. Four new azalea bushes bloomed under the picture window in front of the house, a birthday gift for Donia, who was "most happily rejoicing in April" once again. "I think the dogwood must be blooming with more than ordinary elation just on that account."[11]

Donia seemed much herself again, setting out petunias, candytufts, and geraniums in the garden, pulling weeds and bringing sweet-shrub blossoms to Jane's bedside. Their favorite month brought it's special blessings—golden sunshine over new green leaves, shimmering through rain against a backdrop of blue-gray thunderclouds. "For All the Glory" was in the new book.

> For every April day of gloom and glory
> I thank thee, Lord; for every April day

When storm clouds swathe the world in transitory,
Swift, violent darkness, till a sudden ray
Of dazzling light illuminates the fresh
New buds and leaves adrift in silvery air,
And rainbows, slowly shining forth, enmesh
Our hearts in all the beauty they can bear.

Dear Lord, I thank thee for such days as this
More than for any others I have known,
Days of all earthly days I would not miss.
I thank thee for the sullen storm clouds blown
Across the sky, for silver-misted bloom—
For all the glory, and for all the gloom.

In the meditation she gave thanks for "light that rises in the darkness, and for the darkness that makes us realize how lovely is the light." God, who knew her heart, knew she would not choose the darkness or the storm—or the valley of the shadow. She would avoid all sorrow if she could. But out of experiences she would shrink from had come "the glory of light," the comfort of God's presence, and the sufficiency of his consolation. For that, she was grateful.[12]

The first copies of *In Green Pastures* had arrived, and they were lovely. "My April book—because it *looks* like April," Jane wrote to Kay. The small green volume was her favorite in appearance, so far. Every detail was to her liking.[13]

She had signed two hundred books—in green ink—for an autograph tea at Rich's Book Department. Her mother, Aunt Bess, and Elizabeth were the author's representatives. Donia looked lovely—and completely well. The following Sunday was Mother's Day, and Jane wrote to Gurre: "How grateful I am for a red rose in my hair, only the Giver of mothers can know."[14]

For other mercies, Lord,
My heart could find the word
And music of glad praise;
For orderly calm days;
Evenings that, hour by hour,
Brought little stars to flower
In clusters of delight
Over the breadths of night;
And for much good between
Each dawn, heard, felt and seen,
Multiform, many-hued,
I could voice my gratitude.

But for the life of her
Without whom dawn would blur
And all star-blossoms be
Faded and lost to me—
Lord, for this utmost gift
I have no word to lift.
I watch the dawn skies glow
And know that thou dost know.
"Joy in the Morning"

Critics praised the book unanimously. One described it as "this monumental work," and Alfred Mynders wrote in *The Chattanooga Times:* "Such inspiration as this is rarely found in new poetry nowadays. In the new book . . . there is the same good humor, the same fine sentiment without sentimentality, which has won Jane Merchant a national audience."

Shirley was convinced that Jane was the country's finest poet and would be hailed as such if only more people knew her work. Promotion was the key, and Abingdon wasn't doing enough of it, in her opinion.

Jane thought it best to sound a word of caution. She had been in a writing drought and suffered chronic fatigue since Donia's operation.[15] It could be that she had "no more verse" in her, she lamented to friends. Fortunately, sales were up, though most of her submissions were older works. *McCalls, the Post,* and *The Ladies' Home Journal* had all bought poems lately. They were high paying markets, "persnickety" and hard to please. To Kay she confessed an uncertainty about the future and asked for prayer that she would have an indication of what to do next with her writing.

In mid-August Robert Roy Wright came again. "He wants a book on the Beatitudes and won't believe I'm unable," Jane recorded in her diary. It was too soon to think of another book, even if Donia appeared strong again—strong enough to lift the backrest on Jane's bed. It would be unwise to undertake the extra work with a book manuscript, especially since Jane herself felt depleted and discouraged.

There were several reasons for her despondency. One was the death of Pretty Boy. They would miss his merry ways, Jane lamented to Gurre. If birds could love—and she was certain they could—Pretty Boy had loved her.[16] Another parakeet would mean more work for Donia, and it was out of the question.

Jane would mourn the loss more when she was confined to the bedroom. The family had agreed that Donia's strength must be preserved, and a full-sized crank-up bed would be installed when the summer visiting season was over. There was no other alternative. In the meantime, Jane was able to greet her callers in the dining room without much ado.

A reader in Arkansas had asked permission to pay a short visit in late August. Frances Winter had only recently discovered Jane's books and was anxious to meet their author. Jane consented, and their meeting was of the rare kind, when kindred spirits find each other. Frances was one "who goes into the deep places of one's heart," Jane confided to Gurre *(Noble, Sept. 20, 1959).* In "Note After Meeting," she wrote:

> You were no stranger to me when you came
> Though I had never seen your face before.
> You were an understanding note, a name—
> And then a happy presence at my door.
>
> There were warm smiles of two who recognize
> Mutual acquaintanceship with grief and joy,
> And gratefully I found within your eyes
> A glow of peace that grief cannot destroy.
>
> We talked of books, and it was good to be
> Together till your time was at an end.
> You were no stranger when you came to me
> And when you left you were my steadfast friend.

Frances was a widow, a few years older than Jane, and had returned to school to earn her teacher's credentials. Like Eva, she made no secret of her need for Jane's friendship. The need was mutual. As soon as Frances returned home to Arkansas, they began an exchange of voluminous autobiographical letters, determining common interests and closely aligned views on a wide range of subjects—not the least on literature and religion.

The meeting with Frances had done much to counteract Jane's sadness over other losses. In mid-September she wrote the "Hallelujah" letter to Kay: "I'm happily settled in my green room in what the Sears catalog describes as a 'fashionable piece of furniture'—just picture me being stylish!— with . . . lots of room for you to sit on the foot of the bed, and a crank with which I can easily be wound up every morning and unwound every evening—or any time in between—just like a mechanical doll! And it's much, much more comfortable than my old bed! And people tell me I look better in it, and since any improvement in my looks is cause for gratitude . . . you'd better hop a plane and come and behold the miracle!"[17]

Elizabeth had shuffled the furniture in her own bedroom and made storage space for Jane's small bed so that it could still be used on special occasions for outings to the dining room. But the large bed squeezed out two bookshelves, and Jane with a heavy heart sorted out books to give away. Parting with old favorites was always painful, though she was getting better at not attaching to the physical presence of a book. If she had read it well, the essence of it would always remain in her heart.

The daily view of the boulevard was a greater loss. She was no longer able to watch people pass by her window, "making poems to be written," she lamented to Frances.[18] But the bedroom was cheerful, and the new bed was much more comfortable than her old one. There was nothing to be gained by complaining. Amy Carmichael had taught that joy is "perfect acquiescence to the will of God." Jane would try to practice what she knew to be true.

She had decided that an in-depth study of the Beatitudes was just the antidote she needed to self-pity, whether or not a book came of it. Amy Carmichael had written of the unoffended heart and cited John the Baptist as an example. He had received Christ's words in Herod's dungeon: "Blessed is he, whosoever shall not be offended in me" (Matt. 11:6). John heard the good news that others were healed, raised from the dead, given sight—yet, he was not offended when Christ did not free him from his prison.

The new bed was a wonderful blessing, and the comfortable room with a view to Mother's garden bore no semblance to the dungeon in Herod's castle, but Jane knew the condition of her heart. She longed to attain the ideal—the unoffended heart of John—shining through the Sermon on the Mount. If ever she dared attempt a book on the Beatitudes, she would include "The Unoffended."

> To John, imprisoned for the truth, there came
> No word but this, "Go tell him what you hear
> And see: the blind receive their sight; the lame
> Walk, and the deaf hear words of hope and cheer."
> There was no opening of his iron cell,
> No sudden restoring of his liberty,
> Only the words that others were made well,
> Only the news that others were set free.
>
> And, for the blind who never see the light,
> For all the deaf who never hear the word,
> And all who suffer for the sake of right
> With constancy and patience, undeterred
> By being misunderstood and set apart,
> Christ's blessing on the unoffended heart.

1. Donia Swann Merchant.

2. Clarence L. Merchant.

3. (*left to right*) Ruth, Nelson, Jane, Elizabeth. 1920.

4. Clarence enclosed the porch so Jane could be outside.

5. Jane in Inskip.

6. The family poses with the Model T Ford. (*left to right*) Donia, Jane, Clarence, Elizabeth, Nelson, Ruth, Grandmother Swann. Circa 1927.

7. Jane and Nelson with Billy.

8. The house in Strawberry Plains. 1941.

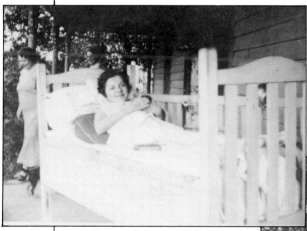

9. On the porch at Dandridge. 1934.

10. At Dandridge. (*left to right*) Ruth, Donia, Grandmother Swann, Jane, Nelson, Clarence, Elizabeth. Circa 1935.

11. Donia, Jane, Clarence in Strawberry Plains.

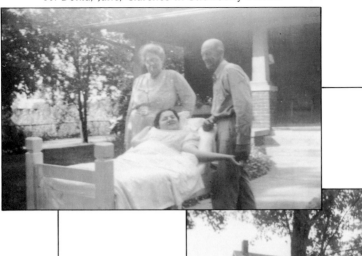

12. The house on Sunset Trail, Fountain City. 1949.

13. Elizabeth. 1944.

14. Jane with nieces and nephews. 1959.

15. The house on Emoriland Boulevard, Knoxville.
Dogwood season, 1970.

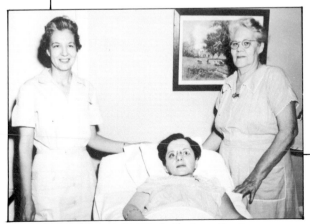

16. (*left to right*) Elizabeth, Jane, Donia.

17. Proud parent.

20. Elizabeth appears in Jane's place at an autographing party in Knoxville. 1968.

21. Jane's books on display. 1967.

22. Jane at Inskip.

12
WITH US
1959–1960

Too stern for us to build on,
This unconditional stone,
Alluring, terrifying—
If we must build alone.

And following this great pattern
For building strong and true
No unassisted spirit
Can ever hope to do.

But when he sees us striving
To live the truth we hear
Always to us the Master comes,
The Lord himself draws near

The carpenter of ages
With skillful, patient joy
Works with us on a building
Storms never can destroy.

For nine years Eva had come twice weekly, bringing encouragement and challenge, people and books, and countless other necessities. Their friendship had grown rich and deep; yet, lately there were differences—and distances—difficult to understand.

The change became noticeable with Eva's growing interest in the Roman Catholic Church. Jane joined her in reading a number of Catholic books and found much true devotion and piety in them, but remained firm in her Methodist convictions.

In 1959 Eva joined the Roman Catholic church and was much occupied with church activities. She was certain that Jane had "prayed her into Catholicism," but Jane would only admit to having prayed John's: "That she may know thee, the only true God, and Jesus Christ." Eva's decision seemed "one of His more astounding answers," she wrote to a mutual friend.[1] In "To Each," she had written:

God speaks to each the language he can hear,
In sermons, or in silence of a star.
In tenement, and temple, slum and cell,
The voice of God calls to us where we are.

Let each of us give reverent care to heed
The voice that speaks to us, from church or clod,
And let us be, oh, very slow to say
Of the voice another hears, "It is not God."

Increasingly there were things the two friends did not discuss. Jane knew the necessity of heeding God's word as she understood it and of respecting Eva's need to respond differently. She must guard against assuming that a way other than her own was wrong.

Amy Carmichael, in her book *Thou Givest, They Gather,* gave a test for a true friendship: to ask who comes first, God or your friend. What is the fruit of your friendship? Does it strengthen or weaken you? The hearts of true friends are bound together by the love of God. Their friendship strengthens, inspires, ennobles them, and lasts forever. A selfish friendship will not last.

Even as she asked herself the questions, Jane was certain her friendship with Eva would stand the test. But this was a difficult time. For so long there had been a comforting sense of understanding and being understood, even when they knew that *complete* understanding between human hearts was beyond their reach. In "The Understanding One" Jane would later write:

"He who understands will understand"—
Quiet words I hold within my mind
That even in thought I may not reprimand
The trusted ones, intentionally kind,
Who do not understand some words I speak,
Who see no reason in some things I do,
Who are not challenged by the goals I seek
Nor stirred by what I feel is deeply true.

Not always can another's heart respond
With ardor to one's best enthusiasm;
Sometimes we venture, unaware, beyond
Our nearest, and must call across a chasm.
Some do not understand us; but the chill
Is warmed by knowing One who always will.

The friendship with Frances Winter, a fellow Methodist, eased the pain a little. Frances had sent on loan her two favorite books: Thomas Kelly's

Testament of Devotion and Antoine de Saint-Exupery's *The Little Prince*. Jane was delighted to discover their common love for Thomas Kelly, but the other book was a new acquaintance. After one reading of it, the little golden-haired prince from a distant planet was "securely nestled" in her heart, she wrote to Frances, and one phrase sparked a poem.[2] The first lines read:

> Having been given, all my years,
> Affection without stint or end,
> His quiet words brought sudden tears;
> "Not everyone has had a friend."
>
> "Friends"

The friendship between the little prince and the fox in the book was a new reminder of Eva, who had "tamed" Jane with dependable visits, as the little prince tamed his wary friend. The fox dared to believe in the little prince's love, and he cried at their parting. But the point of the story was not the pain of losing a friend. The fox was richer now because the essential, invisible truth of their friendship would remain when the beloved presence was gone, even if it was also true that, "one runs the risk of weeping, a little, if one lets himself be tamed," wrote Saint-Exupery.

Eva still came twice weekly, but the visits were more hurried, and Jane blamed herself for the unspoken distance between them. Her deafness and difficulties in communicating were no doubt part of the problem, she noted to Frances.

Her friend disagreed. She compared Jane's writing to Emily Dickinson's and found a significant difference in "what you do with people. You pick the spark that each one has and share it." Emily's poems "reveal her looking in a window so to speak, without being able to take part, communicate." Otherwise, Frances thought that if the two poets had been set in one another's family—and swapped centuries—they might have "written each other's poems"[3]

Jane chuckled at the thought of the exchange and was grateful to have been born the daughter of her own gentle father, not Emily's harsh one. But Frances' description of looking at people through glass was precisely the way she felt at times, watching people talk and not hearing them. If she were able to "get through to and into people," it was surely no special talent of her own, but of the Lord's mercy, she insisted *(Winter, Sept. 22, 1959)*.

Other friends—Eva among them—would agree with Frances. One had noted Jane's "antenna to people's moods,"[4] both in her poetry and letters, a sensitivity and compassion flowing through the words on a page. To her many regular correspondents she was the listener, the one they could confide in, sharing the pain and joys of living, certain of an encouraging response. But that was in *writing,* Jane would argue. She often despaired of the difference between her life on paper and in person. Others didn't seem to notice—her family, Eva, visitors. But they didn't *really* know her, she lamented to Frances. No wonder the Dickinsons failed to understand Emily—they weren't *her.* She was unprecedented. But so was everyone. "When you come right down to it, does anyone ever know just what to make of anybody else?"[5]

The ache of misunderstanding and being misunderstood was universal. Of all Jane's poems in print, none had drawn as much reader response as did "For Those Who Love."

> Have mercy always on the ones who love you.
> Deny yourself the sharp impatient word
> When they are overanxious, overkind.
> Your careless hasty utterance is heard
> Through all the lonely hallways of the heart
> That loves and, loving, yearns. Refrain, refrain,
> In mercy, from self-will, for those who love
> Are desperately vulnerable to pain.

Confinement to the back bedroom increased her vulnerability to loneliness. Jane was shut off from much of the happenings in the rest of the house, and she tried not to take offense. She made light of it to Shirley: "If one is rich in proportion to what one can do without, I must be fabulously endowed!"[6]

Trees were turning to gold in the garden. Jane was notified that the Chattanooga Audubon Society would name a tree in their Literary Acres in her honor on National Poetry Day. Elizabeth would represent her, but Jane ached to see it herself!

Alfred Mynders wrote in *The Chattanooga Times:* "Jane Merchant is by far the most widely read of Tennessee's contemporary poets . . . it will be a tall October day at the Elise Chapin sanctuary, where the foliage is beginning to take on the glory of autumn." He noted that in, *The Greatest of These* "there is a poem which would do for the christening observance"

> A day of wind and sunshine
> And whirling gusts of gold,
> And something more of loveliness
> Than human hearts can hold.
>
> A day of crimson glories
> And tangy tingling air,
> And something more of happiness
> Than human hearts can bear.

Oh, pure must be his spirit,
His tongue well taught to pray
In gratitude, who can endure
A tall October day.
                    "October Song"

The tree was a straight young loblolly pine. Robert Sparks Walker read the dedication: "In consideration of her achievements in the field of literature . . . [we] christen this tree standing in Literary Acres, Jane Merchant."

It was her loftiest honor of the year. The October sky arching blue over her garden also looked on "her" tree, a reminder that even when the bedroom seemed crowded and monotonous, her Father's love was various and spacious.

Her fortieth birthday and a family visit left her worn out. November rain—a source of inspiration in the past—seemed only dismal now. One room "seemed to need sunshine, more than several," she lamented to Frances.[7]

Writing was difficult. Jane described herself as a has-been to Shirley, who came on a quick visit before Thanksgiving, and warned her not to expect any more poems. Shirley took such dire predictions lightly—they had proved false before—but her optimism failed to lift Jane's spirit. It plunged even lower a few days later.

Never before had Jane believed in Friday the thirteenth, she wrote mournfully to Frances. But this day fulfilled all portents of gloom. Eva had found it necessary to limit her visits to once a week from now on. She was overworked and had looked near collapse in the last few weeks. Jane could see good reason for the decision, but she had counted on their visits to relieve the tedium of her one room. Even if Eva insisted that nothing had changed in their relationship, Jane sensed a shift in priorities. She confided to Frances: "I ought not feel like St. Exupery, that I have no one to talk to."[8]

The transition came just at the anniversary of their friendship. Two years earlier, Jane had written to Eva: "It really wouldn't do, would it, to compare the friendship between us to a chain . . . because neither of us would take kindly to chains. . . . And . . . grappling one's friend to one's soul with hoops of steel, as recommended by W. Shakespeare . . . would be an unnecessarily forcible procedure. . . . Would you think I hold our friendship 'dirt cheap' if I said it seems to me rather like the earth itself?—the necessary earth in which all sorts and shapes and hues of lovely things can grow. We're sure of earth as we can be of anything on earth; we couldn't possibly get along without it, we know it isn't apt to cave in under us, and that though it may be muddy sometimes, or dusty, it's there and faithful to the seed we sow. A source of sustenance, a source of joy. And that is how our friendship seems to me."[9]

Now she wondered if her pain was a sign that she had tried to chain Eva to herself and had come to depend too much on a physical presence. Perhaps this stripping was necessary to learn the essential limitation of all human relationships. In her notebook Jane wrote:

> God of my troubled days and anxious nights,
> God of my hidden tears,
> God of my glad hours and my gold delights
> Through varying years,
>
> Teach me, O God, I who am slow to learn,
> Never to seek
> From any other the aid for which I yearn
> When I am weak;
>
> But to rely on thee to lift my care
> And make me strong,
> Thou who hast never failed my reaching prayer
> My whole life long.
>
> "Through Varying Years"

Inner detachment was difficult to achieve when she was physically dependent on others for nearly everything. It was difficult to trust Eva's assurances of continued devotion and not wonder if the visits were only a charity, a troublesome duty. It was difficult not to seek refuge in emotional isolation, hide behind an illusive wall of denial—"I don't need you or anybody!"

In "March Willow," Jane wrote:

> "That willow leafs too early every year,
> And every year its leaves are killed by cold.
> You're like it, child, impetuously sincere,
> Believing every pleasant thing you're told,
> And you'll be chilled by many a snub and slight
> As sure as all those green leaves die tonight."
>
> The young girl listened to the gnarled advice
> And thought how beautiful the doomed leaves were,
> And after stormy days of snow and ice
> She saw the willow's bright releafings stir
> As greenly on the languid sunlit breeze
> As those of any wise untrusting trees.

She wanted to believe Eva. It was better to be hurt by "trusting too much than risk hurting others by trusting too little," Jane wrote in a meditation.[10]

The March willow poem made her hundredth sale to the *Post,* and—at least for the moment—suspended her conviction of being a has-been poet. Her stubborn depression was lifting, and after a quiet, restful Christmas, her energies were returning.

Together magazine for January carried a lengthy feature article by Beatrice Plumb on "Jane Merchant: Poetess of Faith." Jane had consented to it on Eva's urging, but was embarrassed, as usual, to see herself praised in print. The article was factual enough, she admitted to Frances, "but didn't sound a bit like me to me." The Little Prince had said that people never ask the really important questions about other people; perhaps it would be "even more embarrassing" if they did. Having *any* questions answered, in print, was depressing enough *(Winter, Oct. 23, 1959).*

The publicity had boosted everyone's expectations—and Jane's fear of disappointing them. Friends were asking about another book, but her thoughts on that subject were private. She had made no commitment to Abingdon, and she feared it was too presumptuous to tackle the Beatitudes. What did she have to offer on such a vast theme?

Together had printed "For the Seeking," her poem about Jesus' feeding the five thousand with two small fish and five loaves of bread. The last stanzas read:

> "Send them away," I sometimes plead
> When people crowd me with their need.
>
> "They hunger, Lord—and so do I.
> How can I help, or even try?
>
> "Bring me the little you possess
> And give the needy what I bless,"
>
> He says, as He will always say,
> "They need not go away."

There was truth in her words, but living it was harder. Dared she bring the little she possessed in faith that God would bless and make it sufficient? Years earlier she had written that a thing offered would multiply in the very act of sharing it with others:

> With little comfort of my own
> I still may comfort you.
> Scant sustenance for one is full
> Sufficiency for two.
>
> "Sharing"

January brought another tangible encouragement. Gurre and Jack Noble stopped by to visit her on their way to England. Gurre called her poems "mousetraps" for catching people, and Jane quipped, "They snap, anyhow." They all laughed, but the comparison stuck in her mind. Christ told his fishermen followers that he would make them catchers of men, not to ensnare people in their nets, but setting them free in the love of God. That was the higher purpose of her "catchy" poems. For that she had been called to write, and she dared not refuse to try another book if God gave the task.

In preparation for the work, she would read more on the Beatitudes, pray more about it, and write to see if suitable poems would come.

Snow brought flocks of winged visitors to the bird-feeder, and Jane watched a clumsy pigeon trying to perch on the shelf meant for much smaller birds. Its dilemma triggered a sonnet, with the lines:

> It takes a pigeon quite a while to learn
> That one's endeavors and desires should be
> Proportioned to the facts one can discern
> (As it has, on occasion, taken me).
> My sympathy goes with him as he flies
> To find a place where he's the proper size.
> "Outsize Pigeon"

The question on Jane's mind was one of proportion as well: Was she considering an outsize task? It was not so much the physical limitations; Donia's strength seemed adequate for another book project. But as usual Jane questioned her own spiritual preparedness. She was reading Thomas Merton's book *Seeds of Contemplation,* and copied into her notebook words that invariably tugged at her conscience: "A man who is not stripped and poor and naked within his own soul will unconsciously tend to do the works he has to do for his own sake rather than for the glory of God. . . . But every moment of the day will bring him some frustration that will make him bitter and impatient, and in his impatience he will be discovered."

Jane's impatience was carefully concealed, but inwardly her exasperation was easily triggered by trivialities: editorial nitpicking, her own imperfections, and her cramped existence. What did *that* reveal of the true motives of her heart? She had no doubt what Merton would make of it!

Together had printed "If We Ask," with the stanzas:

> Lord, if we ask for patience
> Let us always take
> Quietly each blunder
> And every mistake
> And all the small shortcomings
> Of others and of ours,
> Since from irritations
> Genuine patience flowers.

168

> Lord, if we ask the taking
> Of our trials away
> Teach us that such words as these
> Are what we really say:
> "We have no desire
> For growing, after all.
> Make us selfish cowards,
> Lord, keep us weak and small."

To Frances, Jane confessed that her impatience tended to surface in barbed witticism and scorn, a self-indulgence she loathed. This year during the six weeks of Lent, she would try to abstain from saying or thinking "anything at all uncomplimentary about anyone or anything:"[11]

Merton had unmasked another of Jane's personal traits: excessive modesty. Again she copied from his book: "A humble man is not disturbed by praise. Since . . . he knows where the good that is in him comes from, he does not refuse praise, because it belongs to the God he loves . . . One who has not yet learned humility, becomes upset and disturbed by praise. He may even lose his patience . . . get irritated by the sense of his own unworthiness. . . . The humble man receives praise the way a clean window takes the light of the sun. The truer and more intense the light is, the less you see of the glass."

So much for her illusion of humility! In "Prayer for Discernment" Jane wrote:

> Grant me, O Lord, Thy constant aid
> Against the sly ability
> Of my self-pride to masquerade
> As pure humility.

The insight into the deceitfulness of her heart was both helpful and distressing. Daily she understood more clearly just how much she owed to God's mercy and forgiveness, rather than her own goodness. She tried to put it on paper in four simple lines:

> For all your giving, day by day,
> I thank you Lord; but when I weigh
> The merits of my accustomed living
> I thank you most for your forgiving.
> "With Thankfulness"

The increasing vexations of her circumstances were painful realities, largely beyond her control. But they were not the determining factors of living. Her response to them would make the difference, her grumbling or her gratitude. That lesson she apparently needed to learn again and again. In "Showing Their Mettle" she wrote:

One complained with gloomy eye,
"What a dismal pewter sky!"
Said another, "I've never seen
The sky with such a silvery sheen!"

The three short poems sold together—obviously her painful lessons were useful to others. And so it might be with a book, however inadequate she felt to the task.

The responsibility of writing for a public was still frightening. Gurre had found one of Jane's poems tucked into a Bible in London. She asked if Jane ever gave thought to "the thousands who love and clip your poems."[12]

Jane tried not to think of the reaction of her readers—or of her accountability to them and to God—lest it overwhelm her. Who could ever be sure his or her motives were without self-seeking? She could only trust that if her intention was to do the will of God as well as she could discern it—even if her act was mistaken—he would accept the intention.

She couldn't be certain it was God's will that she attempt another book, but God knew the yearning of her heart and would bring her efforts to his intended end. That much she was certain.

"Dependence" was written with the new manuscript in mind.

Thou knowest, Lord of all, how much I need
Thy wisdom, having little of my own.
Without thy guidance nothing can succeed.
Without thee I am utterly alone.

Without thy constant help I cannot bear
The ever-increasing sorrow of the days,
Nor conquer small temptations to despair
That trip my heart in unexpected ways.

Without thy love I have no love to give,
Without thy spirit I am nothingness.
O fill me with thy life, that I may live;
Give me thy blessing, Lord, that I may bless.

The discipline of Lent was ended, and Easter dawned over Jane's garden. She gazed in astonishment at two small pine trees that appeared to have sprouted overnight. Under cover of darkness Elizabeth had planted them and confessed her part in the scheme, devised by Gurre and Jack, to bring a live loblolly to Jane, allowing her to see what her namesake in Chattanooga looked like.

Her friends had understood the necessity of seeing and touching the real thing. "Bless your tree-loving, bird-loving Jane-loving heart for such a green growing Easter thought!" Jane wrote to thank them.[13] No amount of imagining, reading, or picturing could take the place of experiencing the real thing, as when she could be outside seeing the wonder of sky and smelling the growing things, "And it's just as I dreamed and imagined and wrote, but so much more too. . . . The reality always eludes and surpasses both dream and description."[14]

Gurre would appreciate Jane's "sense of pure incredulity that I'm actually seeing what I'm . . . seeing, if it's just an 'ordinary' Tennessee rainbow, or a glimpse of stars when everyone else is asleep, a feeling as if I've been living somebody else's life all along and have finally gotten into the right one, or an equally strong feeling that I've momentarily slipped out of my own life and am experiencing somebody else's. . . . Usually though, it's more a feeling that I've gotten into the right life at last, which must be a sort of preview of how we'll feel 'when we all get to Heaven'—though I don't much believe I'll 'sing and shout the victory.' I think I'll be too awed and joyous to make a sound, if these previews are any indication."[15]

Spring was hauntingly beautiful outside while Jane wrote "The April Shadow," with thought of the new manuscript.

> Always in April, on her quiet face
> Where calm acceptance of denial rested
> At other times, we saw the shadows's trace—
> The shadow of old patience newly tested.
> We saw how wistfully her eyes would follow
> Explorers of faint winding pathways, bound
> Into the secret depths of glen and hollow
> Where April's earliest blossomings were found.
>
> They brought her wildwood flowers, shy and fair,
> And she would smile, like one who almost sees
> Their forest home, and almost breathes the air
> Where shadows of new leaves on April trees
> She never walked beneath, dance lightly on
> The April earth she never walked upon.

The poem expressed feelings of sadness not likely to be shared by all her readers. But so often the things she thought "entirely too personal and peculiar" to herself turned out to be exactly what others felt, she explained to Frances. "All I know is, I have to be honest."[16]

The poem would go in the manuscript—if indeed there would be one. A sudden crisis had upset the household: Donia suffered a horrifying nosebleed for a full hour and a half before Aunt Bess could reach a doctor. It happened while Elizabeth was gone on a week's vacation—her first in two years—and was a frightening reminder of their precarious circumstances.

Jane's physical dependence on Donia and Elizabeth could not be helped—or could it? She had long contemplated experimenting with a wheelchair. If it was possible to slide into one from her bed without being lifted (and without breaking a bone!) she could do more for herself and be of help to Donia as well. Much of their immediate problem would be solved.

Not surprisingly, Donia and Elizabeth refused to sanction such "recklessness." Even a routine transfer to the small bed was risky. Donia usually left the room while Jane scooted herself over, inch by inch, under Elizabeth's watchful eyes.

Jane persisted, and Elizabeth grudgingly consented to having the chair delivered on trial. Donia tried to conceal her apprehension and fled to the kitchen when it arrived.

The experiment was never carried out. The difference in height between the bed and the chair seat was greater than Jane had anticipated. Getting from one to the other without breaking a bone seemed impossible. The mere thought of trying obviously frightened Donia and Elizabeth more than it was worth.

Dejectedly Jane ordered the chair sent back and tried to make light of her disappointment in "Cure for a Blunder."

> It isn't the first
> And it won't be the last
> And the memory of it
> Will soon be past,
> For I'll forget it
> The minute I make
> Some other stupid
> Silly mistake.

It was best not to dwell on what had happened. Some things—like walking—were manifestly impossible, she admitted to Frances, even if the longing for it never quite died. "It's when things are almost within one's grasp, and yet never quite attainable, that one feels really frustrated."[17]

The temptation to succumb to self-pity was strong, and Jane knew her weakness. "Shall we pray for each other," she suggested, "that James 1:2-4 be fulfilled in us? 'Count it all joy, my brethren, when you fall into divers temptations.' My algebra isn't always up to counting trials as joy, but it should be."[18]

A sure sign of self-pity was inward whining, and Jane was aware of doing too much of it lately. Her poem "Probability" had just been printed. The barb was aimed at herself as well.

> Among five thousand who were fed
> On two fish and five loaves of bread
> Were doubtless several who complained
> About the bones the fish contained.

172

There was pleasant meat on the bones, if she only cared to look. Her "Cure for a Blunder" sold to the *Post* and gave ground for rejoicing, even if Mrs. Redman, the poetry editor, had resigned. It seemed a bad omen, somehow.

The summer was full of tests for her "higher algebra"; Donia was growing weary again. How much longer could she keep on? Jane fervently prayed they would not have to go through another uprooting. Yet, if the worst should happen, that, too, must be borne. Her poem "Alternative" was printed in July, and she sent a copy to Frances with the comment: "I'm afraid most of us lose [the taper] now and then" *(Winter, July 14, 1960).*

> "Better to light a candle
> Than to curse the dark"—
> But if one can kindle
> No enlivening spark
> And has noe smallest taper
> For flame to feed upon—
> One may bless the dark
> And rest in it, till dawn.

She felt bone-weary and hoped to get rested enough to write again. The future seemed an endless uphill journey, and she wrote several friends for prayer support, "that I may know His will and have the strength to do it, if it may be, joyfully."[19]

Slowly and painstakingly poems and prayers for a new book were beginning to take shape, but Jane had not dared commit herself to the publisher yet. One of the poems was titled "High Journey." In the devotion she wrote with it, she said: "Lord, when the way seems very long and very hard and we are worn in spirit, mind, and body, grant that we may not fall or turn aside. . . . Renew us moment by moment, that in thy strength we may go on when all our strength is gone. Amen."[20]

> Up rough roads, in dark weather, we have gone
> For long days, and the journey is not done.
> The raveling way leads ever up and on
> Through forests seldom visited by sun.
>
> Oh, we are weary, weary, and we gaze
> With wondering eyes at those who are not tired,
> Who walk with laughter level sunlit ways
> Bordered by flowers that they have not desired.
>
> But he who calls us to this hazardous
> Steep way has faith in our continuing strength,
> And we may trust in him who trusts in us
> And walks beside us all the road's high length.

13
BOON
1960–1961

New joy
Unfolds; a white
Water lily floating
Luminous on a quiet pool
Of tears.

Jane was flabbergasted to learn that *In Green Pastures* had sold ten thousand copies in its first year. It was both a sobering and an exhilarating reminder of the large responsibility of writing—and of its occasional financial boon.

Frances had asked whether another book was planned, but Jane was not ready to tell yet. She admitted that the publisher was eager for one and that she had given it some thought, but the work was a formidable undertaking, with much tiresome typing and details—reason enough for hesitating.

By return mail came an offer to type the manuscript, and Jane hastened to explain that as long as Donia was able to carry supplies back and forth, it was best for the book—and its author—that she do the typing herself. The very doing of it helped clarify her ideas and usually improved on the long-hand draft.

Writing books must be a little like having children, she often thought. The long process of writing could be likened to gestation and giving birth, from the slow meditating on the germ of an idea, through the careful writing and rewriting, developing poems and prayers. Sometimes a whole afternoon was spent in contemplating and writing a single prayer. The typing was part of the final birthing—it could simply not be done by another.

For months Jane had weighed the pros and cons of another book. Now a verse in her Bible prompted a decision: "But my righteous one shall live by faith; And if he shrink back, my soul hath no pleasure in him" (Heb. 10:38 JBP).

Her main argument *against* the book seemed, on closer scrutiny, little more than a flimsy cover up for shrinking back. A sense of unworthiness no longer had the comforting aura of humility and modesty. True humility, as she saw it reflected in the Beatitudes, was not rooted in an "unworthy" self, but in the saving grace of Christ. With her eyes on him, away from her shrinking self, she could complete the task he had given her.

On September 19 Jane recorded in her diary that she began typing the sample manuscript. The following day she wrote an exuberant letter to Kay, without giving the immediate reason for her elation, but giving thanks for prayers and reporting that she felt "more rested and zestful than in quite a while."[1]

Once the commitment had been made, the paralysis of indecision was replaced by a surge of new energy. Jane trusted herself to the Giver of strength and wisdom for the next leg of the journey.

In the opening poem of the manuscript, the reader is brought to "The Mount of the Beatitudes" where Jesus spoke to the "humble, mournful, meek; the needy, merciful and pure":

> It was a little mountain, with no name
> For overwhelming altitudes, no claim
> To being earth's most majestic, most sublime;
> It was a mountain weary folk could climb.
> And on the lowly mountain small winds went
> Sighing across the grasses meekly bent
> Beneath the weight of many trampling feet,
> And sparrows twittered, finding seeds to eat
> In merciful supply, beneath the pure
> Blue sky, and home trees peacefully secure.
>   And here the searching people heard him speak
> His blessing on the humble, mournful, meek,
> The needy, merciful, and pure, and all
> Peacemakers, and those whom men mistreat, and call
> Hard names for living thus. The startling words,
> Mingled with chirps of confident small birds,
> Brought guilty consternation and disdain
> To many, and to others wistful pain,
> But many hearers, eagerly receiving,
> Found joy beyond belief in sure believing.
>   No inaccessibility excludes
> Us from the Mount of the Beatitudes.
> If we but firmly, finally put aside
> Our anxious selfish righteousness and pride
> And strive in earnest love to do his will,
> Our hearts may hear him saying, "Blessed," still.

In early November, just before election day, the manuscript was in the mail. Jane celebrated by scooting herself onto the small daybed, and being wheeled into the dining room where she could watch the people going to and from the polls.

The presidential race was close, and Jane had watched the debates between Richard Nixon and John F. Kennedy on television—without hearing them. She had voted by absentee ballot for the Republican candidate—not entirely without qualms, she confessed to Frances. She never voted without qualms. The democratic process was not to be taken lightly, and she had found the long and heated campaign embarrassing. The public spectacle had brought out the worst qualities in the contenders and had done little to clarify the issues.

Jane felt uneasy with the kind of rhetoric—written or spoken—that claimed to offer the right answers to all the questions, particularly when a culprit was blamed for all the ills. A complex issue could always be seen from differing viewpoints, and Jane often anguished with those on both sides.

In "Who Is My Neighbor?" she had written:

> Oh, may I never turn away
> From either oppressors or oppressed,
> But ever faithfully work and pray
> That all may be redeemed and blessed,
> Opposing with relentless love
> The wrongs men do themselves and others
> Till by the grace of God above
> We live in harmony as brothers.

The poem, written about the tragedy of racial bigotry, was in her last manuscript, but not because civil rights issues had made political headlines in an election year. Jane's personal concern for the issue was of long standing. If her writing was timely—all her books contained poems of social significance, and her letters often reflected current events—it was because she knew herself to be part of the world she was physically shut away from. She felt its pain and her share of responsibility. And she saw clearly that political solutions, though important, held no lasting cure for its ills.

Abingdon had signalled satisfaction with her first draft, and Jane dared hint to Frances: "I may yet commit another book—but don't alarm *any* of the populace by whispering such a rumor, please!"[2]

When Frances pressed for details, Jane went so far as to say she had promised another book, but repeated the need for secrecy. There was yet much work to be done, and she was alternately pleased and disgusted with the progress, as usual.

The year ended on a good note as one of her best financially. Several magazines had bought poems, raising her hopes for 1961. Any year that read the same "upside down as right side up" looked promising, Jane quipped to Carolyn Ruth. A year turned upside down might prove a considerable improvement over the one just past!

She watched the Kennedy inauguration on television and was elated to see Robert Frost read a poem during the ceremony. Perhaps it augured well for a renewed public interest in poetry!

In February came an urgent request from Abingdon. They would like to have her manuscript ahead of schedule for printing before Christmas. Jane typed for a solid week, beating the deadline. Afterwards she felt the peculiar letdown of having passed a goal with no new aim in view. It was like having the "after-baby blues," without having seen the baby yet—and not knowing if it would do well or poorly.

In the preface she had written of "the higher mathematics" of counting trials and difficulties as blessings, the kind of blessings Christ spoke of in the Sermon on the Mount, when he said: "Blessed are the poor, the needy, the mournful, the persecuted." Jane wrote: "We think of a blessing as something that makes life easy for us; and few of us, however sincere may be our response to the beautiful sayings and life of our Lord, find it really easy to cease being self-centered, self-sufficient, and self-assertive. For most of us it requires constant daily effort to become humbly trustful, receptive, and obedient to the spirit of Christ which alone can make us truly hungry for righteousness, merciful, pure, and peaceable."

It was a daily effort Jane found "more rewarding than any other." Her book was addressed to fellow pilgrims seeking to "draw nearer to the One who lived [the Beatitudes] perfectly."

Once again she had sent the manuscript with the prayer that it not be accepted unless it was pleasing to God. She had done her best; the work she had been so fearful of undertaking was completed. The research and slow writing had yielded much new insight—into her own weaknesses and the mercy of God. Always she saw herself as the main beneficiary of the work, more than her readers, with reason to be grateful, whether or not the book reached print.

Donia's strength had proved adequate. Together they rejoiced in the first signs of spring in the garden. Jane's "Evidence"—later renamed "Reprovings"—was scheduled for printing in April.

> Amazed by the relief
> We feel at fresh re-leafings—
> "O ye of little faith,"
> We hear again.
>
> Though we believe we trust,
> Some unadmitted
> Faint doubt will always need
> These green reprovings.

177

Another reproving of her little faith arrived with the mailman a few days later. Jane had her own system of reading the mail in order of importance. Personal letters were quickly scanned first, to be slowly savored later. Next she opened the envelopes from magazine editors, with their heart-quickening acceptances or rejections. Last she turned her attention to such things as subscription renewal notices, bills, and bulk mail.

That particular day in late February, Jane casually assigned a slim envelope from *The Lyric* magazine to the last stack, thinking it held a reminder to pay her dues. But when she opened it, a check for one hundred dollars fell out, with a citation for "outstanding achievement in the field of poetry"![3]

She squealed with astonishment. The award was totally unexpected, and there was something "deliciously literary" about getting a citation instead of "crassly selling" poems, she exulted to Shirley. "And if there's crass cash along with the glory—'there's glory for you!'—as Humpty Dumpty said."[4]

A note from Robert Roy Wright added to her exaltation: the manuscript had been enthusiastically accepted.

The paper work went easier this time, though Jane never felt quite at ease making her "author's statement about manuscript," trying to explain "what special value" her book had over others in the same category. She usually by-passed the question by quoting what readers had said about her earlier books.

It was easier to fill in the rubrics on education and positions held; she could not resist putting "none" under the first and "mostly horizontal" under the second.

Proofs were done in record time and without the usual neuralgia attack. Although Jane had not taken her task less seriously, she declared to Gurre. With a battery-powered magnifying glass and red pencils and frequently consulting Bible and dictionary, she scrutinized the pages "like an eagle in his aerie scanning the countryside."[5]

The work was back in the mail before Easter, and Jane tried to relax, determined to fight the wave of apprehension that usually followed the final stage of her part in the bookmaking. Had she done her best? Had she caught all serious mistakes? Was her theology sound?

Her latest reading did not help matters. E. Stanley Jones' *Christian Maturity* was critical of Christians who "tried harder," instead of "letting go and letting God." A "religion of duty," placing God as a point of reference rather than a resource, caused the person who tried harder to become self-centered rather than God-centered.

Jane was ever aware of the tension in her own life between trying to do her best and relying on God. She hoped the emphasis in her latest book was not "too much on *trying* to be humble, meek and righteous," she confided to Frances, though trying harder might not hurt some of her readers. "I tried to make it plain that no one attains blessedness by his own efforts alone, nor yet without making any effort whatever."⁶

At the moment she was at a loss about where to direct her efforts in writing. That too appeared to be a common symptom of "postnatal blues" after "birthing" a book. It grew worse with depressing news from *The Saturday Evening Post,* her best—and highest paying—magazine market for more than fifteen years: they would no longer buy poetry, except humorous short pieces for the joke page. Jane would have to work twice as hard to make half as much from other magazines, she lamented to Shirley.

Her complaint fell on sympathetic ears. Shirley was Jane's "self-appointed publicity agent," and she seldom lost an opportunity for promoting Jane—often with happy results. The Kerrs belonged to The Smoky Mountains Hikers Club, and Shirley had donated a copy of *Halfway Up the Sky* to their library. She could report that they had chosen to use Jane's poem "Haze on Old Hills," handsomely illustrated, in their 1961 yearbook.

> A haze, like memories, centuries forgotten,
> Rests on these hills.
> An indistinct, primeval reminiscence
> Eternally distills
> From ancient stone, of faint, uncomprehended
> Truths strangely tall
> We knew long since, and cannot quite forget
> Or quite recall.

But Shirley's latest "good fairy work" had brought a more amazing reward. Jane gasped when she unfolded the clipping from the book page of *The Richmond Times-Dispatch* dated April 8. The lead column, by book editor Dr. Lewis F. Ball, began: "Hardly more than one book in 21 really deserves serious attention. It is the 21st book I want to crown. Mrs. H. J. Kerr . . . has called to my attention a volume of poetry by Jane Merchant entitled *Halfway Up the Sky.* . . . The author is a Tennessean and an invalid . . . she has been totally deaf since 1943.

"Don't think that I praise her work because of her handicaps; it can stand alone on its own merits. . . . Her competence and flashes of insight would do credit to anyone. . . . Her poems sing.

"If she sometimes seems to echo Emily Dickinson, be assured that she has made the divine Emily's processes her own—and she has the same independence."

Dr. Ball quoted "Bookworm's Turning"* and added, "nor can I help quoting 'Scent of Childhood.' "

Dad was the scent of hayfields in the sun.
The faintest drifting fragrances of clover
Undo for me all that the years have done.
While they remain, my childhood is not over.
Dad is beside me, brown as earth, and good
As clear, cool water on a thirsty day,
And all I have experienced and withstood
Is gone, at any whiff of new-mown hay.
And Mother was the smell of new bread, browned
To crusty, crisp perfection. There may be
Some folk whose childhood, lost, is never found,
But mine remains immediate to me,
For always all the years between have fled
At scent of new-mown hay, of new-made bread.

Dr. Ball continued his praise: "One more short poem and I have done. To comment upon the perfection of "For Annie" would be as great a sacrilege as to explain a violet.**

"Of course, I realize that poetry like this labors under one terrific handicap—anyone can understand it. In these days when the cult of obscurity rides triumphant, it doesn't have much chance. Far, far worse—it scans! Yet despite all these deficiencies, I am going to proclaim from the roofs of Richmond that this is genuine poetry. And if Richmond doesn't buy a hundred or so copies . . . it deserves nothing better. . . .

"That so fine a book has been lying around since its publication in 1957 is deplorable, and I take my share of the blame. I just didn't know about it."[7]

Two fan letters from new readers in Richmond soon testified to the effect of Dr. Ball's review, but Jane cautioned Shirley against too much optimism for the future. Her muse was "droopy," and she wasn't doing much writing. Such habitual reaction to praise was hard to break, even if she could unmask it as her old foe: prideful shrinking back.

In the latest manuscript was a poem called "The Hidden Singer," with the lines:

The purest notes belong
To the anonymous song.

*See chapter 6, page 91.
**See chapter 9, page 122.

180

Her meditation was a poignant confession to "God, who knowest all the things we are loath to admit to ourselves, thou knowest the persistent desire of our hearts for appreciation of the good we do. Thou knowest, Lord, our petulance when others seem ungrateful and our inward dismay when our best efforts pass unnoticed. Help us, Lord, to learn from the birds who sing for joy of singing, not for praise; and grant us to find such creative joy in the work we do that we may be truly unconcerned about receiving credit for it."[8]

Jane was deeply grateful for the efforts of her friends to promote her writing, but she still thought of publicity as a necessary evil. It went against her grain to praise her own works, and she did not even refer to them as poems.

"I call mine verse," she explained to Frances, "because poetry is something special, to me. When a young man told Robert Frost, 'I'm a poet.' Frost said, 'That's a praise word. Let somebody else call you that'" (Winter, March 29, 1961).

She had been bold enough this time to suggest to the publisher a few names of people who ought to receive advance copies in order to help promote the book. But the idea of peddling her own wares was distasteful. She even found it painful to ask for money for her handwork, though baby clothes were useful and probably worth the few dollars she charged.

Eva had once chided her for letting her face *show* that she thought a customer felt obligated to buy a set of baby bibs. Ever since that, she had tried to hide her feelings, but had never quite quelled the suspicion that people were buying from kindness, not from need.

The cost of her new book would be $1.75, while the others sold for $1.50. Jane felt dismayed about that. Why should anyone be willing to pay that much for one of her small volumes? Surely the last one wasn't twenty-five cents better, but just the victim of higher publishing costs. How would that affect sales?

Another thought was even more disturbing. She had read a lecture delivered by Dr. Samuel Miller, Dean of Harvard Divinity School, debunking "that whole sickening mess of sweetening piety commonly denominated as devotional literature which . . . continues to make the gospel look and taste like soggy confections of a child's candy store."

Jane hoped Dr. Miller would not lump her books in the category of "sweetened piety," which she herself referred to as "the sincere *skimmed* milk" of the Word. It held little nourishment for Christian readers, she lamented to Frances, and was a stumbling block to those who sought to grow in the faith and who might conclude that the church had nothing better to offer.[9]

Dr. Miller had given an essential reading list of books and authors, and Jane was determined to fill the gaps in her own knowledge. She was ever reading and learning, seldom less than a book a day and always more in the aftermath of a major manuscript, when she felt weary of writing and uncertain of what to do next.

In the summer of 1961, Jane's diary records a substantial, but not unusual, number of books read. They include textbooks on poetry, major works on history and religion, a prose translation of *The Odyssey*, and *The Portable Greek Reader* as well as current fiction and books on theology.

Too much reading could cause an occasional overwhelming conviction that *everything* had already been written, and it was folly to add more. But Jane was willing to admit that such excuses were part of her periodic procrastinations, times of indecision when she would do almost anything *but* write, filling the days with handwork, letter writing, reading, and visitors.

She never entirely ceased her discipline of daily writing, and eventually the dry period would come to an end. Donia had learned to gauge the symptoms: increasing restlessness indicated the "begetting" of poetry and signalled a period of concentrated creativity. Once Jane had settled down to writing, there was nothing she would *rather* do, she confessed to Shirley.[10]

Advance publicity on the new book was out, and the Abingdon salesman came on a surprise visit to let Jane see the book jacket and catalog. Mr. McNish was pleased to point out that *Blessed Are You* was featured on the front page of the catalog.

When he left, Jane browsed through the rest of the catalog and was astounded to find her own name mentioned in another fall release. *Thoughts Are Things* by Graham R. Hodges was a collection of sermons for children, and one of the topics was "Jane Merchant—The Girl Poet Who Wouldn't Give Up."

It was her first introduction to the author—and the book—and she wondered "what might he be telling poor innocent children about me?"

The theme of the sermon was probably inspired by her poem "Answer," beginning with the line *"I can't go on, I can't go on."* It was a favorite of many readers, she admitted to Frances, but she had often wished it had never been printed. It revealed far too much of her private struggles, though it explained why she *had* kept on when she wanted to shrink back; God had kept her going, in spite of herself.[11]

He would keep her from shrinking back in the future as well, even if darkness should enclose her. The family had discussed the thing Jane feared most—and she asked Frances to pray. Soon they must face the reality that Donia could not safely care for Jane alone during Elizabeth's working hours. The only workable alternative seemed to require leaving home and garden, friends, and the beloved hills for the flat West Tennessee. Jane fully expected to live with Ruth and Ed Lee some day—"if I outlive Mother"—but she hoped "against all reasonable hope" that they would move to Knoxville first *(Winter, July 16, 1961)*.

She tried not to brood over her fears. She underlined a passage in *The Divine Pity*, a gift from Eva: "Do not worry. You have or will have your real problems to face, and you must face them squarely. . . . Pray and take advice . . . but . . . when the decision is reached, you must rest in God . . . refuse to keep going over and over the same ground. Refuse to become introspective, and set yourself instead to . . . the active and creative work He has given you to do."

God had given her a work to do, and she was profoundly grateful. Her own strength would fail, but He, who "kept on when I could not," would not let her shrink back.

Blessed Are You was released in time for her birthday. Jane celebrated in the dining room, receiving visitors and autographing books. It was a glorious autumn day, with the sky "a gentle April blue," after a thunderstorm of the night before. It was as if "the blessed Lord were having all my favorite weather on purpose for my birthday," she wrote to Kay.[12]

The book reviews were excellent. W. A. Wright, Jr., in *The Richmond Times-Dispatch* of November 19, 1961 noted that her poems and meditations "probe all the dimensions of human character. They comfort and encourage, but they also seek out those nagging sins that so irritate our souls and are so seldom subjected to divine forgiveness."

Jane was pleased. Few reviewers acknowledged that she wrote to "occasionally afflict the comfortable as well as comfort the afflicted," she observed to Shirley.[13]

Some reviewers missed her point altogether and praised her work for the wrong things, which was worse by far, than not being praised at all, she lamented to Carolyn Ruth. That was happily *not* the case with the column she enclosed in her letter. The clipping was from the *Knoxville News Sentinel*, dated December 3, 1961, and was written by Marianne Tupkin Burke, who "at least understood" what Jane was trying to do.[14]

Mrs. Burke,—under the headline: "Jane Merchant writes poems on the Beatitudes"—praised her "expert handling of verse and meter, cadence and rythm" and called the poems "a meet companion for the message of the Beatitudes . . . written from a heart in tune with the desperation and the aspiration of fellow human beings."

The Arkansas poet Edsel Ford, who had described *Halfway Up the Sky* as "exquisite," wrote about Jane: "Few contemporary American poets would be better qualified to create such a collection of devotionals. This Tennessee poet, who knows the bleaker side of life and yet is able to rise above it and bring her readers with her, is well known for the durability of her inspirational verse."

It was heady praise for a book on the virtue of humility. Could she accept the accolades with simple gratitude and pass them on to the One who deserved the credit? God was the source and strength, the light rising in her darkness. That was the boon she was called to share. In her new book was the poem "To Share":

> Not for my comfort only,
> Not for my aid alone,
> The star-gleam in the darkness,
> The sparkle in the stone.
>
> Not for my single solace
> In ponderous silence stirred
> By inward songs, by gentle
> Small easings of the Word
>
> The dark, the stone, the silence
> Are not mine to explain
> But bear; and mine to share the star,
> The sparkle, the refrain.

14
MEMBERS ONE OF ANOTHER
1961–1963

Whatever gifts we have are of his giving.
Why should we pride ourselves if we receive
Abundantly, the gift of joyous living,
The gift of leading others to believe,
The gift of faith, the gift of cheerful serving,
The gift of speaking, or the gift of song?
No gift was given us for our deserving.
But by his grace to whom we all belong.

Whoever speaks has need of each attentive
Perceptive listener; whoever shares
In ministry requires the deep incentive
Of faithful, sympathetic, fervent prayers.
Let us esteem no service great or small
Since each is needful for the strength of all.

Ever since Eva had cut her visits to once a week, Jane had been extra-sensitive to her own shortcomings in relationships. Studying the Beatitudes had strengthened her conviction that love was the touchstone of faith, but she had grave misgivings about her own ability to love. Frances had sent her Martin Buber's book *I—Thou*. After reading it, Jane asked herself whether she treated others as "thou" or as "it"—as real persons or merely as objects to be manipulated or possessed.

"I think our relationship, yours and mine, is more 'I—thou' than 'I—it,' don't you?" she wrote hopefully to Frances.[1]

But she suspected in herself a desire to dominate those she loved. In "Let Love Be Genuine," she wrote:

> If love is genuine, we must hate
> The evil in our love, that would
> Be first, possess, and dominate

185

Those whom we love. True love of good
And of our brothers, means that we
Are glad to make their goodness known,
And in complete sincerity
Prefer their honor to our own.

In another book on loan from Frances, Jane thought she found an explanation for her difficulties. In *The Struggle of the Soul,* Lewis Joseph Sherrill wrote of those "whose earliest dynamic relationships" had been good, but who were later "underprivileged in giving and receiving the profoundest love." They were capable of having relatively normal relationships, but they retreated from "the emotional costs of profound love."

Here was a perfect description of herself, Jane confided to Frances. Her early childhood relationships had indeed been fine, but later—while her contemporaries were learning how to get along with people in school, on jobs, and in social contacts—she wasn't getting in much practice—not until Eva came, and by then the damage was done. Retreating from close personal love had become a well-entrenched defense posture.

Frances argued the point. Jane's friends knew her as a trusted confidante, who rejoiced in their happiness and shared their griefs. If she were deficient as a friend at times, her failings were of the "normal human cussedness" kind, to be forgiven, not despaired over. She, who so easily forgave the transgressions of others, needed to be more understanding and forgiving of her own.

Frances was reassuring, but Jane was not convinced. She would never be complacent about her relationships, and she feared that her problems of communicating in person were made insurmountable by deafness in spite of her commitment to "keep on trying."[2]

The most frightening aspect of her condition was the realization that her shrinking away from loving others meant that she was holding back from God. Christ had made it perfectly clear that what was done "to one of the least" of God's children was also done to him (Matt. 25:40). Jane prayed fervently to be made capable of the "costly, profound love" Sherrill wrote of.

In his book *Guilt and Redemption,* Sherrill made the same point. He linked our lack of love for ourselves and other people to "an absence of love for God" and "a superficial, often even trivial," concept of redemption, "since the conception of guilt is not radical."

The two books were a succinct summary of Jane's own beliefs, and she expressed her gratitude in "Note to an Author":

Beneath November's meditative skies,
Entirely unobscured by dazzling leaves,

I find a simple grace that clarifies
My view of basic gifts each year receives.
I grow aware of much that will remain
With me now seasonal jubilees are past,
And find your printed words my greatest gain,
A source of vital meaning that will last.

Much that I read gave momentary pleasure
and is forgotten like gay foliage blown
To earth; your book is the essential treasure
Of stalwart trunk and branches clearly shown,
And so I pen this note of thanks to you
Who wrote the words I hope to grow into.

From the opinions of other people, Jane invariably turned for a deeper understanding to Scripture. In Paul's letter to the Romans she found Christian relationships defined: "So we, though many, are one body in Christ, and individually members of one another" (Rom. 12:5 RSV). In that context, self-sufficiency and shrinking from closeness were clearly wrong.

The road to oneness with others led through the narrow gate of self-surrender to the living God. The twelfth chapter of Romans begins with an admonition Jane liked to read from the J. B. Phillips translation: "With eyes wide open to the mercies of God, I beg you, my brothers, as an act of intelligent worship, to give him your bodies, as a living sacrifice, consecrated to him, and acceptable by him" (Rom. 12:1 JBP).

In "The Mercies of God," she wrote:

He made the world in wisdom,
With galaxies of light,
With little blue-eyed grasses,
And birdsong in the night.
He gives to all men freely
Life, breath, and all they own.
In planet and in petal
His deity is shown.

Although men are not thankful,
Refusing to obey
Their inward admonitions
Against sin's dull decay,
Through his excelling mercy
All still may be restored
To health and holy living
Through faith in Christ our Lord.

His grace in every snowflake
And fern and sunset flame
Calls everyone to worship
And glorify his name.
His love poured out in dying—
Oh, Calvary is not far
From us!—calls us to offer
Him all we have and are.

The desire of her heart was to respond in love to God, who loved her, by offering herself in worship and singing poetry. Emily Dickinson had once written the line, "how flippant are the saved." Now Jane wrote "Dissent from Emily."

"How flippant are the saved!" she said,
Hearing the birds her father fed
Sing merrily when he was dead.
Would she have had them sad, in spring?
Salvation is a cruel thing
Unless the saved are saved to sing.

Only those with a shallow, flippant view of salvation would refuse to sing of their redemption when days were dark with sorrow. The faithful were told to worship and adore, to offer a sacrifice of praise in the midst of tribulation. In obeying Jane had found a deepening sense of belonging to the great *Thou* whom her little *i* was drawn to love. In adoration and worship she knew herself joined with all creation, responding in love to its Creator, not losing her sense of self, but being at once in communion and uniquely loved. Her song then was not just for herself, but on behalf of a world awaiting the triumphant completion of redemption—the end of all suffering, the fulfillment of all hopes and yearnings—God's love and glory unveiled.

In "On Behalf of Goldfinches" Jane wrote:

Lord of the golden bird
Whose dancing flight has stirred
My heart to joy that he
So joyously, should be—
I thank thee that he is;
And if there be in his
Being, no conscious praise
Of thee, O let me raise
For all glad things and gay
The things they cannot say.

It was easier at times to feel at one with nature than with difficult human beings. Sherrill had stressed the need to belong to a community of Christians, a church where relationships could be nurtured and unity forged through common worship. Jane was more conscious now of what she missed by being physically isolated. She and Donia were members of Fountain City Methodist Church. They received the bulletin, newsletter, and study books, and they tithed as a matter, of course. Through the Methodist *Book of Worship,* they followed the church services and the annual cycle of the Christian Year. Members of the congregation often visited, and the pastor brought Holy Communion. Jane especially loved the communion service and prayers. Christ was present in the mystery of the sacrament; it was an outward visible sign of an inward, spiritual grace. In receiving it, she knew herself at one with Christ and all who were members, one of another, of his body, the church through all the ages. If she must do without the physical fellowship of a congregation, here was a greater intimacy and a more perfect union than any flawed human presence alone. Through the sharing of the Eucharist, human relationships were transformed, bonded in love.

Jane was encouraged by Reginald Cant's book *Hearts in Pilgrimage.* He wrote that not even the most solitary Christian ever prays alone. If Jane was physically set apart, she was nevertheless joined to Christ's body, a vast throng of worshipers greater than any local congregation or present generation. To pray *"our* Father," not *"my* Father," was a daily reminder that she was not alone. Now she could write:

> To say to God
> "Our Father"
> Is wondering gratitude,
> Is ardent venturing awe,
> Is humble penitence,
> Is reverential praise,
> Is endless fellowship,
> Is all-committing love.
>
> To say "our Father"
> Truly, is
> To pray.
> "After This Manner"

She loved to read the ancient writings of the church, the prayers and hymns of the saints through the ages. Many were still in use, linking the Christian traditions of the centuries, even when denominations divided those who held them in common.

Denominational disagreements were a painful reality. In her isolation from a local congregation, Jane was deeply conscious of her kinship with those in other branches of Christendom. Her sister Elizabeth belonged to the Christian Church, Nelson and Elberta to the Church of Christ. Her closest friends—partners in prayer—differed in denominations, yet recognized the substance of their faith as one.

Jane sold poetry to denominational magazines of nearly every variety in the country, and she read the issues containing her work. They resembled one another in content far more than they differed. Readers who sent thank-you letters usually assumed that she shared their particular beliefs, and they were surprised to learn otherwise. Some wrote again, trying to convert her. She was always saddened by such evidence that many Christians were more concerned with their differences than with their common faith in Christ as Savior.

She suspected that such divisions among those who were "members one of another" in the body of Christ were symptomatic of what Sherrill called "a superficial and trivial concept of guilt and redemption." Jane grieved for fellow pilgrims who used time and energy to maintain their separate ways—and to judge one another. Christ had come to bring reconciliation and love to a strife torn world. His followers were called to spread hope and healing; they were to be recognized by their love for one another. How tragic it was when they fought one another instead.

In "For Unity" Jane wrote:

> O God and Father of us all,
> In all our varied tongues and ways
> Thine is the name on which we call,
> Thine is the mercy which we praise.
>
> Preserve us from divisive pride
> In ceremonials and creeds
> And let our lives be unified
> In faithful service to men's needs.
>
> Let us be one in faith, in hope,
> And love, that all men may believe
> In Christ, and may no longer grope
> Among gross shadows that deceive,
>
> But, coming to the living light,
> May find the grace that sets them free
> And in full fellowship unite
> In all creation's praise of thee.

It was frustrating not to be able to *do* more about the problems of the church and the world. Her never silent conscience accused her of shirking, of not doing enough. She could pray, and from prayers came poetry. She hoped that her poems were what Frances called them: "springboards" for those who were physically fit to take action.

Her editor had hinted for another book. Here again was a call, to present the challenge of living and loving to those who were physically able to act on it. Jane felt a heavy responsibility for passing on what she had learned to others, especially to the younger generation. Her nephews and nieces were growing up. Reese was twenty, towering over her bed. "The Tall Young Men" was written for him.

> Tall deeds become the young men of today.
> Oh, we are proud to see how soon they grow
> Beyond their fathers' greatest height, although
> Our pride is intermingled with dismay.
> Have we so fed their minds and hearts that they
> Will always seek the high, avoid the low,
> And live uprightly by the best they know?
> Will they be always tall, in every way?
>
> False standards, small examples are not few—
> "To get ahead these days you have to cheat,"
> "Whatever you can get by with is right."
> Oh, may we have the strength to be and do
> Our best, that, unbewildered by deceit,
> The tall young men may live up to their height.

Plans for a book could not be made firm yet. Donia had suffered through the winter with ulcerated varicose veins, and she walked with much pain and difficulty. To spare her unnecessary movement, Jane wrote little for editors. Magazine markets were tight, and her efforts earned mostly rejection slips. That, added to her anxiety over Donia's health, did much to muzzle her muse.

In early April the doctor recommended surgery for Donia. Two days before the operation came a letter from Robert Roy Wright asking what Jane was writing. The answer would have to wait.

Donia was hospitalized for a week. Margaret Funk, badly crippled by arthritis, and her sister Trula cared for Jane. Donia's surgery was an immediate success, and she came home walking much better.

In the garden bloomed purple lilac, redbud, and tulips. Soon the window dogwood would be a "full blown Easter angel," Jane wrote to Kay. Her window framed "as much beauty as one window can well hold."[3]

Donia was grateful to be at work among her flowers, and Jane wrote "Custom."

> Always in spring she rises as the new
> Light shimmers through small inexperienced leaves,

Naively not quite green, but dimly gold
And faintly rose, on wakening shrub and tree.

She walks among unpracticed miracles
In the small garden sweet with flowering prayers,
Shining with radiance of dawn-lit dew,
And gathers violets while a robin sings
His ordinary canticle of light.

Hers is a sunrise service every day
And Easter is the custom of her soul.

During the emergency Jane had earned only seven dollars in poetry sales. But her influence as a poet was spreading. Requests for reprints were growing. Her work would soon be in twelve books beside her own. Several of her poems were in textbooks. Beatrice Plumb had included a biographical article about her as a chapter in the book *Lives That Inspire* for the Denison Company. And the publisher wrote to ask if Jane had a manuscript of poetry for submission. She did not want to change publishers, but she admitted to Shirley that it was flattering to have *two* ask for her work.

Donia was ready for another book project, and in June Jane recorded in her diary that she had written her Abingdon editor to suggest two possible themes: Psalm 19, on praise and adoration, or Romans 12, on responding to God's mercies by loving him and one another. Her own preference was the psalm, but the publisher wanted Romans, and so it was decided.

As soon as summer was over, Jane would begin the work in earnest. Her poem "Treasurer's Report" was printed in a denominational magazine in September and would go in the new manuscript.

"How did you spend the summer?"
Friends ask me, and I sigh
At thought of pure extravagance
Of blue in lavish sky,

Of stintless hills and valleys,
Munificently green.
Of flowers and fruits and berries,
All with a jeweled sheen—

And say, "I spent the summer
Accepting thankfully
The overflowing riches
That summer spent on me."

The book would follow the outline of Paul's chapter in Romans that begins with the exhortation to respond with "eyes wide open to the mercies of God," giving oneself as a living sacrifice, an act of worship, and to live in love as "members one of another" in the world. Paul saw that the relationship with God could not be separated from the relationship with others; they were two sides of a coin. Yet, in the human heart—and in the church—there was often a split between them; the cause of much conflict. "It's the Mary-Martha question again," Jane lamented to Frances.[4]

Martha was the always-busy sister of Lazarus who showed her devotion to Christ in action, while Mary loved simply to sit at his feet, abiding in his presence to the neglect of her duties, Martha complained. Jesus gently scolded the grumbling sister. She was "troubled about many things; but one thing is needful. Mary has chosen the good portion, which shall not be taken from her" (Luke 10:41-42 RSV).

Like so many of Christ's sayings, this one was balanced by others that could not be ignored. Love for God was meant to flow into loving deeds unto "the least of these."

How could anyone love God and be indifferent to the need of others? It was a question Jane anguished over. What was faith without action? Could one claim to know a truth without living it? One of her early poems was "Grandfather's Belief." Now she included it in her manuscript.

> "Belief," Grandfather often used to say,
> "Is knowledge people act upon. It's not
> A fine possession you can store away
> To pride yourself upon because you've got
> A better than your neighbor's. You can do
> That very well with things you merely know,
> But if you once believe a thing is true
> That isn't possible. You've got to go
> And put it into practice. Most of us
> Know we should love our neighbors, be forgiving,
> Speak ill of none, be patient, generous,
> And kind to all, in our daily living.
> But if you watch us closely, you perceive
> That much of what we know, we don't believe.

Indifference to others was surely as unloving as open hostility toward them. The first recorded murder in human history was when Cain killed his brother, Abel, then asked, "Am I my brother's keeper?" Cain was made an outcast. No member of the human race could live and die alone. For her new manuscript, Jane wrote "Outcast."

> "Am I my brother's keeper? Shall I care
> If he is well, while all goes well with me?

Concern myself with how his children fare
So long as mine grow healthy, strong, and free?
Must I refrain from living as I choose
Lest what I do harm him in any way,
And even guard the words and tones I use
For fear his hopes be slain by what I say?"

Whoever asks shall never truly know
The strength and joy and beauty earth can give.
Outcast, alone in spirit he must go
Among mankind, a loveless fugitive.
Whoever asks the murderer's question kills
The soul of that humanity God wills.

God commanded his people to love one another, and Christ declared a deeper meaning: love thine enemy (see Matt. 5:43-45). Paul admonished the Romans: "If thine enemy hunger, feed him" (Rom. 12:20). In "Imperative," Jane wrote:

In a far-off land no longer friendly to us
Crops fail, and floods devour, and there is hunger,
Hunger of which we do not wish to think,
Hunger that gnaws at the edges of our easy
Complacent satisfaction in our plenty. . . .

The voices of children whispering to their mothers,
Begging for food, are faint, and do not carry
Through diplomatic channels.

But the word is not equivocal or faint.
The word is not, "If your enemy asks for food—"
But unmistakenly, "If your enemy is hungry,
Feed him."

A believer who complacently closes eyes and heart to the needs of others must also be blind to the true dimensions of guilt and redemption, blind to the mercies of God, Jane concluded. She often wondered how long human beings could continue their destructive ways. "It is of the Lord's mercies that we are not consumed, because His compassions fail not," she reminded her readers in the words of Jeremiah the prophet (see Lam. 3:22). And she added Paul's warning to the Romans:" Do you not know that God's kindness is meant to lead you to repentance?" (Rom. 2:4 RSV). These verses introduced the poem "The Fragile Chain" in her book.

A small boy alone
In a Tennessee meadow

Ponders with satisfaction and esteem
The emerald lusters of a June bug's back.

Another small boy
By a Russian river
Considers at length the design of a turtle's shell
And finds it good.

All over the wide green summer of the world
Children make chains of daisies, chains of clover,
Linking themselves to one another, to earth,
And all earth's novel treasures, little and great,
    with joy.

If a strange pattern appears on a radar screen,
If a pilot is jittery, if a commander panics,
The mushroom clouds may grow in the children's
    sky
By no one's design, but because the bombs are
    there.

It is not by our wisdom, virtue, generosity, and
    brotherhood
That we are saved from accidental doom.
How long will God have mercy on our folly?
How long will the daisy chains hold? The bombs
    are there.

In prayer were no geographical or social barriers, no limits of time and space. Prayer was the most immediate way to put her faith into action, obeying the command to bear one another's burden, sharing in the suffering of Christ. Paul exhorted the believers in Rome to be constant in prayer—for themselves and on behalf of others. In intercessory prayer, Jane experienced the pain of friends who wrote of their personal struggles or strangers whose plight made the headlines. Though she had never seen the concrete slums of an inner city, she knew them in her heart. "The Inner City" was written for the new book.

> Difficult morning
> Blurs squares of finished black
> Into anxious beginning gray.
>
> Slowly, uneagerly,
> Light
> Sharpens edges of thin buildings

Along slatternly pavements
Of broken concrete.

Reluctant eyes hardly
Open on unfinished gray,
Not daring to close.
Arduously, people
Rise in hard dawn
To hard day

Around the world on farms, in villages, or in crowded cities lived those who bore the image of the living God. Surely no single life, no pain, would be wasted, Jane wrote to Carolyn Ruth. However difficult or meaningless things looked now, she was certain that Christ had come "to seek and to save that which was lost" (Luke 19:10). She lived in the hope that, "in the end nothing will be lost; from the dust on a butterfly's wing to all the strivings and griefs of men and women, and the agony and triumph of Calvary."[5]

"In Patient Constancy," written for the new book, expressed the same hope.

O God of hope, teach us to hope in thee
In deep assurance that thy love enfolds
All things that are and have been and will be,
And all is well, although the present holds
Struggle and testing, pain and tribulation.
O make us strong to share the victory's cost
In joyful hope that in thy whole creation
No moment's suffering is finally lost.

Lord, may our longing for the good of all
And our compassion for all earth's distress,
And every daily action, large and small,
By which we seek to give, forgive, and bless,
Unite to hasten victory, as we pray
In patient constancy from day to day.

The manuscript for *The Mercies of God* was finished in January of 1963. In the preface, Jane wrote: "We are 'members one of another,' and if, as I deeply hope, there is help for others in these poems and prayers, I am sure it is due in no small measure to the help others' letters and prayers have given me. My earnest gratitude to all these faithful helpers; may we all be enabled to live the life of self-giving to God and unselfish living with others to which we are called by his infinite mercies to us."

Abingdon's response was quick. Robert Roy Wright wrote that they were delighted with her work. So was Eva, who had followed each book project from the beginning and shared Jane's conviction that one must live the truth one holds.

Eva had brought a petition for immediate desegregation of the city of Knoxville to Jane and Donia, who were both glad to sign it. It seemed a small gesture, but at least it was a public stand against one of the most tragic divisions in the body of Christ and society at large. Jane's new manuscript had poems prodding the conscience of her readers on that issue as well—it was one of her perennial topics.

"I would rather write about redbirds," she explained to Frances, "but I want everyone to have a chance to see redbirds." The summer brought disturbing news of rioting and bombings of black churches in Birmingham, Alabama, and Jane suffered the anguish of guilt. "We are responsible because we didn't protest enough, or love enough, or care enough!"[6]

The Mercies of God was released in September. The work had deepened Jane's sense of oneness with the church through the ages and with all God's creation. She was one with the beauty and joy of it, with the ugliness and suffering, receiving love and giving it.

It was an awesome and wondrous mystery. This year on her birthday she read again Psalm 139, giving thanks for all her blessings and listing them in her diary. She was particularly grateful—and said a prayer—for all who had loved her and showed kindness throughout her lifetime. As she called each name, it seemed that her small room expanded with the presence of a joyous, blessed company.

Her birthday fell on All Saints Day in the church calendar, a fitting day to celebrate oneness with members in the body of Christ in heaven and on earth. It was not a day for feeling lonely. Never had she been so aware of belonging, of being loved. And she prayed to be made more loving.

With six books earning royalties, the three in the Doll House decided to make a long held dream come true: expanding Jane's and Donia's room by eight feet and installing two windows instead of one in the new wall facing the garden.

> Eight feet of outer space are all we need.
> Eight feet of space beyond our present wall,
> Enclosed, roofed, windowed, warmed will be indeed
> A triumph over bounds unduly small.
> Yet to achieve this sublunary aim
> Earth must be deeply outraged with cement
> And garden peace disrupted by our claim
> Much to the birds' astonished discontent.
> We must enlist extensive lengths of pine
> That grew in storm, unhindered, toward the sun
> To keep out wind and rain and to define

The heights to which our fond ambitions run;
But we shall live with added zest and grace
For having conquered even this much space.

"This Much Space"

The contents of the room, including Jane, were "stowed uncomfortably" in the rest of the house while construction was going on. Their new minister, Dr. Thomas Chilcote, came to visit in the midst of the upheaval. "He told someone that my single window was the biggest window in the world because of all I see through it," Jane wrote to Kay. "I told him the builder said that window was worn out. . . . I wonder how many years of looking it will take to wear out these two!"[7]

Moving day was set for Sunday November 24, but the thrill of it paled suddenly two days before when horror struck the nation: President Kennedy was shot to death in Dallas, Texas. The shock and outrage, grief and shame were inexpressible. Jane felt the anguish, the terror, and the lawlessness threatening to rupture the flimsy fabric of civilization. She clung to the hope that love was not dead. "We are surprised and touched to find how many people in other countries share our feelings" she wrote to Betty in England. "James Garfield said when Lincoln was assassinated: 'God reigns, and the Government in Washington still lives.'"[8]

The last poem in *The Mercies of God* was suddenly all too relevant. She had titled it "More Than Conquerors."

We need not fear the death of joyous hope
Within our hearts through life's minute frustrations,
Nor that our faith may vanish in the scope
Of space revealed by cosmic explorations.
We need not dread what future years may bring
To us of loss and pain and helpless hours,
Nor feel despair at any shattering
Of earthly principalities and powers.

For he who loves us well has conquered all
Things that could conquer us, and we may share
His victory, whatever may befall,
Whatever tribulation we must bear,
For nothing in earth below or heaven above
Can ever separate us from his love.

They moved into the expanded room immediately after seeing Lee Harvey Oswald, the accused assassin, shot in full view of television cameras. Then they watched the Kennedy funeral and burial in Arlington

198

National Cemetery—shock upon shock, and still difficult to believe.

It was time to observe Thanksgiving. They had their turkey and trimmings in the new room, and in Jane's mind echoed the words of the psalmist: "He hath not dealt with us after our sins, nor rewarded us according to our iniquities. For as the heavens are high above the earth, so great is his mercy" (Ps. 103:10-11).

Christmas would come in spite of everything, Jane wrote to Shirley—in spite of Herods, the killers of innocents throughout the bloody history of humankind.[9]

Her poem "To Comprehend the Star" was printed in December, and she sent a copy to Kay. Wise men through the ages had followed the star to the Savior. "I hope this nation will be wise enough to follow now."[10]

> Astronomers make reverent surmise
> That the particularly radiant glow
> Illuminating Palestinian skies
> And leading wise men onward to bestow
> Rich gifts on one unrecognized as yet
> As Savior of the greatest and the least
> Was caused when Jupiter and Saturn met
> In rare conjunction in the morning East.
>
> So always men must seek the truth—and whether
> Or not two planets met, superbly bright,
> We know God's love and mercy met together
> To shed upon all men a purer light
> Than any they had ever known before.
> We follow it, to worship and adore.

15
BY ALL THE
RADIANCE
1964–1965

"She seems a bit light-minded," people say
In doubtful tones of many merry ones;
And yet why not be mindful of each ray
Of light that reaches us from distant suns
That spin in tantalizing heights of space?
Why not be keenly mindful of each spark
That, shining down the centuries, lights the face
Of one who walks beside us in the dark?
And who would not be mindful of the shimmer
Of sunlight on clear water, of its dance
On wind-excited leaves, and of the glimmer
Of window lights that greet the homing glance?
By all the radiance of earth and skies
The most light-minded people are most wise.

Several bumps—she called them "worry-warts"—had appeared on
Jane's eyelids, and Elizabeth insisted on an ambulance trip to the
ophthalmologist after Christmas. The chalazions were harmless, but one
was nearly abessed, and Dr. Teague removed two from Jane's right
eyelid. An appointment was made to remove several from the other eye in
February.

Operations on her eyes had been Jane's secret dread since glaucoma
first threatened her sight nearly fifteen years earlier. Since then she had
used hot compresses daily, and she tried to make light of her terror.

> The mountains fear makes
> Of molehills may prove
> Most stubborn of all
> Faith struggles to remove.
> "Obstructions"

She had clung to her faith that God would work in *all* things—even the worst—for good, and she was determined to trust. It was easier said than done, but on the eve of her trip to Dr. Teague's office, Jane had made an inward surrender to the will of God, accepting whatever would come.

Two weeks later her right eye looked better than it had in months, and Jane could write of the ordeal.

> Thou knowest, Lord, I made no spoken prayer,
> Yet in the crucial hour I did not fear
> The thing I long had feared, and I could bear
> Uncertainty and pain and know Thee near.
>
> This quiet willingness that all should be
> According to Thy will; this calm accord
> With what I once prayed might not come to me—
> This was my prayer, and this Thy answer, Lord.
>
> "Thy Answer"

Apprehension for the next appointment had drained her of energy. The good doctor had apparently cut out all her ambition, Jane quipped to Shirley. She didn't mention the work she had just begun, a collection of lighter poems similar to *Halfway Up the Sky*—a favorite of many readers, though not as successful in sales as the devotionals. Shirley was one of the fans who had urged Abingdon to publish a second anthology, and Jane asked offhandedly what she would think of the title *Petals of Light,* referring to "stars and other blossoms"—*if* another collection was ever printed.[1]

Shirley took the possibility for a promise, and she loved the title. "It is ethereal and lovely and speaks to me of inspiration, light-heartedness, and the illumining of dark corners."[2]

That was precisely what Jane hoped to achieve—a book of radiance and light shining in dark places, of joy flowing from sadness, laughter softening a grim reality. In her own dark nights, stars were the sign of God's caring. In a year following the assassination of the president, with the peace of the nation and the world in peril, it seemed especially appropriate to point to the light. "Star Time" would be in the book.

> Now polished seeds of light
> Quicken the deepening night.
> Child watching, alone, apart,
> May a star take root in your heart.

Her appointment with the ophthalmologist went well, but Jane had been terrified while five chalazions were removed from her left eye. After all, it was her "pet"—her good eye—this time, she confided to Frances.

The next day her eye was black and blue, but the vision was fine. Jane was limp with gratitude, and now that the trial was over, she was too exhausted even to read much. For Lent she would meditate on short selections from devotional classics published by the Upper Room. This year she chose *Revelations of Divine Love* by Juliana of Norwich, who wrote that "All shall be well, and all shall be well, and all manner of thing shall be well."

Jane felt a peculiar kinship with this woman of faith who lived in turbulent fourteenth-century England and chose to spend her life enclosed in a small cell attached to the church of St. Julian in Norwich. A small window provided her only contact with the outside world. Another opened on the dim interior of the stone church. Juliana was bound to her cell, not by sickness, but for love of God. She gave herself to prayer and contemplation of the passion of Christ and helping those who sought her counsel at the window. She had learned compassion through suffering, and she wrote of wounds that are seen before God, "not as wounds but as worships."

Even wounds in the eyes—offered to God—were turned to worship, Jane observed to Kay before Easter. God's love was in this, as in all things, enfolding and keeping her.

A month after surgery her eyes no longer required hot compresses—for the first time since 1950! Thanks to the "Father of lights!" she exulted to Shirley.

But her weariness—of mind and body—hung on. She struggled to get back on a regular writing schedule—a much interrupted effort. Frustration was gnawing at her resolve against self-pity. April was surely "by courtesy of God," Jane had written, but it was her month of gloom and glory, with spring tauntingly beautiful behind glass. Marvels of leaf and bloom appeared daily in the garden, and birds returned to their nesting places. "Flying Shadow" was in the new manuscript.

> The shadow of a flying bird
> Has crossed an inner wall.
> To one within, alone, unstirred,
> The shadow of a flying bird
> Has quickened vision sadly blurred
> And cast a new light over all—
> The shadow of a flying bird
> Has crossed an inner wall.

A third of the year was already gone, and Jane was woefully dissatisfied with her accomplishments so far. Not that she was ever fully satisfied, she lamented to Frances. But the discipline of writing must go on, no matter how she felt about the results. And who could draw a line between literary works produced because a writer felt compelled to write them and those written because a writer had to eat? It wouldn't surprise her to learn that Homer had put off composing the *Iliad* until the day before a banquet! "Real" writers were no different from ordinary mortals![3]

Without perseverance there would be no steady results. A book manuscript in process did not curtail Jane's regular submissions to magazine editors—even if the best paying markets had dwindled further. *The Ladies Home Journal* was overstocked and would buy nothing new for two years. *Good Housekeeping* kept sending "little notes of regret," Jane reported to Carl Arneson, a fan-turned-friend in Massachusetts.[4]

Carl was impressed with her 1,200 poems in print and calculated that with an average of five rejections for each check, she had sustained no less than 6,000 disappointments! "I marvel at the serenity which allows you to keep mailing manuscripts."[5]

Jane's records showed in fact a higher average of rejections. Many poems sold on first submission, but others were refused up to twenty times before earning no more than two or three dollars—barely the cost of envelopes and stamps. A few editors had bought poems they had originally rejected when she accidentally submitted them a second time. It had convinced her that "sun spots and blind spots play a large part in deciding what gets published and what doesn't."[6]

She sent Carl her poem "Who May Be a Poet," noting that writing poetry was "searching work, but work one loves."[7]

> The lonely, the rejected
> Who love on, undeterred,
> May speak the unexpected
> Inevitable word.

Her regular markets included several newspapers, and she had just made her first sale to *The Kansas City Times*. The poetry editor consistently printed quality work, wrote fellow poet Dorothy Brown Thompson. She had clipped Jane's "Good-natured" from the paper and encouraged her to submit more. The sonnet was a commentary on Gilbert White's *The Natural History of Selborne* and would be in *Petals of Light* as well.

> "We are very seldom annoyed with thunderstorms,"
> Wrote gentle Gilbert White of Selborne, meaning
> That thunderstorms came seldom. Here, the forms
> And hues of thunderclouds in wild careening
> Are noted with expertly practiced eye
> And something of a connoisseur's approval
> Of quick, dramatic darkening of sky,

Efficient downpour, and abrupt removal.
If White had had occasion to observe
Repeatedly, the swift exhilarating
Glory of thunderstorms, and how they serve
To freshen air grown dully enervating—
Had they come often, I am sure that he
Would have been as seldom annoyed with them as we!

Jane would have welcomed a thunderstorm while trying to complete the new manuscript. Summer temperatures hovered in the upper nineties. The air conditioner was on high, but curtains were drawn against the midday heat, and the bedroom seemed monotonously dreary. Minor irritations and disappointments had a tendency to develop into major ones. "There seems to be an egotism in things as well as people; if objects are given undue attention they assume undue importance," she observed to Frances.[8]

Summer visitors disrupted her schedule, and she was painfully aware of the ambivalence of her reactions. Deafness accentuated the distances—her difficulties in understanding and making herself understood. Yet, she loved her family and friends, and she delighted in discovering new kinships of soul and spirit. In June she wrote "Never by Wishing."

Friendship
Occurs when two people
Momentarily,
Simultaneously
Escape the disguises of appearance, formality, custom
The witch's curse inflicted on them at birth.

Friendship
Is when people
Come true.

With all who came to see her she strove to be open, honest, and true, not to hide behind a mask. Often she saw her visitors as refugees from the clamor of the world. Here in the quiet room, with windows to the pleasant garden, she hoped they would find a few moments of ease and laughter, of renewed strength for their journey. In her manuscript were the lines:

We cannot light the world;
We keep one small room warm
To give whoever comes
A refuge from the storm.
                              "Stormbound"

Jane hoped to do the same for her readers, but even as she worked on her "light" manuscript, she wrestled inwardly with a new surge of depression. It had perhaps been triggered when she read *The New Being* by Paul Tillich. He wrote of healing and psychosomatic illness, of wretched individuals driven by fear and guilt into chronic disability in order to avoid the full responsibilities of living.

Could it be that her physical handicaps masked a desire to escape reality? Jane asked herself in a soul-searching journal entry. Could she have feared life enough to subconsciously will the breaking of bones? She rejected the thought as morbidly perverse.

But what of healing? Her parents had prayed "fervently and sacrificially" for her to be made whole. Surely their prayers had been heard. Even if no startling physical miracle reversed the effects of congenital deformity and disease, she had been loved, and in love there was always healing. Prayers were answered; she grew up "able to love and believe" in God, in life and in people—not warped or embittered as many of sounder bodies.

Her deafness was perhaps another matter. It had come at a time of great emotional stress, and the ear specialist had found no apparent cause. But if she had subconsciously *willed* it to shirk her responsibilities, "it was surely an escape into torment!"

Tillich might see her as someone unable to cope with reality, responding to Christ's question, "Wilt thou be made whole?" with a perennial "No!." Or it could as well be said that she was "one born with defective physical equipment, who by the mercy and grace of God and loving parents, has been continuously healed in the deep rooted places of the spirit, maintained in health of mind and heart, and even of body, despite the basic disability. Able to accept life and affirm it, despite the arrows of hostility, weariness and disgust of life that comes to all" *(Diary, July 1, 1964)*.

To still some of her questions, Jane wrote to the Department of Health, Education and Welfare, asking for information on osteogenesis imperfecta. She knew of only one other case of "brittle bones": one of her less frequent correspondents, Harry B. Ehrstine, a widower in his seventies. Apparently his case was less severe; he was able to use a wheelchair and a specially constructed three-wheel cycle, and he wasn't deaf. He had operated a drugstore and was a lay preacher in the Methodist Church. But he suffered frequent and painful breaks, followed by long periods of convalescence and inactivity. Mobility was obviously hazardous.

The Department of Health replied with little new information. The disease was rare and relatively unknown, though research was underway. The range of severity appeared to be wide, and deafness was "a common feature." At least on that point Jane need not blame herself. But the letter emphasized the importance of avoiding immobilization "whenever possible."

Perhaps if they had not feared so much the pain of broken bones, she would have continued to use the wheelchair instead of settling down in bed at the age of twelve. But at what cost of time, anxiety, and trouble would that have been to herself and those who must care for her while bones were mending? She might have spent all her energies learning to get around awkwardly, instead of staying put, learning to read and write skillfully, she pointed out to Shirley.[9]

There was not much use now in wondering if she had done right. Her circumstances were set and she best stay "light-minded" in the present, rather than brood over past possibilities—if indeed they had existed. Her *Petals of Light* was ready to send to the publisher. In the preface Jane quoted Shirley's response to the title, and added: "It is my hope that she and all friends old and new may find that these 'petals' fulfill their expectations. There are verses here for those who cherish bright blossomings in the earth and sky, for those who practice matrimony and those who merely have opinions on the subject, for parents and grandparents and their friends. If this collection provides a few chuckles when chuckles are most needed, and inspires gentle amusement at the undeniable oddities of ourselves and other people, it may perhaps help to heighten appreciation of all the good and perfect gifts that come to us from the Father of lights."

Among the 195 poems in the book 40 were about children, a favorite subject. "New" was written about a small niece.

> The sky is not familiar yet
> To her, not casual the grass,
> And she is shy with daisies still
> While the new days of summer pass.
>
> I would not be a child again
> To learn the ways of flowers and skies
> But would live always near a child
> With unknown heavens in her eyes.

In the section on marriage was "For Many Wives," a much quoted poem.

> "Taken for granted?" Oh, be glad you are!
> So much is doubtful; let him, in his need,
> Be sure of you with no mistrust to mar
> His faith. What did your marriage mean, indeed,
> Save that you granted him your love for life
> The day he said, "I take you for my wife"?

"Note to Husbands" would appear on the facing page:

> Not always need your love be told
> In shapely words, in seemly gifts
> Of ivory, cloisonné, or gold.
> One surreptitious glance that lifts
> Her from the crowd into your own
> Particulate private realm of mirth
> Does more than words to make love known,
> And more than vast estates of earth.
> But tell your love in words when she
> Has burnt the party roast, or met
> One wearing her hat's facsimile,
> Or supervised a Cub quartet
> And loathes the ghastly race of men—
> Oh, if you love her, tell her then.

The poem had already been printed in the July issue of *The Christian Herald,* and it brought a fan letter from Bruffie Connor, a professor in English Literature at East Tennessee State University and a Presbyterian clergyman. He asked, "Where, in East Tennessee, did you find cloisonné?"[10]

"So far, only in the dictionary," Jane readily responded.

Her correspondence was crowding her writing time, but she found it difficult to resist writing letters. Most of her living was done by mail. In four months she had communicated in person with only twenty-five people but had written to one hundred. Fan letters had sparked most of the enduring friendships she counted as blessings. Carl Arneson and Dorothy Brown Thompson were among the latest. Bruffie Connor appeared to be another kindred spirit. Though her daily living was marked by increased isolation, the circle of faithful friends by mail was growing. There could not be the personal sharing she had once hoped for, but perhaps her hopes had been unrealistic. Through letters she could participate in the joys and pains of active living—an arrangement best suited to her circumstances, and no less real. In "Multiple" she had written:

> One letter brought good tidings,
> Another, news of sadness;
> So my heart is feeling
> Mingled grief and gladness.
>
> So my heart, the whole day,
> Is busy interweaving

> Thanks for one who's happy
> With prayer for one who's grieving.
>
> Seldom does a day come
> Single in emotion
> To one engaged in living
> Life with full devotion.

Life would ever be a mixture of joy and sadness, and she would not have it otherwise. The difficult summer was nearly over, but there had been accomplishments and glad surprises. Late in August Jane wrote "Of Light and Shade."

> "Forget all sorrow," people say, who are
> Considered wise. "Forget each sad event
> That you have known, lest the remembrance mar
> Today's tranquillity and glad content.
> Remember only good." But who has ever
> Found perfect good untouched by any flaw,
> And when was grief so absolute it never
> Held hope of deepening faith and strengthening awe?
> If I forget all sorrow then I must
> Forget friends' understanding, dear concern
> And all the sympathy and patient trust
> That only sorrow helped my heart to learn.
> So mixed are light and shade that if I could
> Forget all grief I must forget all good.

September began in glory, and Jane wrote to Gurre in England, "Today there was a sky that caused me to write a rhyme, beginning:"

> On the first day of September of this year
> At three o'clock in the afternoon, the sky
> Was first created. No blue so purely clear
> As this can ever have met the human eye
> In all past centuries. . . .
>   "Witness"

It was one of her most productive days in a long time. But that evening their friend of a life time, Margaret Funk, died.

"So the beauty and joy and the sadness and the pain of life mingle, and what people mean when they tell you heartily to 'forget the sadness and remember only the good,' I cannot tell."[11]

September 7 marked the tenth anniversary of her first book. Jane noted in her diary that the mail brought two requests for autographed copies of it—one a gift for a high school graduate, the other for a mother mourning the loss of a child. The book she had thought would be out of print within a year of its publication continued to meet the needs of readers in an amazing variety of circumstances. Jane had no illusion that the appeal of the book was due to any great talent of her own. Rather it was the timelessness of the message of God's love.

But she was grateful to have played a part, and she was particularly thankful this year for the tangible rewards of her labor: a wider view of autumn splendor in the garden. *"Another window makes a mighty difference!"* she exulted to Kay.[12]

Her eyes had bothered her again, and she had taken another ambulance ride to be examined by Dr. Teague. Fortunately the problem was only with her glasses—she needed new lenses—but the excursion had turned into an ordeal. She arrived on time for her appointment, but had to spend a full hour in the waiting room with strangers who sat with dead-pan faces, looking worried, tired, and bored. No one even cracked a smile, Jane observed to Frances. Was it "civil good breeding" to pretend that no one else existed?[13]

There had, of course, been curious glances toward the woman on the ambulance cot, and Jane was relieved when it was over and she could return to the sanctuary of her own room. Meeting strangers by letter was much to be preferred to meeting them in public places.

There were happy surprises in the mail that fall. First there was a package from Bruffie Connor containing a lovely enamel-on-silver spoon with the note: "Dear Jane, No woman's life would be complete without at least a sample of cloisonné."[14]

Then came a long letter from a graduate student at Central Michigan University, who wrote that Jane's books had changed her life and opened up a new world of poetry to her. Pat Lassen had found courage to write after reading "Note to an Author." She told briefly of her background as a social worker and missionary in Brazil, where she had adopted an orphaned boy. Her goal was to be an elementary school teacher. She confessed her hope of knowing Jane personally, and she dared to sign herself, "A new friend."[15]

It was one of the rare letters Jane would keep. She agreed to correspond, but could not promise long and frequent letters. There was neither time nor energy to spare. Pat didn't mind. She was grateful to have found a confidante to share her heart with. She wrote to Jane daily, telling of her life at work, in school, and with her mother and young son at home. The warm, exuberant greetings from Michigan soon became the bright spots of Jane's mail, but she hardly dared expect them to continue.

Good news from Abingdon came in time for her birthday. Robert Roy Wright was delighted with *Petals of Light*. The publishing date was set for the following November, "to catch Christmas gift buyers with their sales resistance at low ebb," Jane informed Shirley.[16]

The pre-Christmas season would be busy with book work again, but there was no need to hurry. They planned to have a quiet holiday. Jane had time to autograph gift books for several buyers. Some were intended for people who had been disabled by accidents and bitterly bemoaned their fate. Jane had made a habit of praying for the recipients while signing the books, especially in such cases. She knew well the insidious power of bitterness. Once surrendered to, there was often no stopping place.

"It's only by God's grace and mercy that any of us, however long and well taught of our Lord, would not be bitter in such circumstances," she observed to Kay.[17] Self-pity was always a waste—most sadly so at Christmas—a waste of the light of the star and the song of the heavenly host.

The first frost of the year had brought flocks of birds to the feeder, and she was watching for the cardinal who had inspired "enough poems to deserve several free meals!"[18]

Cardinals come
Day after day
Brushing the dullness
Of life away
With a casual lift
Of a red, red feather—
Red so incredible
Altogether
That I greet its wearers
Each time, with a brief
Glad suspension
Of unbelief.
"Theatrical"

Her expectations of a quiet Christmas turned to naught. It appeared that Elizabeth had conspired with Nelson and Ruth to keep Donia and Jane from wearying themselves with worry and preparations for a family reunion. Once again Donia had all of her children home for the holidays, and she was radiantly happy. "You would think there was something special about the four of us!" Jane wrote to Frances. "The Lord can provide more joyful surprises than Santa Claus."[19]

Kay's latest book, *Psalms of the Heavens, Earth and Sea,* was among the Christmas gifts. It was dedicated: "With admiration and love to Jane

Merchant who rising above physical restrictions, lifts her readers with her in soaring words like these.'' She then quoted Jane:

I have learned well, in tempests and in calms,
The holy beauty of the Shepherd's psalms;
And I have often watched with prayerful eyes
While God writes psalms, with clouds, in evening skies.

"Psalter"

Jane felt unworthy of the dedication, but she needed the reminder that clouds set against the sunset gave glory to the skies. She had best remember that when it seemed that dark clouds loomed on the horizon of living. The three day Christmas celebration had "put a golden period on a leaden year," she noted in her diary on December 30, 1964. But she worried about the future—about her mother's age and health—and had a dreadful premonition that Donia would not live to see another Christmas.

Faith in God's abiding love, not gloomy forebodings, was her shield against the shock of sudden disaster. And Donia seemed less weary *after* the busy, crowded holidays than she had been before.

They had received news that three of Jane's books were being recorded for the blind: *The Greatest of These, In Green Pastures,* and *Halfway Up the Sky.* It was a great honor that her work was found worthy of bringing "light into literally darkened lives."[20]

She was honored as well by a visit from Dr. John C. Hodges of the University of Tennessee. He greatly admired her work and asked to have her book manuscripts for the Library Special Manuscript room. They were safe in an aluminum box under Jane's bed, only because Eva had insisted they were worth keeping. Lawrence Thompson, Director of Libraries at the University of Kentucky, had proved Eva right. He wrote to ask for a handwritten poem for an exhibit, and added that he hoped she would select an appropriate depository for her manuscripts.

Jane would have thought it presumptuous to make the offer. Why should a university want the writings of someone who had never even attended school? But having been asked, she was glad to give her consent.

Shirley was a graduate of the University of Tennessee, and she thought the university ought to award Jane an academic arts degree in recognition of her superior self-education and literary achievements. She suggested as much to Dr. Andrew Holt, president of the university, who agreed that Jane would be a worthy recipient. He would forward the request to the Committee on Degrees, but he warned that the university policy on such matters was very restrictive.

Jane knew nothing of Shirley's scheme and would most likely have discouraged it, just as she was intent on warding off the latest efforts to name her poet laureate of Tennessee. Ollie Barnes Dayton of the state Poetry Society had made the proposal, and Alfred Mynders wrote in *The Chattanooga Times:* "Jane Merchant would richly deserve the honor of being named Poet Laureate of Tennessee. Her books . . . will live long after many of those quoted widely today are entirely forgotten."[21]

The time had come, Jane thought, to make known her thoughts on the subject. She wrote to Alfred Mynders: "I truly appreciate your opinion of my work, but . . . Tennessee, whose mountains and valleys are pure poetry, has many poets, and to single out one would suggest we have only one or few."

Mynders printed her letter with the comment: "This column has never collected autographs, but that of Jane Merchant, signed in ink, goes in the scrapbook."[22]

At the moment Jane felt dry of verse and was writing prose on assignment—a week of meditations for *The Upper Room Disciplines,* for the modest honorarium of $25.00. Her theme was "The Art of God," based on Psalm 19—a favorite.

"The heavens declare the glory of God!. . . . And what are we declaring most of the time? . . . Our dissatisfactions and frustrations. We utter speech from day to day and from night to night, but it declares less the glory of God than the trivialities of man. . . . To the Psalmist the glory of the heavens is . . . immediate and personal, leading him to consecrate all his thoughts, words and acts to the creator of that glory. So may it be with us."[23]

Assignments were welcome in a tight market, and so were requests for reprint rights. But with more poems in circulation, it was not unusual to have them reprinted without credit to the author—or payment. It happened when Jane's shortest poem, "On Reasoning with Any Adolescent: Why/Try?" was quoted by Charlie Rice in *This Week Magazine* as "that perennial classic by Anonymous."

Mr. Rice was informed of his error by Abingdon—and Shirley. Jane noted: "How sad if that verse should be the one for which I'm best known, especially as Anonymous!"

She believed that credit should be given where it was due, though most people seemed to think "poets are, or should be, too ethereal to take any interest in their writing rights!" she lamented to fellow poet Dorothy Brown Thompson.[24]

Proofs for *Petals of Light* arrived during Lent. This time the editor sent along the dummy of the book jacket, and Jane could not hide her disappointment. The cover was purple and white—her least favorite colors for books, she confided to Shirley.

At least she was finished with the work in time for Easter and dogwood blooming by her window—a certainty that never failed, no matter what else went wrong. And things seemed increasingly bent on going that way.

Thank God she did not have to persevere in her own strength, for she felt herself weakening. The future was uncertain, but she had written in "These Usual Certainties":

> For life's continuing amenities
> That do not fail, whatever else goes wrong;
> For grace, in any season, of old trees,
> And every robin's prompt sunrising song,
> For new light on a known view day by day,
> For hills that keep their places year by year,
> And skies where wings flash onward and away
> And punctual stars predictably appear—
>
> I thank our Lord, less with a spoken prayer
> Than with my own continuing endeavor
> To live serenely, faithfully, with care
> That I may be trustworthy, as I never
> Could hope to be did he not always give
> These usual certainties by which I live.

16
OF MARRED CREATION
1965–1966

Done on tired days, as all work now is done
(Eve could converse and act without fatigue
That dulls perceptiveness; now no one can),
This work is flawed as all work now is flawed.

Yet it is done. In spite of weariness
The clouded eye sees form of leaf and wing
The slow hand celebrates in steel and stone.
The frayed mind seeks the fresh, creating word.

Clay cleaves to roots of trees whose tops aspire
To unconditional sky. The cursed ground bears
Sustaining blessings. Laboring, we catch
Glimpses of Eden glimmering through dawn mists.

Donia's "cranking" arm was stiff was bursitis, making the up and down adjustment of Jane's bed distressingly hard. To spare her mother, Jane pretended to be comfortable in one position all day—and suffered in secret. Physical ache was the least of her concerns. Far worse was the awareness of Donia's advancing age and weakness. She was eighty-one. It could only be a question of time—and probably not much time—before the end. Jane tried to prepare herself, but she would rather not think of it at all.

Pat Lassen had sent on loan *On Our Father's Knee* by Fredrik Wisløff, who wrote about the ravens feeding the prophet Elijah in the wilderness: "black, ugly, greedy birds, but they fed him." Troubles were like ravens, noted Wisløff, but "that which God sends or allows to come is always for good, even if it is brought to you on black wings."

Aging and dying were surely approaching on black wings. Their coming was frightening, but a loving God allowed it. They were to be accepted, not resisted. Jane's eyes sought the dogwood blooms pressing against her window.

To see the cross on every blossoming tree
Is, to the careless, stark morbidity;
But those who know the cross through barren hours
Are glad to see how gloriously it flowers.

"Dogwood Blossoms"

Could she not trust her Lord, who by his own suffering had transformed cross into bloom, death into resurrection? Surely the difficult present and unknown future were enfolded in his love.

For now Jane had work to do. Robert Roy Wright had suggested she write a book for children, "with lovely art work." She selected the most popular among several hundred of her poems for children already printed in magazines.

The task was timely; a new generation of Merchants was underway. Reese had married, and his wife, Linda, expected Donia's first great-grandchild in the fall. Jane knitted booties and remembered waiting for the first grandchild in 1941—who turned out to be twins. How dark the future had looked then, with the world at war and her writing career a broken dream.

Twenty-five years—a quarter of a century—how different it had turned out from what she had expected, how unreliable her own predictions had proved to be! But time was irretrievably moving on to an end—that much was certain. Jane was daily more conscious of her need to prepare for it. With urgency she asked Elizabeth and two friends to witness her signature on the form to donate her eyes—when she was through with them—to the newly established Tennessee Eye Bank.

Her fatigue was chronic—or was it sloth, she wondered to Frances. It was likely to be her "besetting sin"—or at least one of them. She was reading Dante's *Divine Comedy* again. In his vision of purgatory the slothful were running for centuries to make up for their sin. That would at least provide a "change from present circumstances," she observed. Dante's description of paradise was more to her liking. She felt at home there. Not to sound "smug and egotistical . . . it's merely a tribute to Tennessee, where I *am* at home."[1]

In the difficult present she had a sense of estrangement, even from the most familiar and beloved. Jane was aware that much of it was her own doing. She tended to withdraw behind the familiar mask of self-sufficiency, her defence against abandonment and loss. The fear of being abandoned had been there—since the childhood experience of waking in an empty house, bound to a bed, with the family gone to the orchard. Never again had Donia left her alone, but for how much longer?

In her notebook, Jane had quoted from Paul Tillich's *The New Being*: "But if we have experienced ultimate acceptance [by God], this anxiety

215

about being rejected by those nearest us is *conquered, though not removed.*" (Jane underlined the last four words.)

There was comfort in knowing that her feelings were typical. The universal fear of rejection was rooted in a deep knowledge that separation was inevitable. Decay, aging, and death are part of the process of living on this earth. They have been conquered by Christ—but not removed. Separation from Donia was something Jane had to accept. Death would come between them, but not forever. Resurrection would follow. It was the moment of severance she dreaded most—and the lonely vigil of surviving. If only she could be spared that. . . .

Her fears, and the physical aches caused by remaining in one position for hours on end, were, of course, hidden. The summer visiting season was especially lively this year. Patricia, Ruth's oldest daughter, was attending summer school at the university and staying at the Doll House. Her riotous golden curls, dimpled chin, and laughing blue eyes were still the same as when she loved to curl up in Jane's bed, listening to favorite fairytales and story books for hours on end or carry on "secret conversations" by mouthing words in silence, shutting out the hearing people in the room. She and Jane lip-read and wrote on slates in delightful conspiracy.

Now Patricia was taking classes in education and children's literature, bringing stacks of books for Jane to read. She even beat her aunt in Scrabble once or twice. But her presence in the house caused more comings and goings than usual, more gatherings of friends and relatives in animated conversation and laughter Jane could only pretend to share in.

After a difficult day she poured her pain into "Inadequate," a poem she thought too private for publication.

> It is raining. The visitors, the kindred, all
>   have gone.
> Rain breaks small crystal fists against the glass
> And throbs upon the roof; an audible rain
> To others, not to me.
>
> Inaudible to me as kindred laughter,
> Inaudible as kindred confidences,
> Inaudible as kindred voices sharing
> The good things that have happened to each one.
>
> The rain makes silent mists upon the glass.
> Trees, flowers, and earth are wavering obscurely.
>
> Silence obscures even the kindred faces,
> Silence changes pleasure to resignation
> On kindred faces when my anxious eyes
> Fail to read clearly a forgetful question.

Their patience, reaching for a pad and pencil,
says silently I am inadequate.

Perennial experience has proven
There is no way of dealing with the recurrent
Inevitable yet always unexpected
Sharp hurt the silence deals, except by silence.

Silence. Accepting, gracious, even humorous
  silence
Even in my own thoughts about the hurt.
Submissive, patient silence. It will pass.
No one was ever required to live forever.

The rain pours down the window. The view is
  drowned.
Floods of silence, in time, may drown the hurt.

Deafness would always be her circumstance, an aspect of marred creation that could be conquered, but not removed. Her choice in responding made the difference between joy and misery. "Accepting, gracious, even humorous silence" could overcome the loneliness of self-pity and despair. In "The Choosers," Jane wrote:

They wander fields where summer strews
Extravagance of petals
And show, with sadly patient smiles,
Their small bouquets of nettles.

Advance copies of her book *Petals of Light* arrived in August. Early purchase orders were promising, wrote the Abingdon sales manager. Jane was cautious, as usual, but anxious: "It isn't poetic to count, or count on, pennies for *Petals,* is it?" she noted to Shirley.[2]

The purple and white volume was more attractive than she had expected—another gloomy prediction laid to rest. Patricia was thrilled. So was Pat Lassen, who came from Michigan the day after the book arrived. She brought an armload of books, pictures, and class plans for her next year in school, so that Jane could better share in her activities. Her letters had come with daily regularity for nearly a year now, supplemented by packages containing stationery, stamps, greeting cards, and small gifts for passing on to friends and kin. These supplies were especially needed now that Elizabeth and Eva had less time for running errands.

After Pat's visit, Jane wrote "Sufficient Cause."

"We met because I needed you," she said.
"Although I did not know it till you came.

Your friendship, like no other friend's has fed
A lifelong hunger I could never name."

And I, receiving from her every day
Affection never given by any other
To fill an emptiness, can only say,
"We met, because we needed one another."

On September 11, Reese called to announce the arrival of Timothy, the first great-grandchild. But soon their joy was mingled with grief. Donia's lifelong dearest friend had died.

"Mother hopes she can go as quickly, without helpless lingering, but who can bear to think of Mother going?"[3] Jane anguished to Shirley. She had written "Unready" a few weeks before.

One golden leaf—and I, whom all
Fall's golden woods elate,
Look at my summer multitudes
Of green, beseeching, "Wait!"

I have not garnered sun enough
To need a harvest moon.
I would not part with hummingbird
And tanager this soon.

And who is weary now of roses
And tired of daisies' pearly
White greetings by abundant fields?
All goldenrod is early.

Amazing fortune plunges us
Head over heels in debt
To fall for gold, but thrifty hearts
Must always cry, "Not yet!"

The next severing pain was totally unexpected. Robert Roy Wright wrote that he was leaving Abingdon. For twelve years he had been her editor and friend. The shock of it inspired "In Time of Shifting."

Now there is change; an unexpected push
Has jostled my kaleidoscope and sent
Familiar forms diverging in a rush
Of whirling colors. I, for long intent
On one design that fully satisfied
My heart with muted brilliances of hues
In rich juxtapositions, must abide
Much less harmonious, much duller views.

> I shall not twist the tube in vain endeavor
> To re-create the pattern that is gone
> For seeking it would mean that I could never
> See beauty in any that I gaze upon.
> If other patterns always seem less fair
> I still am glad my lost design was there.

Later she added a prayer, to the Father "in whom there is no variation or shadow due to change, help us to accept gracefully the changes and shadows of life. If we must lose the friends, relationships, places, or occupations we value most, help us make the most of those that remain and those that follow, assured that with thee there is goodness to be found in every new experience, however unwelcome or demanding it may seem."[4]

Donia's bursitis appeared to be chronic, so Jane decided to invest in an automatic hospital bed. It was something she had long wanted, but thought a luxury they could ill afford. Now necessity turned to blessing; by the touch of a button she could raise and lower herself without troubling others. It was an independence of movement she had never known before.

The screen was off her window. "I'm feeling wealthy today," she exulted to Shirley. "Nearly all the red leaves have fallen from my window dogwood, leaving only the green morning-glory leaves (have you seen blue morning-glories blooming among red dogwood leaves and berries? Everyone should)."[5]

> October dawned upon me with a glow
> Of muted light from sky yet soft with rain
> Shining through crimson dogwoods that bestow
> Their brightness on my room through every pane
> And with a boon of morning-glory blue
> Blooming amazingly high above the red
>   "First of October"

The official publishing date for *Petals of Light* was November 8. The book was dedicated to Nelson, Elizabeth, and Ruth "who share with me a very special Mother." Gurre wrote: "Your 'very special mother' must be very proud being the grandmother of seven such lovely books, and I need not go far to guess what inspiration SHE has been in the writing of all of them."[6]

Gurre was right. Donia was radiantly proud of Jane's latest offspring, but she showed disturbing signs of exhaustion. Elizabeth gave strict orders that Donia was not to lift the heavy boxes of books from Miller's

Book Department; they had ordered 500 books for an autograph tea. Jane signed them in purple ink with pens from Shirley.

The store reported brisk sales, but hometown popularity was no guarantee against a complete flop elsewhere, Jane reminded herself. The first royalty check would tell.

Other worries loomed larger. Her birthday and the new book caused much excitement of mail and visitors. When it was over, Donia looked near collapse. She had lost weight, and she complained of stomach pains. Elizabeth insisted that she go to the hospital for tests. The day before she left, Jane wrote "Respite."

> Escaped again—
> Perhaps.
> More days with sun, with
> flowers
> May lapse
> Before the giant claw
> Descends and rends
> Us and the sun and flowers.
>
> Now nothing ends.
>
> Are mice eluding the cat
> And making merry
> Aware that all escape
> Is temporary?

Even before Donia's test results were known, she vomited blood, and her doctor called to say that an emergency operation must be performed to remove part of her ulcerated stomach.

The family was alerted. Nelson and his family arrived that evening; Ruth came the next day. They spent an uneasy Thanksgiving together, taking turns visiting Donia in the intensive care unit. She was rallying remarkably, and they dared hope for a complete recovery. But the convalescence would be long, Jane wrote to Gurre and Kay. Friends were supporting them with prayers and kindnesses, "and always the Father sustains us."

Ruth would stay as long as needed. Donia came home on December 4. She was weak, but determined to care for her daughter again. Jane had written "Unconquered" of her mother after her father's death in 1949. Now it seemed just as fitting.

> The blow that might have felled her once
> Descends unnoticed now
> Since she received the mightiest stroke
> Of all and did not bow.

220

She lives in staunch unwavering
Uprightness nothing can deform,
Forever greater than any tempest,
Stronger than any storm.

Shirley thought she could best help Jane to get her mind off her troubles by encouraging her to write. With a new collection of poetry in the bookstores, why didn't she press on to new magazine markets as well?

The weary Jane replied. "Each time I think of branching out . . . we have some sort of crisis, and it is all I can do to keep on with the old reliable (sometimes) markets. Perhaps the Lord wants me to keep on with them."[7]

Her friend argued emphatically: "I can't think the Lord wants to limit your achievements or your audience (or your talents!) Crises have to happen just because life is what it is."[8]

Crises had given substance to some of Jane's finest poetry in the past, and they would again, Shirley firmly believed. Her optimism seemed justified by the review of Jane's new book in *The Richmond Times-Dispatch* on December 19, 1965. Dr. Lewis Ball wrote: "For some years I have been an admirer of Jane Merchant's verse. . . . It has a beauty of its own that often suggests the genius of Emily Dickinson. She avoids the cliche and gives her epiphany with economy of effort and with discipline. . . . Her own verse is more eloquent than anything I could say. I particularly loved 'Due.'"

Daily now new jasmine petals
And forsythia blooms unfold,
Paying off, in prompt installments,
Winter's deficit of gold.

He liked even more her "Cardinal Ways."

Well might this ardent scarlet flame,
This bonfire winging by,
Set every garden leaf ablaze
And redden all the sky.

But it is only courteous things
A cardinal can do.
He leaves the trees a freshened green,
The sky a heightened blue.

Dr. Ball continued his praise of her book: "Every page of *Petals of Light* is a thing of beauty and a joy forever. It is metaphysical poetry in the tradition of Edward Taylor and Emily Dickinson— with a heart and perception that are peculiarly Miss Merchant's own.''

Carl Arneson agreed. ''Your *Petals* tell me that evaluation of Jane Merchant will be in the hands of the scholars of the future—specialists in literature, philosophy, religion and semantics.''[9]

Shirley was less patient. She thought Jane ought to let ''a more general publisher'' market her books without the ''religious label,'' a suggestion Jane indignantly refused. Were it not for Abingdon Press, her poetry would not be in the bookstores at all. And the label was accurate enough, she *was* a writer of religious poetry!

Along with her apology for upsetting Jane with her suggestion, Shirley sent a ''meek rebuttal.'' She only wanted to see Jane's work gain the reputation it deserved, from ''college professors and New York Times book reviewers.'' Above all, she wanted it in the hands of readers ''who would not venture near a devotional table,'' but who would love the books if they knew what treasures were in them. These things, she predicted, were bound to happen in the end. The world would catch up. But think what they were missing![10]

Jane was touched, and she confessed that it *would* be nice to have ''literary bigwigs'' use Shirley's kind words. On the other hand, the more she read of books the reviewers *did* praise, the less she valued their praise. Their applause might be greater cause for concern than gratitude.

Any writing, at the moment, was torturous discipline. Donia was able to stay alone with Jane while Elizabeth worked, but it was certainly not a safe arrangement. For the present they were doing fine, Jane assured Shirley, ''but I can't make poems of it all yet, if ever. When I 'look into my heart' to write I find it's still black and blue (I didn't say bleeding).''

At Shirley's request she enclosed a handwritten first draft of her latest poetic effort. ''Experienced'' didn't take long to write, ''but it did to live!''[11]

> We no longer rage,
> No longer protest
> At the torment, the anguish,
> But quietly best
> The worst life can do
> To shatter and scar.
> It's the way life is
> And the way we are

The work was not up to par. Her aching heart was not singing yet. Only determination kept ''the slow hand and frazzled mind'' at labor. But even ''the cursed ground'' of this marred world bore blessings. The crisis had not driven them from home—yet. In late January, Jane wrote a sonnet with the hopeful title "A Place for Spring," with the lines:

> This winter view is desolate enough—
> Swatches of old snow ragged on dun grass . . .
>
> Whatever hard, benumbing storms have crossed it
> This view is still our own; we have not lost it.

Another prose assignment from *The Upper Room Disciplines* occupied most of her writing time. The week's meditations were for Lent 1967, on the theme "The Father's Redeeming Love." "Most of us have felt like worms at times—like giving up," she wrote. "In the Psalm [22:6] Jesus quoted on the cross occur the words, 'But I am a worm, and no man; scorned by men, and despised by the people.' He who in every respect has been tempted as we are, can sympathize with our weaknesses. And He is our Redeemer, even from worminess."[12]

That she felt like a worm, wanting to give up and hide in a dark hole, was understood by her Lord. She had no need to pretend to him. He shared her dread and weariness and would one day lift her up.

A month later she could write to Kay: "Today Mother went outside and picked our first crocus. That is two miracles in one sentence. . . . If the soul of earthly flowers blossom in eternal meadows, I hope this partiuclar valiant crocus finds itself in an especially lovely spot, for the satisfaction it brought Mother and me today."[13]

At last Jane could look into her heart and write in ringing tones of the darkness they had come through. "Correction to Dylan Thomas" was dated March 1, 1966.

> "Do not go gentle"—little matter how,
> Tempestuous or tame, if there is no
> Return; nor do we say, "Do not go now,"
> But simply, passionately, "Do not go."

Three days later she wrote the sonnet "Renewal," with the lines:

> For all that lives in this green world today
> I thank Thee, Lord of life; . . .
> And most I thank Thee for life spared to one
> So much akin to the essential urge
> That pushes grasses upward toward the sun
> And causes buried blossoms to emerge.
> The grave could win no triumph—for one who
> Walks youthful earth again at eighty-two.

The contract for the book of poetry for children arrived in mid-March. The title was *All Daffodils Are Daffy,* named for the poem "Daffy Song," which ends:

> Their petals get frostbitten
> And their cups filled up with snow.
> It's their own fault entirely.
> They haven't any sense.
> There's simply nothing anyone
> Can say in their defense.
> But, oh, it's joy to see them
> When earth and sky are gray,
> For daffodils are daffy
> In the most lovely way!

On the biographical statement Jane wrote at her publisher's request, she could not resist listing her educational qualifications: "From 1919–1934 I majored in being a child, which is a necessary preliminary to writing verse for children. Since 1942 I have majored in being an aunt, which is highly educational and results in various degrees of delight."

In late March came the royalty statement from Abingdon: 2,500 copies of *Petals of Light* had sold in less than two months. Now they could afford temporary cleaning help every two weeks until Donia grew stronger, easing Elizabeth's workload a little.

The crisis winter was over, and Jane dared acknowledge the depth of her despair in her journal. She found it "appallingly painful" to be helpless and a burden when she wanted to be of help. But that was a factor of her existence she *must* learn to accept. "Words that were a special help to me during the hard winter were from 2 Peter 1:19, 'And we have a prophetic word made more sure. You do well to pay attention to this, as to a lamp shining in a dark place. Until the day dawns and the morning star rises in your hearts.' I have tried to pay attention, and this morning day dawned. . . . Enough of the difficulties. God knows them, God permits them, and please God grant me continuing and at last final victory over them. I do not intend to magnify the difficulties. Far better if I can truly say: 'My soul doth magnify the Lord.'"

She could find no words adequate to describe Donia, who had come through the ordeal still "eager to live and anxious to do for others and happy to be outside in warm sunlight. Bert Vincent told Mother last fall he had been hunting a miracle all his life, and thinks I am it. I know Mother is" *(Diary, March 28, 1966).*

Jane herself felt bone weary, and she blamed it on a lingering sore throat and cold. She was "de-composing" tissues instead of composing poems, she lamented to Shirley. Which might be just recompense for writing "Ah, April!" The poem, included in *Petals of Light,* was prompted by the announcement in a newspaper that "during any day in April fifteen million people may be catching cold."

On earth and air has settled
The mystic April sheen.
Now flowers are freshly petaled
And grass is freshly green
And every street is puddled
With pools of azure sky
And birds seem quite befuddled
With rapture as they fly.
On every roof and steeple
The giddy sunbeams play
And fifteen million people
Are catching cold today.
An imminence of roses
Pervades the silvery air
And fifteen million noses
Are twitching in despair.
The robins utter gladly
Their rippling nuptial notes
And gargles gurgle sadly
In fifteen million throats.

Ah, bright the April flowers,
Ah, fair the April blue,
Ah, sweet the April showers—
Ah-choo, ah-choo, ah-choo!

The prospective blooms on her window dogwood resembled "half-popped popcorn," Jane observed to Kay. A stranger to dogwood country might think the tree suffered from "some mysterious malady." "How unfortunate to be anyone who would have such thoughts as that!"[14]

When dogwood blooms are still
Small untouched cups
They are all bruise-brown,
Not white.

But the bruises grow into crosses
Wholly white, save at the very edge,

And all the lowly trees gleam in white glory
Of wounds outgrown.

"Cup Into Cross"

It appeared that the window tree *was* ailing. It had only a few leaves and pink blossoms instead of white. Donia feared it was dying, and Jane quoted a favorite hymn in her journal: "Change and decay in all around I see; O Thou who changest not, abide in me." "I feel decayed too!" she added *(Diary, March 28, 1966).* She had broken a tooth, the bed motor appeared to be failing, and even Elizabeth had slowed down, admitting to a touch of arthritis. Jane had suspected that something was wrong with her—not that Elizabeth complained; the sisters shared the trait of hiding suffering from each other. Nearly twenty years earlier, Jane had written "Confidentially."

"Sometimes I think I can't keep on at all.
I can't help wondering what's the use of it,"
Sue said when times were bad. "But I can't say so.
I just can't let Jim down. He'll never quit."

"A dozen times at least," Jim said, "I've thought,
There's no use going on, I'm licked. I'm through.
But Sue—well, she's so spunky all the time.
I just can't say a thing like that to Sue."

That was ten years ago, or maybe nine.
Yes they came through, of course. They're doing fine.

The poem was printed in *In Green Pastures,* with the meditation: "We thank thee, Father, for others' belief in us, for the trust and loyalty we dare not disappoint . . . for those whose expectant faith in our good qualities calls forth more persistent courage than we dreamed we possessed. For those who keep us at our best—yet love us at our worst. . . . And for all who do not complain, who bear their burdens quietly, with grace and with good humor, we ask, O Father, thy victorious aid."[15]

They would come through the present troubles, of course; her prayer would be answered. Even in the darkest times strength was given to greet friends and kin with warmth and cheer. One wrote on Jane's slate that the three in the Doll House were the happiest people she knew. The remark would have seemed incomprehensible once; now Jane thought it a sad indication of the unhappiness pervading the world beyond her walls. "Perhaps some day I will stop being astonished at how sad and trying some aspects of living are for everyone without exception," she confided to Carolyn Ruth.[16]

Perfect bliss—or any human perfection—could not be expected on this earth. That was a lesson she still struggled to learn. "Why not just reconcile ourselves to the fact that there is something wrong with all of us . . . and go on doing the best we can?" she exhorted Shirley.[17]

In "New Realist," she had written:

> With a few bright threads from a worn-out dream
> She embroiders designs of wings that gleam
> And shimmer, with stitches firm and exact,
> Over the stiff hard fabric of fact.

Her personal doctrine of humanity had not changed since she wrote "Grandfather's Shock-Absorber." Her faith in "the cussedness of man" was in line with the "scriptural and realistic view of man inclined to go wrong," she declared to Frances. Being forewarned that "the nicest people" could behave in "disconcerting ways" made it easier to forgive, but did not remove the hurt.[18] The cussedness of humans caused most of the suffering in this decaying world—and drove hearts into hiding. Jane had written in "To Be Alive":

> Not to withhold the heart
> From the unexpected dart,
> The edged word, keen, unsparing;
> Not to withdraw into
> The peace that once one knew,
> The numb peace of uncaring;
>
> And never to erect
> One barrier to protect
> From any recurrent thrusting,
> But hourly to remain
> Accessible to pain,
> Forgiving, loving, trusting.

And yet, in a marred world, with imperfect people, some things must remain hidden. The deepest secrets of the heart were veiled in mystery. " 'Your life is hid with Christ' [Col. 3:3] are words that are taking on an ever deeper meaning for me these days," Jane confided in her diary. "However much I long at times for a touch of human understanding, a hint that someone . . . sympathizes with the little needless hurts, they are not necessary. These things are to be hidden, not shown. Hid with Christ in God. Surely a safe, unreproachable hiding place where even the most untreasured parts of one's life may be transformed and bring forth strength and even loveliness at last" *(Diary, June 8, 1966)*.

The bright summer days outside her window only seemed to make her confinement more monotonously stifling. She fought against a downpull of despair and dark forebodings. "We are admonished in Proverbs not to ask why former days were better," she wrote in her diary a week later. "I try not to ask, but I know they were. And that present days are better than future days will be."

The harsh reality of decay and death must be faced, but that was not the whole truth. The trials of this world could not be removed, but they had been conquered. In the darkness she had seen glimpses of an abiding light. In "Quest Eternal"—renamed "Intimations"—Jane had written:

> The good for which we search
> Is never wholly known
> A glimpse, a hint, a touch—
> And we go on alone.
> Yet the hint, fleeting, gone,
> Assists us keeping on.

She had sold her 1,600th poem, and from Abingdon came a clutch of fine reviews of *Petals of Light*. One read: "The range [of poetry] is the more amazing when one considers that Miss Merchant writes from the circumstances of a lifetime confinement."

Women used to be confined while having a baby, Jane noted in her diary. A lifetime confinement could account for her being prolific. The reviewer compared her short poems to those of Frost, Guest, and Riley, and Jane commented: "Poor Frost, such company!"

In August came an astonishing announcement from Abingdon: *Petals of Light* had been selected by the American Book Publisher's Council for exhibit at the International Book Fair in Frankfurt, West Germany. It was *the* fair of the publishing industry. To think that her *Petals* would be wafted that far, and perhaps "in a small way" counteract the sordid picture of American life shown in too many books, Jane wrote to Kay Gudnason.

The news had blown away her gloom. Jane recorded in her diary on August 9: "With seven books in print, and the latest going to the International Fair, I am very happy."

The newspaper had announced it on August 8, seventeen years to the day after her father's obituary had been printed. Reminders of death were all around, it seemed. By her window the leaves were turning early and falling from the dying dogwood, while Donia's morning glories bloomed cheerfully among the branches.

> It was a year of trouble; Gran was ill.
> It was hard labor learning not to do
> The gardening for which she had the will
> But not the energy at eighty-two.

She did plant morning-glories, and today
At last a blue one bloomed, frail, transitory.
In all her life, whatever troubles stay,
No year has passed without a morning-glory.
"Fulfillment"

The impermanence of the world was becoming more apparent daily. Jane felt a deep grieving within—and at times a yearning to be done with it. But it was not for her to choose the time or shrink from what was coming. This was her Father's world. Here he had bid her live and work and love until it pleased him to take her home. In "Be of Good Cheer," she had written:

"Be of good cheer, for I have overcome
The world"—this thin, constricted world of mine
With little endless samenesses that numb
My soul even to the wonder of divine
Words of encouragement sometimes, this dull
World of gray problems that can never be
Entirely solved, that, nagging, can annul
Whatever ray of gladness comes to me?

This is the world of which he speaks to us,
The human world of weariness and strain,
Exasperating, irksome, arduous,
With worldly loss for every worldly gain.
This is the world he overcame, and here
He bids us live, and work, and be of cheer.

17
FOR BECOMING
NOVEMBER 1966–
AUGUST 1967

Father,
My trivial Gethsemanes
Seem very great
To one as small as I.

It hurts—the letting go
My well-made plans,
The giving up
My special intense desires
For Thy large unfamiliar purposes.

Help me to pray, 'Thy will be done,'
Now, Lord,
Knowing that as I do so I consent
To enter greater Gethsemanes
By and by.

April, 1967

Watching the dogwood die was like a slow severance from her own earthly self, and as if time was winding down at last. The tree had marked the seasons for fifteen years, standing so close to the window that with the screen off Jane could touch it. She had always felt akin to trees. They spoke to her of faith and fortitude, of hope and grace abiding through every storm, every winter. She had tried to say it in poetry over and over:

So all my songs say only that every tree
That I have known lives evermore in me.
"Theme"

Now, with the tree dying, she felt the grief of parting, as if she herself would soon be leaving this familiar and beloved earth. Her work might be

230

done, her writing outdated. "The publishing world . . . like most of the man made world of air pollution and mind pollution, is not a region where I feel at home, nowadays," she lamented to Shirley.[1]

Her friends and fans thought otherwise. Her newest pen-friend, May Justus, author of more than fifty books for children, had written to express appreciation for "An Array of Terms." She was sure it would be placed in many anthologies, and that Jane's best years as a poet were ahead. May wished her "sunny and starry thoughts" from which to make her "music for the world."[2]

The poem, written in 1961, was one of Jane's favorites, but it had been rejected by "a forbidding array of editors," she confessed to May.[3]

A charm of goldfinches in the sky
And a murmuration of starlings—
But what are the special words that apply
To groups of earth's blossoming darlings?

I shall find a flirtation of violets
And gaze on a dazzle of daisies
And offer a waft of mignonettes
To a lady with suitable phrases.

A blandish of buttercups on the hills
Can delight me over and over,
And I joy in a flourish of daffodils
And smile at a lavish of clover.

A meditation of pansies can touch
My heart and strangely renew me,
And golden the hour when a child brings a
clutch
Of dandelions to me.

May urged her to let a biographer tell her story—or write an autobiography herself. "What a great blessing [it] would be to many people."[4]

Others said the same. Jane noted in her diary that *Guideposts* magazine had asked for material to do a biographical article on her. Since much was already in print—with garbled facts—she wrote her own version, hoping to set the record straight. Eva read it and thought it ought to be expanded into an autobiography, to be sold to a publisher now for publication after her death. Jane's refusal was firm. Under no circumstances would she write what someone had called "an autobiographical ouch!"[5]

All she planned to do in that line was already said in "Autobiographical," in *Petals of Light,* she noted to Frances.

My tale will leave no one aghast,
A simple tale, a true one.
My past is not a purple past
But just a black and blue one.

Several correspondents were saving her letters, and one had asked her consent to publish them. "Unthinkable!" Jane had declared in her diary in July 1966. Fortunately she had the legal right to prevent it. Correspondence belonged to the writer, not to the recipient.

Pat Lassen and a few others had agreed to destroy the letters, but Shirley decried such waste. She treasured hers and was convinced they would someday be published. If Jane insisted, she would burn them, but she hoped for permission to enjoy them a while longer.

Permission was given, with the understanding that the letters would eventually be destroyed. In her diary Jane confessed concern for Eva's and Shirley's stubbornness. They took it for granted that her private life and writings were of interest to a wider public and would not accept the truth—that she was "no part of the literary establishment, just a minor weed in the . . . subculture of popular magazines."

Her own youthful ambitions had once been to reach higher than "the kitchen school of verse," but that was nevertheless where she saw herself belonging now. "The kitchen school helps one keep eating, and I do not scorn it. People in kitchens have as good taste very often (in both senses) as people in the *New Yorker* or *Atlantic Monthly* editorial offices."[6]

Her background was *Progressive Farmer* and *Christian Advocate,* and that was doubtless what God intended. She no longer objected. If the literary establishment never recognized her as a poet, neither would it be necessary to have "one's silliest, least worthy thoughts (in letters) rushed into print, as with poor Robert Frost, as soon as one is dead. It's much more comfortable to be 'just Jane,'" she pointed out to Shirley.[7]

In her diary she wrote: "As for my doing what I've done under difficulties, that's the way most people do what they do. And bookstores are swamped with all the sad details. . . . Let it be forgotten, hid with Christ. I'll probably destroy all diaries before I die."[8]

Or perhaps not all. Too many inaccuracies were in print about her. The *Guidepost* story would be rewritten by an editor, and that was not likely to be an exception. If ever a "highly improbable biographer" should try to compile her story, he or she would have a difficult time verifying facts. In the same diary entry, just for the record, Jane took pains to describe in detail the room where she did most of her living: the electric bed she could control herself—"outrageously" oversized for her small body, but with space for young visitors to curl up at the end; the reading lamp she could reach to turn on and off herself; the hospital overbed table for writing and

typing on—a gift from Eva after Donia's last operation; handwork
supplies in a cloth bag hanging by the side of her bed; "Daddy's" table,
with a glass top protecting the polished walnut wood, holding special
treasures and necessities of fresh flowers, her father's watch, a magic
slate, and a bell to catch her mother's attention; and her writing supplies,
address book, and journal in the table drawer.

Manuscripts and editorial correspondence were in boxes she had
covered with attractive paper, on a shelf near the head of the bed, where
Donia could hand them to her with ease. The old chiffonier beside it held
her clothes and bath things. Books were in the highboy shelf by the foot of
her bed. The office end of the room was better organized for her writing
business than it had ever been. "It's ironic that this should be so, just
when I seem to have least to write. There is of course, a vein of irony in all
of life, which can be met only with a vein of iron in oneself. (I wrote all
that about the room arrangement because I wanted to lead up to that last
sentence!)"

Chronic fatigue seemed to have infested her soul, and the sense of
encroaching decay was reinforced by an ugly, dark blotch on the bedroom
ceiling. The roof leaked, and efforts to repair it had failed, much to
Donia's and Jane's distress. It remained to be seen whether the last patch
would keep the rains out.

Only a few brown and wilted morning glory leaves clung to the
skeleton branches of the dead dogwood. Time, for the tree, was over, and
Jane fought an overwhelming sense of sadness. A friend had
recommended she read *In Green Pastures* when she was depressed, and
she took the advice. The last poem in the book, "Never a Last Goodbye,"
was written after her father's death.

> Somehow my heart can never learn to say
> A last good-by, entirely and completely,
> To anything I ever loved. There may
> Be folk who can accomplish severance neatly
> With no loose ends of longing and regret
> To trip their hearts at unexpected hours;
> But always my heart stumbles, even yet,
> When the shape of hills or the rain-sweet
>   scent of flowers
> Recalls my earliest home, or when the sound
> Of laughter echoes that which used to fall
> From lips long silent to me. I am bound
> By myriad threads of memory, keeping all
> I ever loved so near me still, that I
> Shall never learn to say a last good-by.

In the meditation with it she gave thanks that "through the grace of Christ our Savior we need not say a last good-by to those we love. We thank thee for the promise of eternal life in him, and for faith that all we have ever known of goodness, truth, and beauty shall continue and shall be made perfect. O everlasting God, our faithful shepherd, whose goodness and mercy hath followed us all the days of our lives, we thank thee that in whatever of thy many mansions we may dwell, thy goodness and thy mercy shall follow us forever. Amen.'"[9]

The dogwood was cut down after Thanksgiving, but the stump was left to hold birdseed and a suet feeder. Titmouse, chickadees, and starlings flocked to her window. Where the tree had been was now a more spacious view of sky.

Christmas preparations were difficult. Jane felt unusually tired, but she made potholders and washcloths for several friends, and she wrote cheerful letters. On December 20, 1966, she confided in her diary: "1966 . . . was a difficult year (They all are) and I have reason to believe 1967 will be more so. . . . During the Christmas month, sadly, I had to remember often St. Theresa's 'Let nothing disturb you, let nothing dismay you.' I shall try especially to keep it in mind this year. Not that I may have God, but that God may have me."

To Pat Lassen she quoted Baron Von Hugel: "'I wish you a very rich, deep, true, straight, and simple growth in the love of God, accepted and willed gently and greatly, and at the daily, hourly cost of self.' Of course we're tempted to wish there weren't the cost, but there is. And it's a good New Year's wish for each other, isn't it?''

Snow fell over Knoxville at Christmas, and Jane wrote:

> How vulnerable the small earth lies
> To every wind that blows
> Till heaven wraps it tenderly
> In pure white swaddling clothes.
> > "In December"

She kept her January routine as if nothing were amiss, sending batches of poems to editors and catching up on correspondence. But she had an urgent need to put things in order. Manuscripts were sorted, poems were pasted into scrapbooks, bundles of letters were labelled, and books were marked to be returned or given to friends. Donia was handed stacks of correspondence and diary pages to burn. Remaining journals would be designated for family reading only.

Not until the ninth day of the new year did Jane write a poem—and it "just barely got done," she noted in her diary.

Now I observe
The dimmed, but definite, winter earth still here
Though lacking my attention for days past,
Faint green of winter grass no fainter now
For want of my surveillance, than last week.

Now I observe
The natty two-tone stripes of a sparrow's
Back quite unruffled by my never fully
Noticing them before. Their understated
Elegance is not new, except to me.

Now I observe
How well the world I see maintains its being
Despite my oversights. How well it is
That existence depends much less than I
On my observing.

"The World I See"

Her window view would still be there when she was gone. There was both comfort and regret in that thought.

Two weeks later she could no longer hide her secret. She wrote in her diary: "I had noticed a hard spot in my right breast, off and on, but just couldn't be bothered with it, with a superabundance of botheration already."

Elizabeth was changing sheets on the bed. When Donia was out of the room, Jane indicated the lump to her sister. The skilled nurse's fingers took only a few seconds to confirm Jane's suspicion.

"The doctor must see this," Elizabeth said firmly.

Jane had feared as much, but asked if Donia could be spared the knowledge—at least until they knew the verdict. Elizabeth agreed. It was Saturday, and she would call the doctor early Monday morning from her office.

Sunday was quiet. They had fried chicken and rice for dinner, one of Jane's favorite meals, and she wrote her cheerful weekly letters to family and special friends, saying nothing of what loomed in her mind. If the lump proved to be cancerous, she intended to refuse surgery and insist on keeping her illness secret. Perhaps this was God's provision for the last dark bend in her pilgrim journey. He would give her grace to go through it. She felt better prepared to face death than the hazards—and expenses—of surgery.

Dr. Zirkle came with Elizabeth to the Doll House the following Monday morning. The examination was brief, and his verdict blunt: "It is likely to be cancer. We'll schedule surgery at once," he told them.

235

Donia sank into her chair with a gasp of horror. But she regained her composure quickly, to insist with the doctor and Elizabeth that Jane *must* have the operation. Whatever the risk and cost, it had to be done.

If Jane had thought to rid her mother and sister of a burden by dying, their anguish gave the lie to such a notion. Once the threat to her health was known, there was no turning back. She dared not shrink from living.

Surgery was scheduled for the coming Friday at Fort Sanders Presbyterian Hospital. Jane notified only a few friends beforehand, asking for their prayers. To Pat she wrote: "I'm sorry for the sadness to you and my kin—but remember, 'His way is perfect.' Keep my love for always and always in our Lord, and my gratitude to Him for letting us begin knowing each other here."[10]

Eva insisted that Shirley be told. Jane did it gently, saying, "This is harder on Mother than a hole in the ceiling, but she is being herself and we hope to come through. . . . I love you here and elsewhere, always."[11]

Her private expectations were not optimistic. She prepared herself for the end by addressing a stack of cards to her correspondents for Elizabeth to fill in and mail afterwards.

She packed her New Testament with Psalms (King James Version), Saint Theresa's prayer, and a prayer copied from the Methodist Book of Worship; she would pray it before her operation: "O loving Father, I commit myself with perfect trust into thy loving hands. Watch over me and protect me in my hour of weakness, and grant that as I become unconscious to earthly things my thoughts may be turned to thee. Bless and guide thy servants who shall tend me; give them such success that we may praise thee for thy goodness. And finally grant that I may so bear suffering with cheerful courage that I may be the means, under thy hand, of helping others in their time of trial; for Jesus Christ's sake. Amen."[12]

For her daily meditations she brought *The Upper Room Disciplines.* The meditation for the day she was admitted was a favorite quote from Juliana of Norwich: "He said not: 'Thou shalt not be tempested, thou shalt not be travailed, thou shalt not be afflicted,' but He said: 'Thou shalt not be overcome.'"

The meditation for Friday morning was based on Christ's agony in the garden of Gethesemane. He, too, had known the dread of physical pain and death. In agony of spirit, he sought the will of his Father: "Not what I will, but what Thou wilt."

Surgery for cancer was her own small Gethsemane, and Jane repeated the prayer "Thy will be done" and no longer worried what that will might be. God's will was always best—and so it would be all right, either way.

The operation was scheduled for 8 A.M.. It went remarkably well. The cancer was removed, and Jane woke up in the recovery room at 12:30 P.M. to find a grateful Elizabeth by her side.

She felt great relief, but also an unmistakeable twinge of disappointment at not waking in "the least of many mansions," she confided to Frances. "You say one need not settle for second best . . . but I settled for that."[13]

Her first words to the doctor were; "How soon can I go home?" But she was limp with pain, and not until five days later could she note in her diary, "Feeling better."

Donia was by her bedside during the day and Elizabeth during the long nights. Mail, flowers, and gifts poured in.

Pat Lassen sent a small book by Amy Carmichael; *His Thoughts Said . . . His Father Said.* Jane immediately marked the passage; "His thoughts said, 'I can no longer.' His Father said, '*Thou canst.* Thou canst do all things through Christ which strengtheneth thee. . . . Is it that thou art too weary? Then come unto me and I will refresh thee.'" She was abominably weary, but she had survived, and God, who had kept her going when she could not, would do so now.

On February 5 Jane returned to the Doll House, where Aunt Laura was waiting with Donia. How glad she was to be home! Three days later she could reassure Shirley that she felt "better than seems possible, except that all things are with God!"

The doctor had ordered her to rest, but she worried about Donia and Elizabeth, who couldn't get the rest they needed because of caring for her. "I'm doing so well I'm almost ashamed of myself because Mother feels poorly. Not that she would feel any better if I felt worse!" she confessed in mid-February.[14]

Donia's arthritis had flared up, and her hands were painfully swollen. The doctor said it was probably aggravated by stress, and Jane tried not to blame herself for it. The crisis was safely behind them now, and she prayed that her mother's suffering would diminish soon. In "These Gentle Hands," she wrote:

> There are no hands more beautiful than these
> That through the years have helped small things to
>   grow—
> Babies and chickens, flowers and dogwood trees—
> And shaped uncounted loaves of bread from dough
> Mixed with unerring art to satisfy
> Deep needs, and sewn neat seams, and hammered
>   scores
> Of nails with deft precision, and hung to dry
> Clothes scrubbed and boiled in kettles out of doors.
> These hands have kept their gentleness of touch

Through years of working with untiring skill
To feed and bless and comfort, and though much
Swollen and often painful now, they still
Devotedly persist in serving others.
There are no hands more loving than my mother's.

The bout with cancer was still too fresh to examine closely—or write about.
So far, "by the mercies of God," she had escaped an emotional reaction. At
least she knew not to indulge in self-pity. The writings of Juliana of Norwich
were a continuous comfort, and she quoted from *Revelations of Divine Love* to
Frances: "He sustaineth us within Himself in love; and travailed, unto the full
time that He would suffer the sharpest throes and the most grievous pains that
ever were or shall be; and died at the last. And when He had finished, and so
borne us to bliss, yet might not all this make full content to His marvelous
love; and that showeth He in these high overpassing words of love: 'If I might
suffer more, I would suffer more.' "

Jane added: "Christ doesn't want pity for His suffering. He *for the joy*
that was set before Him endured the Cross. I think contemplating the
crucifixion is meant to make us realize, and respond to, the vast reality of
His love—and incidentally to keep us from self-pity."

She was still weak and shaky, but she was back to her daily routine of
dressing and bathing herself, reading, and doing handwork. Her writing
time was filled with answering an extraordinary amount of mail. "I've
been so showered with kindnesses that I don't seem to get anything done
but write thank you notes."[15]

It wasn't time yet to consider the ramifications of what she had been
through. In one of her poems she had written:

We turn back to our ordinary tasks
From things too vast for us to understand,
From the stupendous happening that asks
Us what we are, and makes supreme demand
That we confront ourselves and our denials
Of what we thought we were, and meant to be—
Courageously undaunted in all trials
And showing utter faith and loyalty . . .

We turn back to the little things we know,
Convinced that they are all we dare to do;
But Christ comes to us even as we go
About our petty duties, to renew
Us in his love, and call us, till we hear,
To greater tasks than those we failed through fear.

"To Greater Tasks"

All Daffodils Are Daffy was launched in mid-March with little fanfare. The publishers knew Jane was not up to autographing and interviews. But the reader response was gratifying. Whole elementary school classes of children wrote to thank her, and *Publisher's Weekly* described the book as, "A light and varied collection . . . which can serve as a reassuring introduction to poetry for the children who have heard some-one . . . dismiss its glory with 'It's fine, but it's kind of hard to understand.'"

Edsel Ford, who had called her *Petals* "one part thorn to two parts roses," wrote: "I'm so glad to see this side of my much admired poet put between covers. . . . It's a joy to have and to hold. . . . Warm good wishes for *another* shelf of books."[16]

Live daffodils in the garden celebrated spring, and the Doll House was being readied for Easter—and Patricia's graduation from the university. The family would arrive in full force, and Jane bemoaned her own—and Donia's—weariness. "Perhaps we are unduly ambitious for this present, imperfect world," she conceded to Eva.

Abingdon had already asked for another devotional book. Jane was conscious of her debt of gratitude to God and those who cared for her—a far greater debt than she had been aware of before. There had been times in the past when she had indulged in the self-pitying image of herself as an unwanted burden. The recent events had shown just how wrongfully she had judged those who loved her. In a Good Friday journal entry, she confessed: "I give thanks to God for the kindness that has been shown me. I was wrong in thinking people do not care enough. May I accept God's pardon, and put from me . . . the doubts of what I should and should not have done for the good of others, and may I die unto self and live unto righteousness" *(Diary, March 24, 1967).*

She prayed daily Mary's words of surrender to the will of God, "Behold the handmaid of the Lord; be it unto me according to thy word" (Luke 1:38). She asked Pat to pray with her, that she "might know and be willing to do and write what God would want now."[17]

In "On Recovery," she wrote:

> What shall I render to thee, Lord of all,
> For family and friends' staunch tenderness,
> For kindnesses too numerous to recall
> Or even to note in pain-confused distress?
> What shall I render for the warm concern
> And skill of many before unknown to me
> And of helpful ones whose names I did not learn
> But who are surely known and dear to thee?

For all thy bounties well administered
By thy own patient ones without cessation
Through prayer and healing touch and strengthening
    word,
I will take fully the strange cup of salvation
By pain, and call upon thy name, O Lord,
To give to each abundant rich reward.

It seemed reasonable to assume that she ought to do a devotional, but she was not yet sure. The *Guidepost* article had been printed, and she bemoaned the simplistic treatment of her facts to Frances: "I've never been as single-mindedly sure of what God wants me to do as this sounds." A week later, she wrote: "I suppose I was kept here for a purpose. I have inquired of the Lord, but the answer so far is 'wait.'"[18]

In doing devotionals, she was always aware of the great benefit to herself, and she wondered if she wasn't doing it more for her own sake than for God's. "It makes me squirm [to think that] the most popular poems in my books are . . . centered on the person's self and not on God. *The Mercies of God* is the least popular of my books, possibly because most people feel no great need of mercy."[19]

There was no way of settling the question of motives entirely to her satisfaction. When she prayed for direction, the quotation that came most often to mind was from Luke's Gospel: "Whoso putteth his hand to the plough—let him not look back" (Luke 9:62, paraphrased).

For now she would pray for honesty and courage to face the truth about herself and ask that her heart and intentions be purified. "Until Thy Love" was written with the new book in mind.

If it is true Lord, that in serving others
I merely serve myself, and merely seek
My good in gaining approval from my brothers—
Forgive me, Lord. I know that I am weak,
Vain, selfish, wayward, in myself unable
To do the smallest good for good alone.
My motives are all mixed, my heart unstable,
Thou knowest, Lord, and thou hast always known.

Yet, Lord, thou art all love, though I am not.
Thou wouldst not have me anxious and afraid,
Searching my soul for every hidden blot,
Bewailing every blunder I have made.
Thy love accepts marred love and works, until
Thy love conforms me wholly to thy will.

In mid-May Jane began in earnest going through poems, trying to plan a devotional, but she noted in her diary that she felt "as weak and shaky" as when first coming home from the hospital. Perhaps she was in too big a hurry to get over the operation, she wondered to Eva.

But in June, in the midst of a demanding visiting season, she got off a letter to the publisher, suggesting a theme from James 1:17-27, to be titled *Every Good Gift*. James spoke of God as "The Father of lights from Whom every good gift comes." Jane had searched the Bible and found it virtually blazing with light texts. And the letter of James had always seemed to be personally addressed to her.

The light James spoke of illumined the soul in darkness, like the warmth of the sun reaching the seed buried in the soil. It was not a visible light, but an unseen presence; nurturing and giving strength to grow. It was the light of faith, not sight.

Abingdon responded with enthusiasm to her suggestion. In late June, Jane recorded a "back to normal" day in her diary. She wrote two poems, crocheted a baby bib, washed her hair, and helped snap green beans for the freezer. But she took a tranquilizer on Elizabeth's advice—without much faith in the results.

Daily living and future projections were precarious, the dark soil her seed of faith must rest in. In July, Dr. Hodges and Carl Sandburg died within a week of each other. Jane noted to Shirley: "In the midst of life we are in death, but surely the reverse is true also."[20]

She sent a note of sympathy to Dr. Alwin Thaler, who had lost two close friends within such a short interval. He wrote back immediately, telling her of when Carl Sandburg had last visited him: "I read him some of your poems. He said he liked them much better than Robert Frost's."[21]

It was a gratifying endorsement from such a noted poet, though it brought the familiar fear of future failure. It was best not think of it, but do her best and be satisfied that perfection was neither required nor expected.

Pat Lassen came again in August for five days, the last of their summer visitors. Her daily letters had arrived as regularly as the United States Postal Service allowed. Donia considered her almost a part of the family. Pat took a room at a nearby motel, but she spent the entire day at the Doll House, where she was allowed to make herself useful. Donia could catch up on her rest while Pat cooked, cleaned, baked for the freezer, and "did" for Jane. She found time for long talks, games of Scrabble, and even an outing on the small bed on wheels. Pat was astounded to learn that Jane had never actually *seen* the bathroom and Elizabeth's bedroom, so she insisted on a journey of discovery through the unknown regions of the Doll House.

When Pat left, the house was strangely empty. "If I hadn't learned not to weep when I felt like it, I would have washed away by now," Jane wrote to Pat on the day of parting.

It was time to work in earnest on the new manuscript and to meditate on "light" texts rather than on the loneliness she felt. In her notebook, she drafted the prayer poem "The Fruit of Light":

> Father of lights,
> Light of the world,
> I wait before you.
>
> As a seed in sunwarmed earth
> Receiving
> Light that empowers the tentative stem to thrust
> Through softened earth in search of light, more light,
> That swells the bud, that opens the flower, that forms
> Slowly from day to day, the fruit of light—
>
> So, Light of all life,
> I wait.
>
> There must be the response of the seed to the sun,
> The thrust of the stem through the earth,
> But always, first, the complete acceptance of light—
> No turning away from the light, no hurry to grow
> By one's own efforts, alone.
>
> What any have not received they cannot give,
> There is no fruit of light
> Without concentrated acceptance of light.
>
> Father of lights,
> Light of the world,
> I wait.

God's light was a gift, most mercifully wrapped in the disguise of darkness lest human eyes be blinded or the seed of faith scorched. It was a gift to be accepted joyfully.

Jane suspected that this book would be her last, and she meant to make it her thank offering. The biographical articles she was almost ashamed to read, had too much emphasis on her difficulties and said little about all the help, the kindnesses, and the care given her. She wanted readers to know and share her gratitude for life, for light in dark places, for every good gift. One of the poems she would include was "Far More Abundantly," written for Pat's birthday.

> I could not think to ask that hills should be
> Wreathed always in blue mists of loveliness.

I could not have desired that any tree
Be staunchly graceful through the violent stress
Of icy storms. It would not have occurred
To me to pray for skies blue as they are
Or seek creation of a crimson bird,
A violet or a snowflake or a star.

Especially I never could have sought
For one most loving friend who treasures all
I do and am, and takes unstinting thought
To give me pleasure in large ways and small—
And yet God gives all this! I can but bask
In love that gives far more than I can ask.

18
EVERY GOOD GIFT
SEPTEMBER 1967–
AUGUST 1969

Giver of every good and perfect gift,
Giver of life and breath and everything,
Giver of rains and fruitful seasons that shift
From glory into glory and always bring
Renewal of gladness to our restless hearts
And freshness to our discontented days,
Give us, who live by fickle fits and starts,
The grace to live in constant peace and praise.

Thou in whom there is never variation
Or any shadow that is due to change,
Give us, in every trial and each temptation
When darkness gathers and light seems a strange
Impossible illusion—give us still
The power to live in love and brotherhood
And radiant joy according to thy will,
Father of lights and giver of all good.

The past year had been full of apparent contradictions, Jane thought, God's love disguised in difficult circumstances. It was beyond understanding. Faith alone could accept it.

But so it was with God's greatest gift to humankind: the gift of himself in his Son, wrapped in the dark mystery of crucifixion, an apparent failure, a tragic end to the bright promise of a Messiah king. Yet the slow dying on the cross won the gift of life, the victory over darkness and death.

Faith made acceptance possible, but not easy. To say "Yes, Thy will be done" when pain and doubts clouded the mind was always a Gethsemane experience. Jane had wrestled often with self-will. She found, in the darkest moment of surrender, a oneness with God the Son in his suffering, his compassion, and his love. Afterwards, as in the garden following a summer storm, all seemed brighter, tinged with joy and gratitude as with sunshine. From deep within had come a fresh outpouring of poetry.

Years earlier she had written of the source of her poems:

> Mine are from a hidden heart
> Where the tears are.
>> "Source"

A biographical article about Jane, "She Teaches in Song," in the October issue of *Light and Life Evangel* said the same. The author, Marie Chapman, borrowed her title and theme from the words of Percy Bysshe Shelley, who said of poets: "They learn in suffering what they teach in song."

In her new book, Jane would try to encourage her readers not to despair at disagreeable circumstances, but to accept them as an offering of sealed treasures from the Father of lights. In "The Peaceful Fruit" she wrote:

> This undesirable present
> With innumerable snarled strings of frustration
>> attached to it
> Must be accepted thankfully, with grace.
>
> There is no pleasant chastening
> In any now.
> The wincing of raw pride
> Is not now soothed into humility.
> The sting of shame for little testy sins,
>
> The red remorse for whip words of denial,
> Are not now eased with comforting forgiveness;
> But when meekness and repentance come
> There is yielding.
>
> The peaceful fruit of righteousness
> May be round lustrous apples of good will,
> Sound well-ripened peaches of gentleness,
> Bland soothing pears of patience,
> Rich flavorful grapes of joy.
>
> Of these we may be producers and partakers
> If we take graciously the chastening
> Unacceptable present.

Work on a book manuscript intensified her perennial frustration of not knowing whether the results were good or bad. Publication—and reader reaction—was a long time off. Occasionally a poem brought a "fleeting glow of satisfaction," but that was deceptive. She knew that the true worth of her work was beyond her knowing, that perhaps it was best she didn't know.

Yet, when she most despaired of failure, but resolved to struggle on in darkness, there often came a glimmer of encouragement—usually from an unknown reader. While typing her manuscript, Jane received a long thank you letter from Ruth Northcott, a missionary in Africa. She had cherished Jane's books for years, but only now found time to write: "I wonder whether you know how very wide and deep your ministry is. . . . I have rejoiced in your knowledge of the scriptures and even more in your acquaintance with the Author. I am sure you have lifted the load of many of your kinfolk in Christ, and for some who do not know Him, you have planted the seed of desire. . . . Thank you for what you are and for the way in which you use your talent. . . . May God bless you and continue to use you for His glory."[1]

Jane was grateful, but she knew where the credit belonged. She had written "Of Work Approved" earlier:

> "Thank you," the letter said,
> "Because you have not wasted
> The talent given you."
> I, knowing how I tasted
> Failure and doubt and fear,
> Seeing many a shrug and nod
> As I worked on, say only
> "Thank God, thank God, thank God."

Her ninth book would give a starker picture of "this undesirable present." It was inevitable; the world within and without the Doll House walls was overshadowed by darkening clouds. The news was filled with reports on the Vietnam war and riots at home and abroad. No matter how familiar Christ's warning "In the world you will have tribulations," the events still had the power to shock and surprise, Jane noted to Bruffie.[2] "The Morning News" was written for the new book.

> The jungle headlines tighten on my heart.
> It seems gross tentacles of greed and lust
> Writhe from the page and follow through the door
> Striving to squeeze all hope of life from me.
>   In the young garden where the early light
> Treasures the tender green of every leaf
> I ponder headlines snakily threatening

Destruction of all gardens. None are safe;
Yet in this garden all is perfect praise.
The latest robin, totally unaware
Of triteness, sings his immemorial song.
A robin's song cannot defeat the jungle
Or guarantee that robins long will sing
In any garden. Yet the song is true,
And hate cannot destroy what love creates
If we can love—if we can love enough
To give compassion, understanding, help
To those lost in the jungle they create.
    If all our gardens are Gethsemanes
Wherein we learn to say "Thy will be done,"
And give ourselves to doing of His will
At any cost, at any sacrifice
In absolute obedience—only then
The garden, not the jungle, will prevail.

In the jungle of humanity, men and women thought less of their neighbors' need than their own greed. God's will was scorned. "*My* will, *not* thine," cried angry voices. Seeds of selfishness produced the bitter harvest of violence and destruction.

There was no remedy in our blaming one another. One alone was without fault, and he came not to condemn, but to forgive and call to repentance and stewardship of life on this fragile planet.

Jane had written "With Faithful Awe" several years before, but she included it in her "thank offering."

Oh, let us make an altar of the earth,
Tending entrusted land with faithful awe,
Mindful of human need and human worth
And of the grace and terror of the law
That as men sow, they reap; then let us sow
All fields of earth, the fertile and the lean,
With earnest care that none alive may know
The pangs of hunger, desperately keen,

And let us sow compassion and respect
For every person of whatever race,
Color or rank or creed; let us neglect
No thorniest bramble patch till we efface
The weeds of hate, and make, with one accord,
An altar of earth, devoted to the Lord.

The manuscript was off to the publisher in early November, gratefully dedicated "to my sister Elizabeth, a very special nurse, and to all faithful physicians and nurses who help preserve the gift of life." In the preface, Jane expressed her hope that the book would help others to "trust in the unchanging Father of lights even when there is darkness in their lives, with gratitude for the gift of life with all its lights and shadows."

Now she could relax with a one-volume edition of Shakespeare's plays, a gift from Dr. Alwin Thaler, who had used it and made copious marginal notes—an extra bonus. "I am wealthy!" Jane exulted to Shirley.

Dr. Thaler had followed up their correspondence with several cordial visits, and now Shirley was emboldened to ask his help in getting a degree for Jane. He responded with enthusiasm, but could only report that the university policy was still rigid: "I am *sorry!* . . . Jane Merchant deserves such an honor, and would honor the bestower—much as when Harvard awarded Miss Keller an honorary degree."[3]

Shirley would not give up her efforts to alert the academic community to Jane's work. She sent *Halfway Up the Sky* to Dr. Rosemary Sprague of Longwood College, who wrote: "I shall treasure that small volume . . . and look forward to anything else [Jane Merchant] publishes. And see that our library gets copies. She really is a good *poet.*"[4]

Jane was grateful for the endorsement. She was even more elated with news from Abingdon that her latest manuscript had been accepted. The contract was signed before Christmas, and so a difficult year had yielded much fruit, she noted in her diary. Physically she was stronger than before the surgery—she had produced a book and written fifty poems and sold seventy. The family had also been prolific; Donia had two new great-grandsons, Randy and Joseph.

There had been worse years than 1967, Jane concluded, but not many. "However evil the days and the years, the Lord is good to all, and His kindness is over all that He has made" *(Diary, Dec. 1967).*

"For Lesser Blessings" was in her new manuscript.

> For these I thank thee, Lord, again and always;
> For merriment of snowflakes disappearing
> As soon as seen; for rapid perky small ways
> Of chickadees; for unexpected clearing
> Of clumsy thicknesses of clouds to show
> Blue deeper than the skies of summer dream;
> For gleeful rush of waters eager to throw
> Sparkles of gladness from a wayside stream;
> For vibrant scent of mint leaves intermingled

With fugitive sweetness of faint purple flowers—
If these seem lesser blessings I have singled
Out for my praise, O Lord of all my hours,
I thank thee for small joys that I could do
Without, because I have not needed to.

Magazine markets for poetry were slow and showed no signs of improving. Jane sold a piece of adult fiction for $25.00, but that was not her forte—or inclination. What to do next? She suffered her usual anxiety over not "using her time and talent to best advantage," she confessed to Frances.[5]

Her January gloom was considerably lightened when Nelson and Elberta came with Joan and three-month-old Joseph for three days. Jane was wheeled into the kitchen to witness her grand-nephew take his bath in the sink. She celebrated with a sonnet:

Seeing your smile of rapturous approval,
Your happy approbation of the world,
Feeling my finger clutched beyond removal
By wee rose-petal fingers tightly curled
About it, gazing deep in joyous wonder
At the enchanted wonder in your eyes. . . .
                    "To Joseph at Three Months"

The poem sold quickly, and so did two poems about winged visitors to her winter garden. One was "Dialogue":

"Thanks, Lord," I said, "for sudden, absurd
Joy in the antics of one small bird
Flinging itself from tree to tree
As if nothing were wrong with the world or me"—
Then I, in thankfulness, almost heard,
"Not joy, but your lack of it is absurd."
                              "Dialogue"

These sales boosted her morale, and now it was needed. The day after returning galley proofs to Abingdon, Jane was notified that *Blessed Are You* would go out of print due to rising costs and low sales. "The first of my children to die," she lamented in her diary on February 23, 1968.

The news put an immediate damper on her ambition. Why should she spend her energy (and Donia's) on something so temporal? How long would the other books, including the new one, last? Was this proof that her work was outdated—in spite of fan mail from high school and college students, and even from young soldiers in Vietnam?

Time was irrevocably passing. Her generation was now the "older" one, soon to become the "oldest," whose ranks were rapidly thinning. A new generation was already taking over. They seemed preposterously young for the responsibilities of a world ripe for disaster. Did they feel, as her generation had felt a lifetime ago, confidently optimistic of righting the wrongs committed by their elders? Or had the nuclear age exploded that illusion? Jane asked herself these questions as Ruth's son, Edwin, in Army uniform, came by on his way to a tour of duty in Turkey.

1968 was a presidential election year, and it promised increased turbulence. Robert Kennedy, brother of the assassinated president, was a candidate in the presidential primary. The campaign had already incited anti-war violence (a curious contradiction, Jane thought) and fanned the smoldering fires of the civil rights movement. Student unrest was fermenting world-wide, with campus riots spilling into city streets. It was not a good year to be an American in uniform, at home or overseas.

It was a wonder the world had not been caught in a nuclear holocaust yet, Jane observed to Frances. "Maybe we need to become aware of how often fire and brimstone doesn't rain from heaven."[6]

The trumpets of daffodils greeted April, but the fourth day of the month brought horrifying news: Martin Luther King, Jr., had been shot to death in Memphis.

Eva came directly from school to report the mixed reactions of the students. One incident prompted Jane's angry retort:

> The news has spread.
> The clergyman, Nobel Peace Prize winner,
> Who dreamed that the American dream is for all
>   Americans,
> Is dead,
> Shot in his dreaming head
> Almost as if he were a president.
>
> In the library,
> Surrounded by the works of Jefferson, Lincoln,
>   Thoreau, Whitman, Sandburg,
> Students tell the gentle darkskinned assistant,
> "I'm glad that fellow's dead,"
> And grin at seeing her wince
> At their mannerly endorsement of murder.
>
> The same students see, on the television screen,
> Rioting, looting, black

Smoke rising around the white
Dome of the Capitol
And, outraged, cry, "Why
Do they want to act like that?"

Incredibly, hopelessly
They really wonder.
                    "In the Library, April 5, 1968"

Incredibly, the Easter sun shone undiminished over the lilac scented garden where Timothy hunted for Easter eggs. Jane's mail brought another bright surprise: a gem stone award for poetry—a jasper bird from India. Now she had two "chips from cornerstones of the New Jerusalem," she noted to Shirley.[7] The first was a carnelian, set in a plain silver ring on her finger.

The heavenly city seemed much preferable to this world of terror and lawlessness. "I have kept a certain amount of sensitivity to life, and I don't feel happy," Jane lamented.[8]

Work was slow while grief was raw. She found relief in reading biographies of Emily Dickinson—always a fascinating subject. She was particularly interested in finding clues to Emily's faith, and she thought she found one in Emily's poem:

"Tell all the truth but tell it slant—
Success in circuit lies
Too bright for our infirm Delight
The Truth's superb surprise,
As Lightning to the Children eased
By explanation kind
The truth must dazzle gradually
Or every man be blind."

"To tell all the truth, of course, is beyond even Emily," Jane observed to Bruffie. "But that's better than libraries of explanations of why Christ taught in parables."[9]

Faith was a gift from the Father of lights. Was is so surprising that it should come wrapped in darkness of doubt? Honest doubt, Jane was beginning to think, did not prove the absence of faith. The whys were inevitable and unanswerable in times of suffering. Those who endured in trust, confessing their doubts, surely bore witness to an abiding faith. Did not Christ himself cry on the cross: "My God, my God, why hast thou forsaken me?" (Mark 15:34). Yet he breathed his last in trust: "Father into thy hands I commit my spirit " (Luke 23:46 RSV).

Biographies of staunch defenders of the faith revealed their familiarity with doubt. John Wesley, founder of Methodism, wrote to his brother Charles after years of fruitful labor: "I am only an honest heathen, a proselyte of the Temple. . . . I have no proof of the eternal and invisible world, unless such as shines from reason's glimmering ray. And yet I dare not preach otherwise than I do . . . and I feel an increase of zeal for the whole work of God."

Jane would once have found this quotation "most disillusioning," she confessed to Bruffie. Now she believed that God said "Well done," to Wesley in the end.[10]

She was not afraid to admit her own doubts and questions, but there was a firm line of trust she refused to cross. When Bruffie asked her to comment on apparent contradictions in the four Gospels, Jane was quick to retort: "Christ speaks to me so personally in all four Gospels that higher criticism of me drowns out higher criticism of them."[11]

Within days her faith received another shockwave of whys. Robert Kennedy, brother of the assassinated president, and winner of the Democratic presidential primary in California, was himself shot down in front of television cameras in Los Angeles. He was killed only two months after King's murder in Memphis.

Jane watched the televised funeral and agonized to Carolyn Ruth: "Was that clumsy, mismanaged burial in wet gloom the symbolic end of life, liberty, and the pursuit of happiness for a nation that, never as great and glorious as it fancied, had elements of greatness?" She could not bring herself to answer yes.[12]

In her poem "More Than the Hills" in *Halfway Up the Sky* Jane had asked: "Loving America, what do we love?" The last stanza read:

> We love the land because we love the dream
> Of justice and of liberty for all,
> Of each heart free to follow its own gleam
> To its own victory, erect and tall.
> More than the hills, the rivers or the loam
> Of any region, the vision is our home.

The nation was in dire straits, and that year's fourth of July called less for celebration than for sober reflection, Jane declared to Bruffie. She quoted her favorite passages from the prophet Habakkuk's lament over lawless Israel: "For still the vision awaits its time. . . . Though the fig tree do not blossom . . . yet I will rejoice in the Lord" (Hab. 2:3, 3:17-18 RSV). The words inspired trust, but Jane confessed that when her private "fig trees" occasionally failed to bloom, she usually didn't rejoice.

The great affirmations of faith through the ages were trustworthy. Jane deplored modern writers—especially theologians—who cast them aside, choosing instead to live entirely from their own "core of nothingness." She had found it necessary at times to repudiate her own dark experience with the positive words of the Bible, "Believing the Twenty-third Psalm and Romans 8:37-39, even when I didn't, has helped me survive."

Much of her writing, she feared, was based less on personal experience than on "paper grace and hearsay evidence."[13] "If we hear only a small whisper of Him, is it because we aren't really listening?"[14]

In her new book was "My Search for Him."

> I strive to keep inviolate
> A time each day in which to wait
> In faithful silence for his word,
> But silence often is unstirred
> By one response my heart can hear
> Or any sign that he is near.
>
> Yet never is the lonely cost
> Of patient listening wholly lost,
> Nor must I feel he doesn't care
> Or heed my deep, attentive prayer;
> My search for him could never be
> Unless his love were seeking me.

Bruffie sent on loan Elton Trueblood's *Company of the Committed.* Jane responded by quoting her favorite sentence from the book: "We can bear witness to the truth without claiming to be possessors of it." She added, "I tend to let my books witness for me—sometimes I fear I contradict them in person."[15]

Advance copies of her "thank offering volume" had arrived. It seemed even more apropos of the state of the world than when she wrote it. Would her readers be helped to trust God's loving presence when all experience seemed to deny it? Accept his gifts of light in dark disguises?

Jane needed the reminder herself at the end of a summer of national trauma and grief. The future, private and public, seemed frighteningly uncertain. In her devotions she turned to the communion service in the Methodist Book of Worship. Much of it she knew by heart, and she quoted to Bruffie: "It is very meet, right and our bounden duty at all times and in all places to praise Thee." Often she repeated the prayer "so constantly necessary these days; 'O lamb of God, that takest away the sins of the world, have mercy upon us . . . Grant us thy peace.' "

Pat Lassen came again in August, this time to stay at the Doll House for a week while Elizabeth took a much needed vacation. Pat had energy for housekeeping, canning, and freezing, with time left over for pure enjoyment. With her camera she took pictures of Jane and her window view for Bruffie, who responded with a sketch of his house in the country and an invitation to visit. Pat offered to hire an ambulance to take her there, but Jane and Donia said no. Even an outing to the dining room was exhausting these days. Jane was content to stay home and grateful that her friends cared enough to wish she could go.

In "Apart" she wrote the lines:

> If ever it might have been
> I should have been glad.
> That you wish it might have been
> Makes my heart less sad.

Bruffie had long wanted to visit Jane, and she assured him of a welcome. But circumstances repeatedly interferred, perhaps to their mutual relief. Emily Dickinson, an oft quoted subject of their letters, had preferred not to meet her correspondents. Could it be, Jane wondered, that Emily feared "embarrassment at meeting face to face after meeting heart to heart"?[16]

Bruffie wrote in advance of a planned visit: "Can you see past this dust?"

"I can, if you can," Jane responded, but she warned of the unreliability of lip reading and limited conversations on magic slates. "Most things in life are hazardous, of course."

Letters were less so. Both had confessed to a once-a-week 'down' day, and timed a light-hearted encouragement note accordingly. Bruffie's Mondays could be glum, while Jane knew occasional low Fridays— usually her deadline for completing poems to be typed Saturday, when Elizabeth had time to carry the typewriter. Lately the accomplishments of the week often fell short of Jane's optimistic intentions.

They planned a visit for November 1, and Bruffie intended to bring *The Complete Poems of Emily Dickinson* as a combined birthday and Christmas gift. But in early October he mailed the package with a Christmas card. "To withhold it a moment longer would be a sin and a crime," he declared.

Jane's reply was dated "Christmas, October 10th. In Emily's words, 'To thank you is impossible, because your gifts are from the sky.' . . . At first, on this dumbfounded morning, I must admit my own Merchant words were, 'Oh, he ought not to have done that!' . . . but there are enough 'Thou shalt not's' in the Decalogue already; and if the Heavens open who am I to tell them to shut up? . . . I offer reverent thanks!"

Emily could always spark poetry, and Jane's output in October rose markedly, she acknowledged to Bruffie. She sent "Temples" as a commentary on their latest theological discussion.

"The heaven of heavens" is no exact
Location anyone can place.
Illimitable, infinite—
Minute confines for Grace.

And yet the everlasting Lord,
Constricted, cramped within the wide
Heaven of heavens deign to enter
The lowliest heart and to abide.

"As to the current anxiety over getting one's God in the proper size . . . I've tentatively decided that my God is big enough for me, but I'm not big enough for Him."[17]

A quotation in the Methodist study book on loving success more than God had pricked Jane's ever sensitive conscience. "Security is most people's idol, and enough mammon to avoid being a burden to others would tempt any invalid," she confessed to Bruffie, "but my intermittent muse located my love elsewhere." "Immeasurable" was another October production.

"He that loveth father and mother
More than me," I flinch to hear,
"Is not worthy of me,"—having
Parents excellently dear.

Yet I need not stint my loving;
Let me love them as I may,
Christ must love them more than I do—
Can I love Him less than they?

"Do I need spanking for that?"

The spiritual and social challenges of poverty were hotly debated by theological factions, and Jane found herself "constantly squirming in the middle between the prodigal liberals and the hold-everything fundamentalists."[18]

The prevailing attitude toward the issue set the trend in poetry, as well, she noted. "It might be comforting to read that we are going to have cradle-to-grave security, and our children will have enough even if they don't lift a finger, if only I believed it . . . I can't conscientiously quit preaching the virtue of hard work and doing things properly (I'm tired of overcasting improperly sewn seams in expensive clothing) and that very emphasis on hard work apparently makes my work obsolete. Peculiar, isn't it?"[19]

Her readers in both camps—and points in between—claimed that her poetry expressed views that sounded just like theirs. "I *hope* Christ thinks I sound like a Christian," Jane lamented. "Pigeonholes are strictly for the birds!"

She could only hope that in the end all Christians who were unwilling to get along on earth would find themselves in one inclusive Heaven, with "as many as possible of the hurt, cranky, impossible people, and those who helped make them that way . . . with all hurts and tensions healed, and tears wiped away. Or what's a heaven for?"[20]

In her out-of-print, *Blessed Are You,* book was "The Lavish Lord."

> How prodigal the Savior is,
> Sowing the poorest land
> With rich abundances of seed
> With an unsparing hand.
>
> How prodigal the Savior is—
> And yet he cannot spare
> A single lamb from all the flock,
> A bird from all the air.
>
> And never can the lavish Lord
> Of galaxies above
> Afford that one bewildered soul
> Be stranger to his love.

The spring 1969 issue of *Mature Years* featured a five-page illustrated article, "Enjoying Jane Merchant's Poetry," by Marion Armstrong. Jane found the last paragraph embarrassing reading: "Jane Merchant . . . senses life with her heart and lives it to the fullest. She is clean and pure and radiant; she is a petal of light!"

Her friends, predictably, thought the description apt. Bruffie suggested that she consider an illustrated collection of poetry. Abingdon had signalled their interest in a book similar to *Petals of Light,* but Jane was not ready for another project yet.

The pale green walls of the room she shared with Donia were being painted bone-white. The brighter color, they hoped, would help Donia's weakened eyesight, but Jane admitted that she loathed the disorder—and the new color. "Skeleton-white," she described it to Bruffie.

A few days later she apologized for her crabbiness. Within the "bone white walls" bloomed April bouquets of tulips, pansies, roses, azalea blooms, sweet shrub, narcissus, trillium, and pink dogwood. "I think these bones shall live!"[21]

Spring and news that two great-granddaughters had been added to the latest crop of Merchants buoyed Donia and Jane, but when they were offered an ambulance ride on the dogwood trail, neither of them felt strong enough to go. Saying no hurt, even with the windows open to spring. "If April in Palestine resembles April in Tennessee, it must have made the cross just a little harder to accept, I think," Jane observed in a letter to Bruffie.

An ambulance trip to the ophthalmologist for a check up in May brought her out of the house for the first time in two years. Her eyes were fine. Jane rejoiced in a glimpse of open sky, but it took an entire day for her to recuperate from the trip.

So far the year had yielded little in writing. Much of her sales were old works, dug out of her small chest of "editorial rejects" and things she had once thought too personal for publication. So much of her mind was "auctioned off" that it was small wonder there was little left, she lamented to Bruffie.

She told him of Abingdon's request for another volume, and her doubts of whether it was worth doing. Her readership, at least, was growing and eager for more. Jane was listed in Foremost Women in Communications 1969–1970. Her fan letters came from every continent. The latest, from Rita Snowden, a New Zealand author, suggested they exchange books.

Bruffie asked point-blank about Jane's new book project, and she confessed that one-half of her was still wondering, while the other half had procured a ream of paper and new ribbon for the typewriter and was hard at work. Anything else would have been out of character with "Merchant mulishness." She and Donia would work as long as they were able. And what Eva called "the fortunate need" to earn money was still a factor. Elizabeth had taken a side-job every other weekend at St. Mary's hospital. Jane could not push herself less, no matter if her efforts brought rejection slips and her books went out of print.

A suggestion for a title and a theme for a new book was already in the mail. *Because It's Here* was inspired by the Apollo 11 moonshot, scheduled for July, and the current fascination with space.

> Men travel to the moon because it's there
> And dance upon its dust because they can—
> And in forbidding bleakness note how fair
> The little flowering habitat of man.
> Yet many of us need not go beyond
> One tiny tended garden spot to gaze
> At earth with grateful wonder and respond

With interest to its creatures' varied ways.
We honor valiant astronauts who test
Man's skill and knowledge in fantastic flight
Yet follow any redbird's course with zest
And feel immediate intimate delight
When minor galaxies of blooms appear
On earth we cherish well because it's here.

Abingdon's quick response was enthusiastic, but Jane was not so sure that she and Donia were "fitten" to do a book. Summer visitors would interrupt on and off until mid-September, and time slipped away quickly now, with so little accomplished. Or did it just take longer to get things done?

"Whatever happened to old-fashioned durable summers" that lasted "approximately forever?" Jane lamented to Dorothy Brown Thompson. Modern summers were "instant" and "perishable."[22]

When would there be time to get a manuscript together? She cautioned Bruffie to keep the project secret. Nothing was certain until it was done.

A special visit preempted all other happenings in late June. After thirty-three years of corresponding with Jane, Carolyn Ruth came to Knoxville for two days. "She has probably done more than anyone outside my family to educate me," Jane acknowledged to Bruffie. "It seems unlikely that a really meaningful friendship could be carried on . . . by letter . . . for that length of time, but it happened. We are very different . . . yet the friendship lasts."[23]

The meeting could have been disappointing, Jane confessed afterwards. Gratefully it turned out to be very satisfying. Eva joined in welcoming Carolyn Ruth; the friendship had been a threesome for much of the past eighteen years.

Their joy in being together was touched with grief. Eva's mother had died only two weeks before. Other friends, as well, had lost a family member in the last few months—Frances' mother, Kay's father and Carl Arneson's wife had died. Jane shared their anguish. She had written "In Sympathy" for *In Green Pastures:*

I know that all is different for you now,
There is a strangeness in the earth and sky
And all familiar things when one we love
Is dead. We look at those who did not die
With wonder, and at those who are not sad
Uncomprehendingly. I know, I know,
When hearts have followed loved ones to the grave
Return to life is difficult and slow.

Oh, in the lonely strangeness, feel it true
There is no difference in my love for you.

Not many of Donia's contemporaries were left, and she seemed to think that her turn was imminent. With aching heart, Jane pushed herself to complete the manuscript and was able to work steadily only "with time off to go to the moon" on July 20. She watched the moon landing on television. "I stay up till midnight for nothing less than dancing on the moon!" she quipped to Bruffie.

"View from Earth" was in her manuscript.

Since conscientious astronauts have told
The nitty-gritty truth about the moon's
Dull granulated surface, will its gold
Aspect be one of our unvalued boons?
When Luna, changeling orb of mystery,
Is base for automated laboratories
For cosmic data, will it cease to be
Acknowledged sovereign of our harvest glories?
Of course it will not. Any lightest fluff
Of new moon in a peachbloom evening sky,
Or full moon gilding clouds, has power enough
To capture any earthling's heart and eye
And to dispel with immemorial glow
All drab unlikely facts our minds may know.

The draft of the manuscript was finished a week after the moonshot. It needed extensive revision, but she was grateful to have come this far. Magazine sales had picked up, too. "The day after *we* walked on the moon, *Good Housekeeping* bought a . . . verse. I haven't come down to earth yet," Jane exulted to Shirley.[24] *Good Housekeeping* bought a poem from her again before the month was up; so did *McCalls,* making her feel as if she were "still functioning."

In August, Elizabeth took a ten-day vacation, leaving Pat Lassen to care for the Doll House and assist Jane with fetching and carrying. The typing could go quickly now, and by the end of the month the manuscript was in the hands of editors, and the hands were "probably shaking," Jane reported to Bruffie.

Physical circumstances were becoming more painfully "perishable," but her task was to voice gratitude for the ongoing gift of life. Most of the 204 poems in her new book called attention to "the small delights (and exasperations) of life on this irreplaceable earth rather than on the remote possibilities of life on other planets," she wrote in the preface. "Our own small earth is here for us to treasure and tend. . . . All the resources for joyous human life for all . . . are here, if we will conserve and use them wisely instead of wasting them. Even when one's personal situation here is discouraging—and whose is not at times?—we can still 'make it do' well with . . . patience and humor.''

The book was dedicated "to my friend Eva Venable, because her friendship is always, in sorrow and joy, sustainingly here.''

Like all her books, it was offered to the Father of light in gratitude for every good gift. Her unchanging theme was praise for the repeated wonders of each day and each year of living. "Repeating Marvels" was in the manuscript.

> Sometimes I wonder if the Lord grows tired
> Of praise expressed in my accustomed phrases
> Of glorious skies and woodlands wildly fired
> With passions of pure color and of hazes
> That, half-concealing old, beloved hills,
> Reveal new loveliness with every hour.
> I would create fresh terms for joy that fills
> My heart these glowing days, had I the power.
> Yet since the sky is blue, predictably,
> However unbelievably each year,
> And oaks are red each fall, it well may be
> That He, repeating marvels out of sheer
> Delight in them, is pleased with gratitude
> Expressed in old ways vibrantly renewed.

19
GIVE THEM
TO GOD
SEPTEMBER 1969–
DECEMBER 1970

God needs the lonely places in your heart,
God needs the desolate, the unshared hours
Of loss and pain and friends' misunderstanding,
The weary hours when all your strength is spent
And all your wisdom is not wise enough.

Give them to him, the hurt, forsaken hours.
He will receive them lovingly, and give
What you at last are ready to receive,
The fullness of his comfort and his grace,
The encompassing presence of his love.

God needs the hours you know your need of him,
The lonely places only he can fill.

Abingdon's acceptance of the new manuscript came almost before Jane had time to worry. Her editor, Robert J. Hill, Jr., was pleased and wanted no changes. Could they be hard up for something to keep the presses rolling, Jane wondered to Bruffie. Her contract arrived only days later. First proofs were due by her birthday and page proofs by Christmas—Bob Hill offered to gift wrap them! Everything about this book had gone faster than her others. She hoped it wouldn't turn out to be "premature"!

The outlook was not so good for a second collection of children's poems, tentatively titled *Sparkles*. It did not suit Abingdon's marketing needs, and three other publishers politely rejected it. Jane did not want to try again.

It was a small consolation to receive a purple orchid and an engraved silverplated tray from the Tennessee Women's Press and Author's Club at their October convention, but Jane remained discouraged about her writing.

Her mind was wearied by anxious thoughts. Donia, who on "poor" days could get around only with a walker, was distressingly preoccupied with death; she hoped to "fall asleep" quietly without a long period of helplessness, Jane confided to Kay. "I pray that above all things for her, but always, 'not yet, not yet.'"[1]

Bruffie hinted of giving Jane a concordance of Emily Dickinson's poetry, but she reluctantly explained that the book would be too heavy for Donia to carry. There would be little room for books later, "when I move to Ruth's . . . when Mother is no longer here to tend me." She did not want "more treasures" to dispose of when she wouldn't care "much about anything—when Mother isn't here."

She apologized for burdening Bruffie with her troubles, but she wanted him to understand the situation. "You won't mention—my . . . going to West Tennessee. After all, it may never happen."[2]

His visit to the Doll House was still pending. Donia had remarked that if he waited too long they might not be there. Of course, no one could tell for sure, but it seemed wise not to make long-range plans.

Bruffie understood and confessed to having serious trials of his own. He quoted Elijah in the wilderness, who cried under a juniper tree, 'It is enough; now, O Lord, take away my life" (I Kings 19:4 RSV).

"While no Elijah," Jane replied, "I've been under the juniper before . . . [and] been tempted to say, 'It is enough'—and been replenished. . . . There will be sustenance for you."[3]

When Bruffie asked forgiveness for adding to her concerns, Jane assured him: "The barren days of friends are not to be forgiven, but shared. May the wilderness . . . soon rejoice!"[4]

Other friends suffered and confided their anguish. Jane would keep their secrets and did not condemn a failure. To one correspondent she wrote: "I have read your letter . . . and duly destroyed it. . . . I hope it did help you to write it down. . . . Friends are friends, no matter what mistakes or sins they fall into, and until such time as I make no mistakes and fall into no sins myself, I don't condition my friendship on others not doing so. . . . I'm sure you know that I wanted you to tell only what you wanted . . . if you wanted to tell it. In that case I'm glad to listen. I love you without knowing what the trouble was, and I may love you even a little better for knowing."

Jane was grateful that Pat routinely destroyed her letters. Others would, on request, and she could confess the molehills of worries that tended to become mountains in her mind.

But Donia's strong premonition of dying was no minor matter. Jane sought pastoral advice from Bruffie. What should she do when Donia needed to talk about her approaching death? Should she let her talk or say, as people often do, "Oh you'll be here for a long time yet"?

Bruffie confirmed what she had been inclined to do all along: let her mother talk and just listen. But Jane had "got to wondering" whether she was giving Donia sufficient assurance. "The less I think about some things, the better I manage, it seems. Living hurts too much for thinking how much, at times."

Her confession of pain was typically cloaked in humor. The week past had been like "the dumb day" described by Charlie Brown in a recent "Peanuts" cartoon. Jane begged Bruffie to refrain from going into shock over her "having weeks like that, as some dear sentimentalists" would, who mistook her public image for the real Jane. "One visitor confided to Eva . . . that I have the look of 'fragile porcelain,' which was news to everyone else who has seen me."[5]

Bruffie howled over the "fragile porcelain" comparison and compared her instead to cloisonné—porcelain backed up with metal—"I rather think stainless steel!" Sensitive people, he averred, were bound to end up with an occasional "dumb day," which accounted for the gift of humor. Comedy was tragedy too deep for words. Her "dumb Friday" letter had made the manse ring with laughter.[6]

Jane thought it funny herself now. But to Carl, who suffered the unaccustomed loneliness of a widower, she wrote: "I don't expect life becoming any easier; rather it seems to get harder as one goes along, but at least one isn't quite so painfully astonished, and cares less passionately, and so makes the best of what is given, 'Because It's Here.'"[7]

Proofs for the book had arrived on time for her birthday. She was fifty, though according to her calculations—horizontal years being "twice as long as vertical"—she was one hundred. The celebration lasted for days, with visitors, flowers, presents, and greetings. Nine Pen Women provided her very first surprise party, with a fancy cake and gifts. Elizabeth had to work on the day, but Eva brought fried chicken for lunch and stayed to look over the proofs, as she had done with each book before.

Nineteen years earlier, at Thanksgiving, their friendship had begun. A year later Jane wrote "To Eva," a poem not intended for publication. Now it was in the book dedicated to her friend, and it was "even more true than when it was written," Jane declared.

> Now as I name the blessings of a year
> Most mercifully blessed in many ways,
> A year in which harsh undertones of fear
> Changed into gentle symphonies of praise,
> A year of work rewarded far beyond
> Expectancy, a year of dreams come true—

I count as richest gift of all the bond
Of comradeship uniting me to you.
Because the grief and laughter we have shared,
The sympathy by which our love has grown,
Have given me greater joy than I had dared
Believe could possibly become my own,
All this Thanksgiving Day my heart shall spend
In offering thanks for you, my friend.

Bruffie sent Jane's Christmas gift, *The Complete Letters of Emily Dickinson,* early in December. She was thunderstruck: "Dear Miracle Worker, the mailman came attended by angels today. . . . I simply don't believe it—and yet 'my soul doth magnify—'. . . . This very morning I wrote a friend, and mentioned . . . that, if I do nothing else in 1970, I would try to read ED's *Complete Letters.* And then the mailman came."[8]

She woke the next morning, relieved to see the *Letters* on her table. So their coming had not been part of her recurring nightmare of being in a "library full of beautiful, fascinating books" only to awaken just as she had begun to read.

A comparative study of all her Emily books would provide an antidote to January. Lately they had gone "from Christmas tree to juniper tree" each year. Aunt Laura was visiting for the holidays. Like Donia, she was no longer able to do what she had once been capable of doing. "I hurt at the thought of what age does to people," Jane lamented to Bruffie.

The juniper month fulfilled her predictions. Donia was exhausted, and she spoke of her funeral as if she felt it would be "very restful, which wearies me so that I don't know what to do from day to day, but perhaps it is only January," Jane wrote on the last day of that month.

In her new book was "Mild Defense."

> "What good can be expected of a year
> That starts with January?" one demanded.
> "If we can live through it we're in the clear
> To weather all the rest," I said with candid
> Assent to her distaste for heating bills,
> Post-Christmas letdown, bitter winds, and frozen
> Dangerous streets, and various virus ills—
> "Although it's not the month I would have chosen."
> But after all a year must start somewhere
> And January calls us to renewed
> Resolve just when we need it most, to bear
> Grim days with humor, grace, and fortitude—
> And all my life I have discovered very
> Good things in years that start with January!

February brought relief, at least, from the weather. "Tennessee returned to us this week," Jane announced to Kay. She had seen a robin, and "like Paul upon meeting his friends, 'I thanked God and took courage.'"[9] Snow flurries, like "little torn paper scraps," had greeted the robin, and inspired Jane to write "A Parade of One."

> One robin, improbably,
> Joyously here,
> Creating a summertime
> Atmosphere
> On frozen dullness
> With breast aglow
> Is greeted with flurries
> of ticker-tape snow—
> Which, flurried myself,
> I soon discern
> Suitably welcomes
> A hero's return.

The poem sold on first submission to *The Christian Science Monitor.* Another poem earned her $60.00 from *Good Housekeeping,* and Jane won first prize and $25.00 in the national Pen Women contest for a haiku written in October 1967.

> Red and yellow leaves
> Drift slowly earthward; falling
> They have forever.

Outside her window a soft spring rain fell on the greening garden, and Jane sent Bruffie her poem printed in *The Lyric* for spring.

> Bright rains that pour from springtime skies
> Soon float away all troubles
> As on earth's surface arise
> Grass foam and crocus bubbles.
>   "Effervescence"

Review copies of *Because It's Here* were sent out in March. Her friends who received copies from the publisher sent comfortingly laudatory comments. Jane had worried more than usual about this book, "aware of defects, like the mother . . . of a cross-eyed baby," she admitted to Shirley. The sonnet "Shirley" was a favorite, but it was still not good enough for Jane!

She cherishes, as women do, her own,
And yet with a child's deep wondering respect
For bloom on butterflies, for silver blown
From dandelions; she would no more expect
To make her husband, child, or friends conform
To any design of hers than she would try
To dictate color to a crocus corm
Or teach a hummingbird which way to fly.
She seeks, with gentle ardor, friends who share
Her treasuring sense of life and gives them each
Complete acceptance, unremitting care
In the lonely places love can seldom reach,
And the greatest gift the loving can confer;
The boon of being totally safe with her.

Bruffie thought he recognized himself in the book. "Page sixty-three is just like me!" he wrote. "Signed, 'Stale Dew.'"[10] He was referring to "Conversational Pause."

"I loathe cliches," he said in confidence,
At which my conscience started in dismay
And scared from mossy corners an immense,
Exhausted, sagging, spiritless array
Of terms that I had used in talk with him:
"She might have healed the breach; she might have
      broken
The vicious circle; now it's sink or swim"—
How pitiful the phrases I had spoken!
As memory, meanly faithful, shuffled all
The superannuated workers past,
The worn enfeebled figures, ready to fall,
And blank expressions left me shamed, aghast.
"That's why," my friend resumed, "I'm thankful you
Use language sparkling fresh as morning dew!"

Had he *really* used "fresh as morning dew"? Bruffie wondered. Jane assured him she had only used her poetic license to make a spoof of her fear of offending him with stale phrases.

Soon she would be able to talk to him in person. They had set a new date for his visit: April 15, two days after the launching of her book and Apollo 13. By then the dogwood would be in bloom. Jane thought that for anyone to leave earth in April was "surely a mistake!"

Miller's Book Department wanted to have an autograph party, and Pat Lassen came the week before Easter to help lift the heavy boxes and place five hundred books, one at a time, on the overbed table for Jane to sign. It was at such times that she was grateful that her sister was named Elizabeth, while she "escaped with plain Jane."

Elizabeth was her representative at the autograph party, looking radiant, Jane thought, in a new dress. She was surely exhausted with her grueling routine of two jobs and doing most of the Doll House chores. She never complained, and Jane did not pry into her feelings. They did not talk of the difficult things both were aware of.

"We can't know all and share all with those we love," Jane had written to Kay on Palm Sunday 1967. She had said the same in "Give Them to God." Now she prayed for her own and Elizabeth's unshared hours of weariness and pain, asking that comfort, strength, and grace would be given to do the difficult things that must be done.

There was a loneliness—even in the most intimate human relationships—that could not be eased by anyone but God. To try would only inflict more pain. The human heart was a sacred place. Jane had copied for Pat a passage from *The Purpose of the Church and Its Ministry* by H. Richard Niebuhr: "In love there is an element of 'holy fear' which is not a form of flight but rather a deep respect for the otherness of the beloved and a profound unwillingness to violate his integrity." It was a truth they knew and practiced in the Doll House.

Elizabeth was off work the week following the book launching, so she could be home to greet Bruffie. Jane was, frankly, relieved. She was a little jittery in advance of his visit. So was he, and to draw attention from "this poor dust," he arrived with a basket of golden apples, polished to perfection. The gift was a reference to "Apple Tree," one of his favorite poems in the new book.

> This is the tree that every child climbs first.
> This is the tree we can't remember learning,
> The tree we always knew. Its name is a burst
> Of juicy tartness in our mouths, returning
> To us the tang of earliest delight.
> Its name is April and a lyric foam
> Of delicately wistful pink and white.
> Its name is another synonym for home—
> And yet a synonym for places where
> We never were at home except in dream;
> The gardens of Hesperides, the fair
> And unknown isles where golden apples gleam;
> Tree of familiar noons and fabled dawns,
> Of vanished Edens and suburban lawns.

Bruffie apologized for apples that didn't quite fit her tree. Jane assured him that his offering, and even more the giver, had been received with gratitude. She was deeply relieved to find that he was "as real in person as in letter," a brother in spirit with whom she could share joy and pain.

Two days after their visit, she had horrifying news to convey: "You may not believe this—I don't. . . . Yesterday, without any warning, Elizabeth doubled up with pain . . . [last night] she had surgery for a perforated ulcer and is in the Intensive Care Unit . . . and may be home in a week. Mother is holding up well. A friend is staying with us. Aunt Laura comes tomorrow . . . after that my sister-in-law if necessary. Ruth and her husband have come four hundred miles. . . . Praise be for kin!"[11]

Complications set in. Elizabeth remained in intensive care for six days, and her recovery was slow. Jane sent emergency bulletins to friends, asking for their prayers for "my lovely, brave, essential sister."

She could do little more for Elizabeth than write a daily note of encouragement. She confided to Pat: "I feel I can't do anything really to help, and that everything I say and do is the wrong thing to say and do. . . . I feel I might jump out of my skin if anybody touched me now!"[12]

Jane's fear of being touched was well founded. Aunt Laura and Trula, a friend who had come to help, were changing sheets on her bed when she cried out, "Please don't anybody touch me!"—just in time to keep from being hoisted up by one arm. The consequences could have been a broken bone—a dreadful complication of the circumstances.

Elizabeth phoned from the hospital twice daily, but Aunt Laura and Donia were nearly deaf. It was difficult to get any news straight. "I said this feels like a comic opera," Jane observed to Eva. "Actually it feels more like a Hardy novel . . . characters are doomed by missed encounters and letters arriving . . . late. I trust the comic opera aspect will prevail. My attempts at keeping communications open [with the rest of the family] seem . . . at times to do more harm than good; but I suppose I'll keep trying no matter how trying others find me."[13]

She confided her despair to Pat: "I'm not letting myself wonder if Aunt Laura and Mother can hold out till Elberta comes. . . . I shouldn't say [it], because you'll worry . . . but I can't seem to keep from telling you the truth. Don't tell anyone or try to do anything, sweet, just love me and pray for us as you are doing."[14]

Pat's letters brought daily reminders that all would be well in the end. Jane re-read Amy Carmichael's *His Thoughts Said*. Afterwards she admitted that expecting perfection of herself or of others was foolish. "What kind of egotist would hope not to make any mistakes anyhow!"

She could best help their situation by accepting her own limitations and being grateful that help was given. This crisis, too, held a gift in a difficult disguise from the Father of lights. Her part was to obey the command she knew by heart: "Rejoice always, pray constantly, give thanks in all circumstances; for this is the will of God in Christ Jesus for you" (I Thess. 5:16-18 RSV).

In "The One Thing" she had written:

> Sometimes, perplexed and shaken,
> Uncertain of His will,
> In dread lest my mistaken
> Unguided act bring ill,
>
> I find I've been remiss
> In the one thing I must do;
> "Rejoice, give thanks, for this
> Is the will of God for you."

Elberta arrived on May 7, the day Elizabeth's temperature and blood tests registered normal. Perhaps she would be home in a week. With such reasons for rejoicing—tentative as they were—it might at last be safe to cry, Jane confided to Bruffie—if she could without being caught at it. In her last book was the poem "Poise."

> I must move softly now,
> My face composed and still.
> My heart is a flagon filled to the brim with tears.
> I must move softly lest any spill.

A month after her collapse, Elizabeth came home. She was not fully recovered, but she looked better than Jane had feared. "As we Methodists don't say as often as we should, 'glory be and also hallelujah!'" Jane exulted to Bruffie.

Through it all, Donia had remained calm. Jane had written of her strength in "Unfading," printed in *Halfway Up the Sky:*

> I wish I knew from what material God
> Fashioned the sky. It shows no sign of wear
> In spite of all the years of sun and storm
> That it has weathered. It is pure and fair
> In its unfaded brightness, as when new.
> I don't know what God used for it, but I
> Have always thought he made my mother's soul
> Of something that stands weather like the sky.

Jane felt less fit, and she dared admit to having pain in her right arm and shoulder and rapid heartbeat. The doctor insisted on a trip to the hospital for X-rays. To Jane's relief, there was no sign of recurring cancer. The pain was probably stress related, caused by pressure on a nerve. Rest and aspirin should cure it.

Her windows framed the many miracles of May in the garden, and Jane let her eyes and mind find restoration there. In "Remedies," in her latest book, she had written:

> When wounds in the being are raw and new
> Lay a web daintily cool with dew
> Over them or a delicate mist
> Of snowflakes caught in an amethyst
> Tulip chalice, or bind the gauze
> Of a rainbow over the mark of claws.
> By noon and dawning take scrupulous heed
> To gather simples for mortal need.

Elberta left in early June, and Ruth's sixteen-year-old daughter, Peggy, came to stay for a week. When she left, the three in the Doll House were at last alone. Elizabeth was slowly regaining her strength, but she would not return to work until August. Jane tried not to think that far ahead. The acute crisis was over, but it had resulted in an immediate benefit: Donia consented to using a hearing aid and was able to hear on the phone and in normal conversation again.

For two months Jane's typewriter had been on the shelf. Now she could at least type old poems for submission to editors. The thought of writing something new was as alien as if she'd never written a poem before. The difficult happenings had not yet settled down in her she confided to Frances. But so many people had been kind and helpful, and maybe there would be "time and opportunity to make some constructive use" of it all. "One hopes, anyhow."[15]

Critics were saying nice things about her latest book, and Carl Arneson declared it her finest. He singled out "Words" as his favorite poem, saying that it was outstanding in "perfection of form, simplicity and universal appeal," in what he termed "the twilight of poetry." "[It] belongs to the era that gave us the classics," he declared.

> I am sustained
> In soul and mind
> By great words, spoken
> To all mankind.
>
> But the best words
> My heart has known
> Were small words, spoken
> To me alone.

Arneson felt certain that other readers would be prompted by her poem, "and many meaningful small words will be spoken instead of dying in the aridity of good intentions."[16]

Jane wanted to believe him, but in the aftermath of Elizabeth's collapse old fears of rejection and abandonment had surged with new force. Perhaps the kind words and assurances of friends and relations were only gestures of consolation. The cussedness of people gave good reason to suspect even the most sincere promises. There was no guarantee against a change of heart, and the most faithful love could not keep death at bay. All earthly ties must one day be severed.

Such thoughts could be dangerous—self-pity was a familiar short-cut to depression. Jane fought the temptation to withdraw behind the barricade of self-sufficiency. Shutting others out only increased the distance and pain.

Patricia was married in June, but her cherished plan for a wedding in the Doll House garden had to be cancelled. Jane, who had never witnessed a wedding, hid her disappointment. The newlyweds came instead with the rest of the family for the annual fourth of July reunion.

It was a joyous occasion, but Jane wrote to Carolyn Ruth: "If I feel more than ordinarily alienated after a visit from these whom I love and who love me, it shouldn't be reason for wonder, I suppose, but it will always be reason for sadness."[17]

It grieved her to feel most inadequate with those she loved best, those for whom she was and must always be a burden. Could she trust their assurances that she was a much loved, *wanted,* burden? What of the day when Donia would be gone? And perhaps Elizabeth—and even Ruth? Would anyone else have time to care for her? Their lives were full of urgent demands; other obligations, other priorities. She could not blame them if they abandoned her in a nursing home some day. It was a possibility she rarely allowed herself to dwell on, but it *did* lurk in her gloomiest thoughts.

Almost everyone, it seemed, had suddenly developed serious health or other problems. Living had always been precarious, but she was more acutely aware of that fact now. "I do not cease to marvel at how much some people can bear—and yet continue to live constructively," she observed to Carolyn Ruth. "Nor . . . how little [others are] able to endure before freaking out" *(Reynolds, July 7, 1970).*

She prayed for strength to endure and not give in to the terror of abandonment by rejecting those she feared to lose. She wanted to accept instead the loneliness of heart only God could make bearable. In the hurt, forsaken hours she could turn to him and receive grace and comfort enough to share. "Repayment," was in *Every Good Gift.*

I would not weary others with my sorrow
Who are already weary with their own,
And so I shall endeavor now to borrow
A glint of gladness from a sunlit stone,
A little gaiety from waters going
Precipitately down a woodland glen,
Enthusiasm from winds' zestful blowing,
And sparks of glee from an impetuous wren.

These borrowed qualities need no returning
To any stone or brooklet, wind or bird.
It is enough if I am mute concerning
My woes; and if I speak a helpful word
Of healing merriment to troubled friends
The loan is paid with ample dividends.

In all her books she had urged her readers to think the best—not the worst—of others' intentions. Yet, she deplored how easily she forgot her own advice. In the future she would try harder to put "the best construction on other people's actions," a quotation from her poem "Builder," in her latest book.

She cannot drive a nail
Nor put a shelf together
Nor even assist with castles
In child-and-seashore weather;
But her upbuilding talent
Yields endless satisfactions;
She puts the best construction
On other people's actions.

The summer had gone much too quickly. Elizabeth was rested and fully recovered, eager to return to her job. Pat came from Michigan for two weeks to help ease the transition. It was a happy visit. Elizabeth had found a stack of old records, and she played songs Jane remembered. "Pat was impressed at my being able to sing 'Hand Me Down My Walking Cane,' among others," she reported to Bruffie.[18]

Before leaving, Pat conspired with Eva to have a small telephone installed on the wall by Jane's bed. Elizabeth called from work at noon, and Jane could feel—with her hand on the phone—when it rang. She would pick up the receiver and, while Donia made her slow way across the room to respond, Jane related their morning activities and any news from the mail. So far she had not told anything to "somone who is not Elizabeth," she wrote Carolyn Ruth.

Now Jane had a link to the outside world and a list of numbers to dial for help if anything should happen to Donia while they were alone. Even without knowing whether anyone heard her, she could keep calling one number after the other until help arrived. Their situation was perhaps neither "sane nor safe," she admitted to Carolyn Ruth, but with the phone, she felt reasonably secure. Perhaps now she could get back to work.

Pat had brought an anthology of poetry by Robert Frost, and Jane copied several poems into her notebook—an old ruse for priming her own production. Several poems had sold during that summer, and Jane had won two poetry prizes. Rosemary Stephens, a speaker at the Mid South Poetry Festival, wrote to ask what she was writing "in the '70's that she wouldn't have written in the '60's," and named her "foremost among Tennessee poets, the unofficial state poet laureate."[19]

In her reply, Jane pointed out that the issues of the seventies promised to be those of the sixties intensified and that she had written "on conservation, space travel, and racial justice" in the fifties and sixties as well. Dr. Stephens had asked for an unpublished poem, and Jane sent "In Time of Testing," written in 1969. It indirectly expressed her feelings on the issues of the day.

"DO NOT BEND"
The envelope was marked in blue
Block letters, and I knew
The photograph inside would show
Miss Constance Donahoe,
The upright sister of a wavering clan,
Who taught the alphabet of rectitude to thirty classes
Of awed and temporarily
Behaving children.

"The teacher with the backbone"
So she was known.
Children grew into the beginnings of
Accuracy, Bravery, Character
Before her keen
Serene requiring gaze.

The student lettering the envelope
Was well aware no one and no event
Of public or private woe
Could bend Miss Donahoe.

The admonition is for the rest of us.

By the mercy of God she would not bend. The daily discipline of prayer and study, work and rest continued, and Jane was writing again. "I'm beginning to feel like myself and not a stranger—though oneself, no doubt, is always strange enough," she observed to Carolyn Ruth in September.

In "Prayer After Rest" she wrote:

I have been weary, Father, long, how long;
Too weary to do more than pray Thy grace
To help me through tense nights when fears were strong
And through the waiting days I had to face
With patience and serenity; and though
Thy love was present always, Lord, to heal,
And friends' dear kindness should have brought a glow,
A worn relief was all that I could feel.
But now, O Father, Thou hast given rest
In one untroubled day, entirely fair,
Thou hast fulfilled my soul's intense request
And spared life to the one I could not spare.
For all Thy grace and mercy through hard days,
At last, at last, O Lord, my ardent praise.

In late September, Ruth and Ed Lee came from Union City to install their daughter Sara in the dormitory at the University of Tennessee for the fall semester. Nelson and Elberta were due from Maryland the following week, but Nelson called instead to say that Elberta had an emergency kidney operation and that Reese was recovering after back surgery. Joan's husband was scheduled for back surgery next. Jane wrote to Bruffie: "Salutations from under the juniper tree. Any shade is welcome. . . . We're a concerned and disappointed bunch."[20]

A combination of work and prayer was the best antidote to worry. Jane had an assignment from David C. Cook Publishing Company to write an Easter service for their *Leader Guidebook,* comparable to the Thanksgiving Service they had bought earlier. It was the kind of challenge she relished, requiring research and meditation on Bible passages. She put the work aside to celebrate her birthday—with three cakes, visitors, and much mail. Frances hoped that her birthday wishes would come true, and Jane replied: "My main wish and prayer at present is that Mother may live out her days in peace here, without more operations on herself or her family, and without becoming deaf or blind or helpless, all of which I know she dreads. After that—well, I wish I'll manage to make the best of Union City."[21]

They expected Aunt Laura for Christmas, but before Thanksgiving came word that she had fallen and broken her hip and wrist. She was recovering nicely after surgery.

"This must be the year of 'Operation Merchant,' " Jane lamented to Bruffie. "Five among our kin . . . and I am plumb tired of shocks."

Jane sent him the Thanksgiving service in which she had written: "Perhaps on this Thanksgiving . . . we are more aware of problems than we are of anything else . . . The effort to deal bravely and responsibly with them can sap strength and eat away at energy so that we are not always the best advertisers of the abundant life Jesus offers. All the more reason, then, to do what Psalm 103 says: Bless with our whole being the holy name of the Lord."

Donia was saying that she wished Christmas would hurry, Jane confided three weeks later. "I think she has a notion of this being her final one on this particular sphere, but I hope not."[22]

Her Christmas mail brought thank you letters from old and new readers—students who were writing papers on her poetry, a woman's church circle named after her, a pastor thanking her for sermon inspirations. Carl Arneson told of a young Sunday school teacher in New York City who tamed his unruly class by reading aloud from *Halfway Up the Sky*. "You have a wonderful gift," he concluded. "It is a great privilege to make Jane Merchant known to 'those who are weary and heavy laden.' "[23]

Her own weariness mattered less when others found help through her work. The peace and rest she wrote of and yearned for—and knew moments of—was not an absence of turmoil, shock, and grief but the presence of God in the midst of it.

Snow fell gently over the garden before Christmas. After a "lifelong enchantment with snowflakes," Jane was shocked to read a "Peanuts" comic strip about polluted snowflakes. The two words side by side said "more than volumes of sermons and lectures on the sins and stupidities of humankind."[24] The condition of the planet—and the human heart—was likely to deteriorate further, but Jane had done "much living" on Jeremiah's Lamentations, especially: "But this I call to mind, and therefore I have hope: The steadfast love of the Lord never ceases, his mercies never come to an end; they are new every morning" (Lam. 3:21-23 RSV).

She had written "Old Prayer Renewed" in September.

> "Peace at the last," the ancient prayer requests;
> But, O God, grant us peace along the way
> To meet each moment's unexpected tests
> With equanimity each crowded day.
> Grant us tranquility abiding still

Within our hearts and the incessant rush
Of many obligations to fulfill,
Not only in starred evenings' final hush.
"Support us all the day long," Lord, indeed.
Support us with serenity unmarred
By sudden crisis, overwhelming need,
And hours of helpless waiting, tense and hard.
Lord, grant to us who love and hope and fear,
Peace at the last, and even now and here.

20

BRIGHT FLOWERING

JANUARY–AUGUST 1971

Why am I happy, suddenly,
As if good fortune had come to me?

It's not for tidings that I have heard;
It's not for sunlight or singing bird.

The weather's dismal, and my affairs
Are full as ever of irksome cares.

It's all of the thankfulness—out of season—
That I couldn't feel when I had reason.

It's all of the cheer, now real and glad,
That I tried to show when my heart was sad.

All glory to God for prayers that flower
In an unexpected, unlooked-for hour.

The juniper month required all the fortitude Jane could muster. Donia wanted to make advance funeral arrangements, and with heavy heart Jane informed their pastor, Gordon Sterchi, of her wishes. Once the matter was settled, Donia seemed almost cheerful, but Jane wondered to Bruffie how she herself could keep on acting as if anything else mattered. But "hearts continue bearing the thing they could not bear," she quoted from her own poem "Afterward."

Daily, hourly it seemed, Donia's hearing, vision, and walking became more difficult. Time and age advanced relentlessly.

Jane found it nearly impossible to write new poetry, but she kept trying and sold of her old store. In late January she took stock and counted 2,080 of her poems in print, with several more sold. Over a thousand were in manuscript form; many had never been submitted to editors, 150 were currently in circulation. Of her more than 3,300 poems, only 1,100 were in her ten books, leaving a goodly number to work with for any future collections.

It was hard to imagine ever doing another book. Monotonous rain drenched the dreary garden, adding to Jane's dejection. She felt empty of poetry, as if she had written all that could be gleaned from the few square yards of her private world.

Carolyn Ruth was in Europe. She wrote vividly of visits to the Hague and London. Jane answered her letters with an apology: "Perhaps the reason I haven't written the letter I *want* to write is that I *don't* have new scenes to write about!"[1]

Self-pity was treacherous consolation, but she had never felt so alone and isolated—even from her own household. Donia had been Jane's "ears" to a world of sound for nearly thirty years, but now her vision and hearing difficulties blocked much communication between them. Jane had read *Deafness,* a new book by the British poet David Wright, who had lost his hearing in childhood. She learned that chronic fatigue and a sense of alienation was common among the deaf. Now Donia was experiencing it as well.

"It hurts to see her feeling the hurt and loneliness I feel most of the time, about deafness and others' exasperation with it," Jane confided to Bruffie. "But we get our wires crossed, and sometimes I'm surprised into seeming exasperated myself, and then loathe myself for it. It seems to take all I've got, and sometimes more, just 'To Live Humanely', these days."[2]

The poem she had quoted was in *The Mercies of God.*

"Oh, I am only human," so we say,
Excusing, with the words, our negligence
Of ordinary duty, and our intense
Deep ire at being wronged in any way.
"I'm only human—" seeking to repay
With double weight some word that gave offense
Or any slight to our own consequence;
While praising all the values we betray.

We must be more than human; we must call
Upon resources far beyond our length
And height and depth to be what we should be.
True life demands the utmost of us all,
And it requires a more than human strength
To live humanely with humanity.

Now that Donia could do little fetching, carrying, and hearing messages, Jane felt the physical restrictions of handicap with undiminished force. The reality of her circumstances had always been there, but never had her options seemed so limited—or the need for a positive response so great.

Nearly thirty years earlier she had first understood that circumstances alone were less the determining factors of her life than how she chose to respond to them. She was not a helpless victim of handicap (she hated the word *victim*). Handicap was part of the raw material she was given to work with; the gift of life in difficult disguise. The Father of lights was the giver who loved her and asked only that she trust and daily accept what he gave. Somehow she had imagined it would get easier toward the end. Now she must accept that it could get worse.

Aunt Laura had sent an article from the *National Enquirer* about famous personalities with physical handicaps. There were many, according to the writer. He named Jane as an example and declared that everyone has handicaps; either physical or emotional and "every handicap is a potential incentive to achievement."

Tennessee author Wilma Dykeman touched on the same idea in her column in the Knoxville *News Sentinel* in August 1970: "Jane Merchant is one of the physically handicapped who helps the spiritually handicapped. Many . . . who seem sound in body . . . have a more crippling sickness of mind and attitude. Jane is one of the healthiest people I know. We are glad 'because she's here.' "

Jane sent both clippings to Shirley, who was quick to note that adversities had given "great authority" to Jane's writings on suffering. Affliction could have silenced her or impelled the writing of "tortured or torturous" things. "Instead you chose to sing and soar and speak with great clarity and precision—and beauty and joy—so that the contrast is a very noteworthy thing."[3]

The reminder was comforting. The choice between torturous and joyous responses to painful circumstances was a daily, sometimes hourly or moment by moment, challenge. The end of the pilgrim road was nearer, but not yet in sight, and the last stretch loomed steep and dark. Jane prayed for endurance to finish the journey; failure was possible to the end. She could yet choose to shrink back in fear, give in to hopelessness and self-pity and burrow into the darkest corner of her dungeon of despair.

Her own strength was insufficient against the lures of self-centeredness. Her prayers, these days, were for help. In "My Name Is Legion," she had written:

> By day and by night
> Among old tombs,
> In mountainous
> Fantastic glooms
>
> Crying and cutting
> Ourselves with stones,

Re-echoing echoes
Of our groans—

O thou who bade
The storm be still,
Drive out the fiends
Of our self-will,

Of our self-pity,
Our self-pride,
All self-indulged,
Self-multiplied,

And grown so strong
No man can bind.
Restore to us
Our rightful mind,

And send us home
To friends, to tell
What mighty kindness
Made us well.

Jane yearned to accept the will of God with gladness. She whispered her weary surrender of self-will with a prayer that in time she would be given grace to do it joyfully. Meanwhile she could voice gratitude without feeling it, offering "a sacrifice of praise" with a sorrowful heart.

The seed of faith had been planted long ago, nurtured by a persistant trust that it would flower brightly even after the darkest winter. "As leaf and bud [grow] unobserved in silent darkness," Jane had written in a meditation, so would obedience through the winter season of the spirit produce renewed and fruitful lives through Christ.[4]

"Metaphors" was written nearly twenty years before.

Faith is a light?
But eyes may be
Too full of tears,
Sometimes, to see.

Faith is an anchor?
But the strain
Of storm may snap
An anchor's chain.

Faith is a seed.
In dark and storm
It grows, unseen,
And safe, and warm.

It will bear harvest
For your need.
Plant deep and well.
Faith is a seed.

Faith, like a seed, must grow in darkness. And so it was with other growing things at their often hazardous beginnings. The child is conceived and nurtured in the dark womb, the pearl in the oyster. Jane had put it concisely in "Price," from *Petals of Light.* A thank you note from a reader, an eighty-three-year-old nun, called the four short lines "a Bible of trust—a theology in itself."

Exasperated? Irked? Impatient?
Ponder this, when reason whirls:
Only irritated oysters
Ever manufacture pearls.

But it was difficult, in the darkness, to trust that the suffering was not meaningless or wasted, to remember that, just as the embryo plant or child could not survive outside the protective confinement of soil or womb, so must she consent to rest in darkness until her faith had grown to its intended glory and her eyes could bear the brighter lights.

Jane had written of "the amazing meekness" of God, who would not force his heavenly will on his children, but left them free and waited patiently for their consent. Freedom was an awesome responsibility, and she thought often of the terrible consequences—the loss to self and others—of not responding to God.

She prayed for grace to accept the particular darkness chosen for her and to believe that Christ was present, however lonely and abandoned she might feel. She prayed for faith to trust that through the darkness God was drawing her closer, holding her securely, forgiving her faltering and her doubts. That was the hope she lived by and would cling to.

Things looked dark, as well, for her writing. Reliable markets continued disappearing. *This Day,* a Lutheran magazine, ceased publishing and returned a poem they had bought earlier. The editor hoped Jane would keep on writing her "very fine" poetry and collect it in books. He wished her "continued . . . strength and inspiration for the feeding of others."[5]

The next blow was harder. On a "glum Friday," when "daffodils blooming in the gloom'' outside her windows were the only encouraging signs of spring, Jane informed Bruffie of ''wintry tidings'' from Abingdon. They ''must reluctantly'' let *Halfway Up the Sky* go out of print. The book was the favorite of several friends, as well as her family, and Jane intended to ask if it could be reissued in paperback with a livelier cover. Though she doubted that the request would make a difference.

Her friends joined in the plea, but in vain. Bruffie, Eva, Shirley, and Pat offered instead to pay for a private printing. Jane was tempted to allow them, but she could not ignore the publisher's contention that reader interest was waning. She had long suspected that poetry lovers were a diminishing breed.

Dogwood bloomed in the garden. In Jane's latest book she had included the poem ''Again the Dogwoods.''

> Again the dogwoods lift white ranks of crosses,
> Memorials to battalions of the slain,
> Memorials to our spirits' myriad losses,
> The white transfigurations of our pain.

Halfway's demise was a painful loss, but it, too, could be transfigured by the cross—if she would only let go all her resentment and anger toward the anonymous ''they'' of the editorial board who had passed the death sentence. Could they not have launched a promotional campaign instead?

Easter was imminent, and Jane tried to still her churning thoughts by reading the Gospel accounts of Christ's passion, suffering, crucifixion, and resurrection. In ''The Easter Story,'' she had written:

> Lord, I rejoice in all the Easter glory
> Of Christ triumphant over death and gloom,
> Reading again the old, beloved story
> Of grieving women—and an empty tomb,
> Of men who walked a lonely road in sadness,
> Men rendered desolate by loss and fear,
> And how their grief was changed to holy gladness;
> These are the stories that I love to hear.
>
> Yet, Lord of love, unless I learn to say
> With all my heart, ''Forgive them, for they know
> Not what they do,'' when others hurt, betray,
> Or mock me, and unless I whisper low,
> ''Thy will be done,'' when I must suffer pain—
> I know I hear the story all in vain.

Measured by the cross of Christ, her pain at the loss of *Halfway* was infinitely small. Christ had said, "Thy will be done." In her small Gethsemane, she must let go of every fugitive vestige of rebellion and say the same.

April was glorious, and Jane had been outside on an ambulance ride to the ophthalmologist for her annual check-up. The doctor declared her eyes the best he had ever seen them. On the way home the driver chose a longer route so that Jane could see more of spring in bloom. It was balm for her grieving soul, and it inspired a sonnet, one of the first poems written that year.

> Today the lilacs blossom, queens of spring;
> Most cherished, most beloved for color and scent
> Of all the blooms that all the seasons bring,
> Their fragrance is a healing sacrament
> Cleansing all memories of loss and pain
> From bitterness, and making doubly sweet
> Remembrances of joys all hearts retain. . . .
>
> "Time of Lilacs"

Jane was ready to make peace with her sorrow and relinquish the desire to keep *Halfway* in print. The poetry had touched many hearts and would live on in her readers. So, too, must she live on and not cling to what was gone. When Bruffie asked what she intended to do about the book, she replied; "I think I'll just let it go quietly, though not without a tear."[6]

In "Good Afternoon," in her other out-of-print book *Blessed Are You,* she had described the yielding of her will to the Father of lights.

> Alone on a hill,
> Resting in sun,
> Grass-silent, rock-still,
> These things I have done:
>
> Outgrown a resentment,
> Made peace with a sorrow,
> And laid by contentment
> For many a morrow.
>
> Being silent and small
> And letting light through
> I have done all
> I most needed to do.

Easter brought encouraging news that *Together* magazine had accepted "A Calendar of Haiku"—one for each month of the year—and would print them illustrated in their January 1972 issue. To sell haiku was a happy boon. "They seem more like milkweed seeds, to waft abroad without money and without price," Jane wrote to Shirley.[7]

Donia turned eighty-nine in late April. Her birthday was so well celebrated that she seemed willing to have another, Jane reported to Bruffie. Spring had rejuvenated both mother and daughter once again. "Birthday Lady," written two years earlier, was still true.

> Though her hair is silver, her laughter is gold,
> And her eyes are merry and keen.
> She says with a twinkle, "I'm only as old
> As the rainbows I have seen."

The April issue of *The United Methodist Reporter* of the Holston Conference arrived in time for Donia's birthday. In it was a feature article on Jane, entitled "My Heart Shall Keep a Song." The author was Donna Bradley, a friend of the family. Jane had agreed to the write up, hoping to surprise and please Donia and acknowledge her share in the work. The article concluded: "Jane and those who know the Merchant family well, insist that great tribute must be paid to her mother . . . a gentle-strong teacher who has shown Jane a way to love without giving up."

All spring Jane had spent much of her writing time answering an increased volume of correspondence, caused by a sudden public interest in her bone ailment. Osteogenesis imperfecta had been spotlighted in an article in *Redbook* magazine, written by the mother of a boy with the condition. Response to the article led to the start of a foundation, to facilitate research and to establish contact with patients.

Jane immediately sent a contribution and was pleased to hear from Gemma Geisman, the author of the article. She had enjoyed Jane's poetry for years without suspecting her condition. "I thought you to be a perceptive, lively and energetic person who had seen the world close-up," she wrote. "Now I realize that it is your spirit that is perceptive, energetic, lively. . . . You have seen the world as very few people have, and through your magnificent gift you have brought it to others. You can be such inspiration to young sufferers of OI."[8]

Gemma was the editor of *Breakthrough,* the OI Foundation publication. She asked for a poem and a biographical sketch from Jane, who was glad to comply. For once she didn't mind revealing details of her invalidism. The poem was "Prayer for Mothers," from *Think About These Things.*

> Thy grace to every mother;
> And oh, thy special grace

To mothers of the children
Whose feet do not keep pace

With the running of their playmates,
Who do not hear, or see;
Thy grace to all the mothers
Whose wounded hearts must be

The source of reassurance,
Encouragement, and power
To children who are different.
Lord, give them, hour by hour,

Good cheer and faith and courage
And steadfast self-control
To help their helpless children
Grow strong in heart and soul.

Through the foundation, Jane heard from several mothers of children with OI and was alerted to two recent books on the subject: *Give Every Day a Chance* by Beverly Plummer, whose daughter had OI, and *Letters to Polly* by Melvin Schoonover. Both Schoonover and his daughter, Polly, had OI and were wheelchair users. Jane reviewed the books for *Life and Health* magazine and wrote a brief article on the OI Foundation. It had come too late to help her, but perhaps she could do a bit to help them, she noted to her friends. Many of them responded with contributions.

Jane empathized with Schoonover's anger at the lack of privacy suffered by those who must depend on others for basic needs—and his humiliation of being treated as mentally defective because he was physically crippled. No human being could be dismissed as "defective" in Jane's view. She had sent Bruffie a quotation from her notebook, copied from C. S. Lewis' *The Weight of Glory*: "There are no ordinary people. You have never talked to a mere mortal. . . . It is immortals whom we work with, joke with, marry, snub and exploit. Immortal horrors or everlasting splendors. . . . All day long we are in some degree, helping each other toward one or the other of these destinations. . . . Next to the Blessed Sacrament itself, your neighbor is the holiest object presented to your senses."

It was always a bit unnerving to be reminded of the awesome responsibility she had toward the ones she lived alongside. In her letter to Bruffie, Jane enclosed "Hopeful of Being," written "in protest against people's habit of dismissing others as 'trite,' 'ordinary,' and 'merely.' "9

Hers was a trite life—
ABC's and the other children making fun of her
    clothes.

She knew the ABC's were old but not that tears
Had splashed in dust as a child ran home alone
Ever before.

It was all quite ordinary—
The shame of not dating and the stiff silence of the
    one date she had,
The typing job and the apartment she tried to brighten
With condensed books and paint-by-number pictures;
She learned that tears were never unusual.

She died, crippled by arthritis, in a retirement home,
Saying, "Father, into Thy hands"—
Timidly hopeful of being, out of all the millions of
    trite people,
Considered unique by One.

The Upper Room Disciplines had asked for another series of seven daily meditations. Jane was preparing herself by reading the Psalms from the Good News Bible. The language was "plain and fresh," she noted to Kay, but it lacked the "surge and thunder" of the King James Version—still her favorite. In places there was a shift in meaning as well: "Compare Psalm 104:31: 'The glory of the Lord *shall* endure forever, the Lord *shall* rejoice in his works,' and '*May* the glory of the Lord last forever! *May* the Lord be happy with what he made!' The change from prediction to prayer is probably suitable for an age when the Lord must be unhappy with what happens to much He has made. At least we do well to pray for His happiness rather than our own."[10]

For her meditations, she chose the theme "His Words and Ours." The draft of the first four went quickly. Even so Jane explained to Bruffie that her work was not up to standard, "but the standard does seem to lean toward the ponderous rather than the meditative—that 'ponder-ous' is a pun, but not premeditated—and can I help it if premeditated also sounds like playing on words? When I work with them why not play with them? As I noted [in "Exception"].[11]

There is no man
But will admit
A pun's the lowest
Form of wit—
Unless, of course,
He uttered it."

A week later she was less exuberant. She wrote to Carolyn Ruth of having spent much time "waiting to be waited on" while trying to finish

286

the meditations, answer several letters, wrap a couple of gifts, knit a pot holder, and prepare for an evening visitor. The circumstances no longer allowed much constructive organization of her day. She felt more a captive of time than in control of it.

The meditations reflected her exasperation. How could it be, she wrote, in an age when men on the moon could communicate with earth, that people in the same household, city, or nation suffered a break-down of communication? How had words come to mean such different things to different people?

Could it be an attempt to return to Eden by naming things anew? There God brought every beast and bird to man to "see what he would call them, and whatever the man called every living creature, that was its name. An engaging picture, reminding one of young parents showing their child a flower or an animal, saying, 'What will he say when he sees this!' One senses the Creator's pleasure in His creation and His desire that man share in it."

But no one could return to Eden by denying the reality of evil, "calling things by new names that please us better than the old. . . . We cannot recover some lost state of bliss by words affirming our own worthiness. We are guilty, for we have transgressed. . . . We regain Eden only by trust in the 'second Adam,' Jesus Christ."

Individuals were still held responsible for their use of words—a sobering thought in an age flooded with words. When Jesus called Simon "Peter"—rock—the impetuous Simon became rock instead of quick-sand. "Any effort we make to call another by his name, to speak to the person he is and can become, may make a redeeming difference in him."

Those who boasted of telling it all, telling it like it is, were more often telling it as they think it is, doing much harm by "dwelling exclusively on the most horrible aspects of life."

In an age of excessive and noisy communication, "many people, young and old, experience a poignant, silent loneliness," she concluded, especially children alienated from their busy, working parents and the retired, "useless" elderly, set aside by a fast-paced, changing society.

Mere human words could not heal wounded hearts and link them together. Christ was the restorer of broken relationships. "In a caressing touch, even in a smile that recognizes a stranger's personhood, we may testify to the Word that was made flesh and dwelt among us."[12]

The meditations were sent off in late May. In early June came the acceptance and a $25.00 honorarium. They would be printed in 1973, "if the world holds together that long," Jane wrote to Bruffie.

The temporariness of earthly matters—including her own body—was much on her mind. Donia was content to think of herself—and her daughter—buried in their Bookwalter Cemetery plot beside Clarence, but Jane had other plans. If she outlived her mother, as she expected, she would donate her physical remains to the University of Tennessee Medical Research Department. It seemed sensible now that Osteogenesis Imperfecta was being researched.

The legal form she had obtained from the university advised consultation with a pastor. Jane turned to Bruffie and hoped he had no objections. "I feel it is an entirely moral thing to do, I know it isn't illegal, and it certainly isn't fattening," she quipped. "I'm not expecting to 'put off this mortal' for some time yet, in case you wonder."[13]

Bruffie's answer came in a box marked fragile, delivered by the mailman. He had risen early the day before to cut five long stemmed yellow rosebuds, wet with dew, from his garden. They were carefully wrapped in moist cotton and sealed in plastic. They filled Jane's room with their fragrance.

"Dear Bringer of Golden Apples and Sender of Golden Roses!" she wrote to thank him. "In a certain renowned poetry contest, so I've read, the second prize . . . is a golden rose . . . made of precious metal. The first prize, of course, is a *real* yellow rose. And here I have five of them dropping from Parnassus . . . without entering any contest for them, either."[14]

The plans for her earthly remains were not mentioned again. Jane revealed that Abingdon had asked for another devotional book, and she would think about it. The time was "not yet—if ever." Summer visiting season made serious study and writing impossible, but it was good to know that a book was wanted. It was something to pray about and wait for a clear indication.

In the meantime, she was busy with a favorite pursuit: reading literary classics. Some she knew almost by heart, books by Dickens, Sir Walter Scott, Jane Austen, the Brontë sisters, and, of course, Shakespeare. There were voids in her acquaintance with books, perhaps because she had not made a systematic study of them in school, but she was determined to fill the gaps. Her education would go on as long as she could hold a book and see to read.

That summer Carolyn Ruth was taking a course on George Eliot, the nineteenth-century English author. She sent her books to Jane, who was "promptly enchanted." *Adam Bede* "came just when I was feeling special need of escaping into a saner world than the present," she confessed. "I . . . turn thankfully to George Eliot as to someone my obsolete consciousness may be able to comprehend. . . . I suppose the chief charm of troubles of characters in novels is that one doesn't have to try to do anything about them . . . [they at least take] my mind off the constant awareness that Mother is very frail . . . and the burden of responsibility heavy on Elizabeth. And the faith and patience exemplified by Dinah and Adam are very needful to me. I am somewhat like Adam in one way—'A nature like Adam's,' " she quoted from the book, " 'with a great need of love and reverence in it, depends for so much of its happiness on what it can believe and feel about others!' . . . I suppose that's the reason I prefer to read books with characters I can admire rather than characters for whom I feel only mingled disgust and pity, as in most current novels."[15]

To Bruffie, she declared: "thank Heaven for nineteenth-century novelists, and may twentieth-century ones be forgiven!"[16] She had spent happy hours searching out references to George Eliot in Emily Dickinson's letters, and she confessed that there had "been moments since 1967" when it would have seemed "less trouble . . . to self and friends" if she had "evanescenced then." But "how wasteful . . . to die without reading ED's [Emily Dickinson] letters and B.C.'s [Bruffie Connor]. Every good and perfect gift . . . cometh down from the Father of lights, but nothing hinders my gratitude to the earthly transmitter of light."[17]

Health problems beset the family again. Elizabeth had surgery to remove calcium deposits from her shoulder, and Ruth had charge of the Doll House for a week. Ed Lee came with her—on crutches, his leg in a cast. Nelson's visit was delayed; he had chipped a bone in his hand. What next? Jane lamented. Some of her friends held that positive thinking would ward off all calamities; for her part, she seemed to "handle life better with a cross."

All was not dark. Their apple tree produced "an embarrassment" of small, faulty fruit, delicious in apple sauce and pie. "So much, at least, of Eden remains to us," Jane observed to Bruffie in late July.

Terry and Linda, Nelson's son and daughter-in-law, brought the three children on a surprise visit, and Jane took a whole roll of pictures of the little ones playing outside her window. She had described an earlier generation of young visitors in poetry:

> Today the lemon lilies bloomed
> And a yellow warbler flew
> Across the morning, and a small
> Impulsive zephyr blew
> Small Peggy's curls about her face—
> Was ever day so fair
> With golden petals, golden wings,
> And golden baby hair!
> "Golden Things"

More and more Jane felt "adrift in an alien atmosphere," she wrote to Carl Arneson. They had watched the televised splashdown of another space capsule returned from the moon, and Jane felt seasick at the sight of the small craft bobbing helplessly in giant ocean waves. It was too much like her own life at present. She could only trust that "heavenly space watchers" would not let it sink.

Pat came from Michigan in August, while Elizabeth went to Asheville on vacation. Jane had hinted to Bruffie beforehand that he would be most welcome while Pat was there. They planned a party with Eva for the coming Saturday. Bruffie came with his wife, Marie, and their daughter Janie. They brought a handmade wooden tray laden with cake, cookies, and preserves from their kitchen and Michigan blueberries and seedless grapes.

The friends already knew one another through Jane's letters and from corresponding directly. Bruffie was greeted by Pat and Eva as a long awaited brother at a family reunion. Donia beamed on the happy gathering, and Jane was radiant. "It's blissful when one's special people enjoy each other," she wrote afterwards to Bruffie.[18]

Pat left the following week, but the Doll House was filled with family: Nelson and Elberta, with Terry, Linda, and their three small ones en route to Arizona for the winter.

They were reluctant to leave. Donia seemed noticeably weaker, and they were afraid she would soon be unable to stay alone with Jane, even though Elizabeth could readily be reached through the phone by Jane's bed. Something would have to be decided—soon. Perhaps they could wait until Christmas, but no longer.

Jane hid her fears, but she marked a passage in *The Imitation of Christ* by Thomas à Kempis with the date; "Aug. 1971": "It is temptation that troubles you, and a vague dread that makes you fear. But of what avail is such fear or dread of things that perhaps will never come, save that the spiritual enemy desires that you should have sorrow upon sorrow. Bear your present troubles patiently, therefore, and do not fear overmuch those that are to come, for sufficient to the day is the day's evil. . . . Trust strongly in Me and have perfect hope in my mercy."

She marked another passage a few pages further on: "An hour will come when all your labors and troubles will cease—and truly, that hour is at hand, for all that passes away with time is short. Continue therefore as you are doing. Labor busily and faithfully in my vineyard, and I will shortly be your reward. Write, read, sing, mourn, be quiet and pray, and suffer adversity gladly, for the kingdom of heaven is worth more than all these things, and is much greater than they."

The difficult present could only be lived moment by moment. Deliverance would come in God's time. Until then he would keep her "keeping on." Nearly ten years earlier, Jane had written "For the Oppressed," in *Every Good Gift*.

The promise of deliverance came—
And each believed and bowed his head
In reverence of the holy Name
That Moses and his brother said.

The promise of deliverance came—
And harder tasks and heavier toil,
And they, in weariness and shame,
Were still the tyrant's helpless spoil.

The promise of deliverance came—
And after many an anguished hour
When hope was faint and faith was lame
Deliverance came with mighty power.

The promise of deliverance came—
Oh, never let your heart grow numb
If added burdens seek to maim
Your faith; deliverance will come.

The burdens seemed bound to get heavier. Jane clung to the promise that strength would be given when it was needed, and she tried not to think ahead. She felt like a coward, but she knew that fear was no proof of cowardice. Her prayer was for courage to accept the dreadful uncertainties and remain faithful to the end. "I'm standin' in the need of prayer especially just now," she confessed in a letter to Eva on the last day of August 1971.

Eva suggested that she might find encouragement in some of her own books, and after reading *Every Good Gift* Jane felt much better. There was "The Sower and the Sea," her poem about the seed of faith sown and nurtured in the heart by the same One who could still the storm of uncertainties that threatened her frail craft of life. In the meditation she had written: "Forgive us, our Father, for our panic in the sudden perils of life. Forgive us for our unbelief in thy caring when unbelievable disasters come upon us. O God, whose eternal care for every one of us our finite minds cannot begin to comprehend, help us so to receive and care for thy truth implanted in our hearts that in our worst hours we may not doubt thy care for us. In our Lord's name. Amen."[19]

He had cared all that hotly dusty day
For all the importuning multitudes,
Teaching the truths of Heaven to allay
Their stormy fears and heal their inner feuds,
Teaching them that the kingdom, like a seed,
Must grow in secret quiet, no man knowing

291

How it is formed, and urging them to heed
How they themselves received the lavish sowing.

Worn out with care, he slept till many a wave
Beat on the boat. "Do you not care" awoke
Him, "if we perish?" He who came to save
All men from perishing arose and spoke.
If we had listened carefully would we dare
In storms, to say to him, "Do you not care?"
                                "The Sower and the Sea"

21

ONE GRACIOUS TIME
SEPTEMBER 1971– JANUARY 1972

No doubt, no doubt the vivid days
Were marvelous, were splendid,
But now the flame of red, the blaze
Of gold and orange are ended.

Now there is unassuming brown
Of resting earth receiving
The final dull leaves drifting down
Without aspect of grieving.

Now there are soft harmonious hues
Of gray, serenely gentle,
And nothing that we need refuse—
Oh, nothing detrimental

At all in the explicit bough
And introspective sun.
One gracious time has ended now
And one has just begun.

There was a sense of finality as the last summer flowers faded in the garden, as if time itself was nearing the end. Ruth's daughters Sara and Peggy were installed in their dorm at the university for the fall semester. Their young exuberance burst into the quiet rooms of the Doll House like gusts of spring winds out of season.

The contrast between the nieces—bubbling with energy and optimism for the future—and Donia, whose days were rapidly waning, struck Jane with painful force. "All things temporal seem to become more temporary all the time," she noted to Dorothy.[1] Things temporal had a beginning and a definite end. So did her strength, which seemed to have run out.

Work required an immense effort, and in weariness she longed to say, "It is finished!"

Things temporal seemed more and more like pale shadows of a reality beyond time and decay. The familiar wonders of her garden—grass, flowers, trees, birds, and sky arching overhead—were fleeting reflections of eternal glories. The earth itself, in marred loveliness, was transient against the backdrop of eternity.

How much longer would earthly pilgrims enjoy the fragile marvels of a disposable world? In Jane's last book was "Unless We Guard Them Well," now to be reprinted in a Kendall College publication and recited at an environmentalist convention.

> Perhaps the children of a future day
> Between picnics on Venus and the moon
> And explorations of the Milky Way
> Will come and spend a summer afternoon
> Among the quaint old-fashioned people, asking,
> "And did you really see a robin, sir?
> And even a clover field with cattle basking?
> And could you tell us just what daisies were?"
> Let us speak carefully of the long ago
> Lost days when earth was green, and country air
> Was filled with winging song and petaled glow
> Lest any yearning listener may declare,
> "Oh, I would give the moon if I had heard
> A thrush, or ever seen a hummingbird!"

Her words would perhaps inspire *some* to take more seriously the task of caring for this perishable planet. Jane had rejoiced in the beauty of it, but she longed for the day when the veil would be lifted, and she could see clearly the glory only dimly perceived now, when she could love and adore the Creator without restraint or limitation.

Till then she must live and give thanks for the present. "'What a wonderful day the Lord has given us, let us be happy, let us celebrate!' So let's!" Jane exhorted Frances on September 7, the sixteenth anniversary of the publication of her first book. She had expected it to be out of print within a year—one of the glum predictions she was most happy to admit was wrong. In the book was her own paraphrase of the words from Psalm 118:

> This is the day
> Which the Lord has made
> From dazzle of sun
> And dapple of shade

From joyous green
And rapturous blue
And gold light making
All things new;

A sample of heaven
Floating free
To stay us till
Eternity.

"Bright Day"

The prayer she had penned then was perhaps more needed now: "Help us, Lord, to perceive thy steadfast love in dark days as well as in bright."[2] But over the years she had also learned better to depend on the Father of lights in deepest darkness.

Her work was still in demand. A new poetry magazine, *Old Hickory Review,* asked for a contribution. Jane sent "Five Haiku for Spring." The editor, Kathryn Robbins, was delighted: "I have enjoyed your poems for a long time. . . . I love the things you write . . . and give you a BIG welcome to our ranks."[3]

There was only one poem in the entire October issue of *Good Housekeeping*—Jane's "Rain Clouds," inspired by a remark Eva made about "a gray flannel sky."

Gray drapery fabrics
Flannel, in winter;
Gauze, in spring;
In summer, plush;
In autumn, silk.

Fall was unusually warm, and the leaves did not turn until late October. Outside Jane's window the colors were growing "richer and more vibrant by the moment," she reported to Bruffie. "The morning glories have filched *all* the blue from the sky, 'and I can't chide this larceny as wrong/When they bloom blue and lovely all day long.'* I suppose I'm really a has-been when things remind me of what I've written instead of causing me to write something new, but today is created for contentment, and I'll be concerned about my own deficiencies some other time—most other times—but not today."[4]

This was a day for storing up bright wonders of October, as she had written in "This Soaring Day" in *Every Good Gift.*

I know that I cannot entirely keep
Undimmed in memory this soaring day.

*From "Grand Larceny" in *Halfway Up The Sky.*

295

I shall forget just how the huge clouds sweep
Through high enormous blue; I'll lose the way
Their rushing shadows on rich autumn hills
Make ever-changing tapestries of light
And shade—I cannot keep this day that spills
Its thousand glories on my dazzled sight.

Yet though I cannot memorize the hues
And shapes of every cloud and field and wood
I think in darkest times I shall refuse
Despair, in confidence that life is good,
Long after I have quite forgotten how
Vivid the leaves are on each shining bough.

"Glimpses of radiance," treasured in the heart, helped sort out her thoughts from darkness, Jane stated in the meditation accompanying the poem. She needed her store of light the next day. Abingdon had decided to let two more books, *The Mercies of God* and *All Daffodils Are Daffy*, go out of print. Her mail also brought back a losing poem from a contest. It was titled "History of Grief," which sadly fit her mood.

"An empty doorway and a maple leaf"—
     No,

For grief
A few charred timbers
Where no doorway is, no house.
And one blackened
Leafless
Tree.

Four books out of print seemed to be a strong indication that her type of writing was losing ground in public popularity. On the eve of her birthday, Jane confided in her diary: "It is dismaying to have the work I've put so much into being devalued . . . when so much else is slipping away. But I must remember that the books did much better than anyone expected. . . . And that they may still do good. But what am I to do now in my 52nd year of life? I still have unused potentialities, but how am I to use them? 'Behold the handmaid of the Lord; be it unto me according to thy word' [Luke 1:38]."

The future looked uncertain, indeed, but her faith was in an unchanging God. His loving purpose for all creation would ultimately triumph. In *Every Good Gift*, her thanksgiving volume, was "For All Healing."

For broken things:
Moth wings,
The fleeing hare's snapped spine,
The swooping owl's limp pinions,
The child's first doll, the woman's heart, the man's
Life work
Broken—shattered—spent—
For every individual crushed hope of this moment,
    this hour, this day,
And of all moments of all past centuries;

Lord, we repair
To thee in prayer
That all life's brokenness
At last, at last
In thy time, in thy way
Be healed through thee, by thee—be wholly healed.

We trust that this may be
For thou art holy.

God had kept her from shrinking back in the past, and Jane would not give up now. The "Merchant mulishness"—whether it was perseverance or stubbornness they had never determined—was still a dominant characteristic in the family. More than twenty years had passed since Jane wrote "Definitions," about her father.

"Your dad's a very stubborn man
    Indeed," our mother said.
He said, "A persevering man,"
    But Mother shook her head.

"That's what you call it," she observed.
    "A man who'll work away
Till grass is growing where it won't
    Is stubborn, I should say.

"And yet I reckon any man
    Who's fully set to win
Can't tell where perseverance stops
    And stubbornness sets in."

In her notes was the outline for a devotional book based on the Lord's Prayer, 114 poems arranged in five sections. It might meet with Abingdon's approval. But writing new poems and meditations was not feasible yet. Donia could not handle the materials. Perhaps later, with Ruth, in West Tennessee.

Thought of the move, with all its implications, filled Jane with dread, making it nearly impossible to "make herself available" to poems waiting to be written. She kept busy instead typing old works for editors, writing letters, and knitting or crocheting Christmas gifts.

Carl wanted to give her a Christmas amaryllis, but Jane explained that Donia could no longer care for plants, and Elizabeth had her hands full. Even the garden was diminished; Donia did not venture outside, and her flowerbeds were pulled up or mowed down.

Jane was loath to contemplate a view of spring without her mother at work among growing things, but she was writing poetry for April already. Lucille Turner, of David C. Cook Publishing Company, had asked for an Easter service for their *Leader Guidebook* again. The deadline was February 1, and Jane thought it best to get it done now. Setting her mind on the events leading up to the resurrection helped still her dread for the future.

The anguish of Christ in the garden of Gethsemane and His cry 'Thy will be done, not mine' were constantly in her thoughts and prayers. Was he tempted at the last to refuse the bitter cup of death? To cling to earthly life and loves? If so, Jane could understand his torment. She felt ready to face her own dying—but not Donia's. Her earliest memories of love were of her mother's gentle face and soothing hands. Why could they not be her last? Why could she not be granted to die first? The selfishness of her wish haunted her as she watched Donia move slowly and painfully across the room. She was nearly blind, nearly deaf, and still determined to keep on. She needed rest—the final, peaceful rest. Jane could not pray other than the words of Christ: "Father, if it be possible, let this cup pass from me—but nevertheless, not my will, but thine be done" (Luke 22:42).

Christ accepted death and in so doing conquered it—the last enemy. He died alone, forsaken, so that none of his followers would face death alone. He would be there. "I am the resurrection and the life," he declared. "And whosoever liveth and believeth in me shall never die" (John 11:26).

Beyond the wrenching separation of physical death was a greater reality of resurrection and oneness in Christ for all believers. That promise made the rest bearable. In gratitude Jane could pen the triumphant theme of her Easter service: "Christ has conquered all these things." That hope was alive in her heart and her writing. She aimed to proclaim it as long as she had breath. God willing, there would be a market for her work.

Her preference was to write just for self and friends, but that was a luxury she could not afford. What Eva called "a fortunate need" had spurred her on to defy rejection slips and humiliation and drove her now to overcome weariness and feelings of inadequacy.

Good Housekeeping, one of the few high paying markets left, bought one of her poems in late November; "a lachrimose little lyric" written ten years before, Jane reported to Carolyn Ruth. The check was most welcome before Christmas, and the sale was a boon to her writing morale. The poem was "Untold," and it would be printed in March, which seemed a long time off. Where would she—and Donia—be then?

> A burden to bear,
> A sorrow to quell,
> And no one at all.
> Whom I can tell.
>
> Some griefs are shared,
> Some woes are known,
> And some the heart
> Bears all alone.
>
> Time moves in silence,
> And even I
> May not remember
> By and by.

The November weather remained the warmest in memory, and Jane was grateful for a reprieve from ice and snow. The winter would come soon enough, and she tried to prepare herself. In a prayer she had written: "Our Father, thou knowest what is in the darkness; . . . Thou with whom light dwells, grant us to dwell with thee, blessing thy name at all times and in all seasons."[5]

The first Christmas greeting had arrived, a card with her own "I Wish You Christmas" poem. Several people had paid for the privilege of using it in the past. She had never got around to it herself, and doubted whether she would. It was painful to think of Christmases beyond this one.

Peggy and Sara were bubbling with ideas for the holidays, Jane observed to Bruffie, "which is suitable for their ages and conditions, but a little Christmas-dis-spiriting, somehow, for mine."[6]

She hid her despair and prayed for grace to focus on the Giver of lights. They were determined to make it a joyous Christmas. Nelson would come first, then Ruth's family, while Elberta went to visit her aging father in Kentucky. If this was the *last* Christmas for the parents, it would be a time for love and gratitude. To enjoy—not bemoan.

"It seems wise, if very difficult at times, for us to enjoy this Christmas as much as possible," Jane confided to Carolyn Ruth. "For I'm sure Mother doesn't expect to *see* another Christmas, her eyes are so poor, even if she is with us next Christmas. . . . But she still enjoys the sight of snowflakes and sunshine, and the slender pine tree blowing in the wind."[7]

In "First Snow" in *Think About These Things,* Jane had written:

> No one is old
> Who lifts his eyes
> And sees descend
> From busy skies
>
> The season's first
> White flakes of cold.
> Whatever his age,
> He is not old,
>
> Because he knows
> One heaven-sent
> Moment of pure
> Astonishment.

In spite of the happy anticipation, Jane sometimes wondered whether her mother would make it until Christmas. Sometimes she awoke before dawn and strained to see Donia's sleeping form across the room. Was she too still? Jane's heart beat a staccato of fear. Her hand, nearly paralyzed with dread, fumbled in switching on the lamp. In the flood of light her anxious eyes sought the familiar presence on the other bed. Limp with relief she watched the measured rise and fall of the blankets. Thank God—thank God. Donia was breathing. All was well.

Wind and rain whipped the bare trees in the garden—a "Winnie-the-Pooh blustery day" to be sure, Jane noted to Bruffie. But a chickadee on the "bird-parking-meter" was unruffled, feasting on seeds and suet in ample provision.

How grateful she was for birds—messengers of grace—demonstrating trust as they launched themselves fearlessly on flights through unknown skies, as if to say, "Watch us fly into the sky till we are lost to your sight. We are not lost, but enclosed by our Heavenly Father, hidden in Him. So will He enfold you in Love when you abandon yourself to His mercy. Trust and let go your fears. The future that is unknown to you is known to Him. Watch us and don't be afraid!" In "Bounty" Jane had written more than twenty years earlier:

> God could have left the sky
> Empty of wings,
> Empty of lilting
> Swift motion that sings.

White stars to measure by,
Clouds, sun, and moon;
Grace need have added
No lovelier boon.

But out of his bounty
He uttered sure words,
Fulfilling the heavens
By giving the birds.

Christmas packages were arriving daily at their door. Many of Jane's friends remembered Donia and Elizabeth with gifts, as well, and the spirit of happy expectation grew with each brightly wrapped addition to their pile of presents.

One box was marked for opening before Christmas. Irma Lidner, a new correspondent since summer, had been in Israel and sent an olive wood vase filled with frankincense. "I shall treasure it as long as I live," Jane wrote to thank her. At fourteen she had read and cried over Sidney Lanier's "Ballad of Trees and the Master." Now, for the first time, her hands held the wood of the trees that grew in the garden of Gethsemane—the trees that gave oil for anointing and for light in the lamp, the trees Christ knew and loved.

Never had she seen grain so "richly, *quietly* beautiful." Jane touched the graceful vessel and thought of the hands that had shaped it. Had Christ the carpenter run his hands over pieces of olive wood? Surely he had, just as he knew frankincense, the sweet smelling resin of the balsam tree. It was the traditional symbol of divinity, presented to the holy Child by Melchior, wise king from the East. "This will be the Christmas of olive wood and frankincense to me, whatever else the season may bring," Jane rejoiced to Irma.[8]

Another reader sent an arrangement of artificial holly and pine cones. Elizabeth hung it on the front door in time to greet Shirley, who arrived with an armload of gifts. The days were full now, and Jane had much to do just to cope with mail. It was not yet time to suspend her submissions to editors for the holidays. There were some pleasant rewards: a check from *Jack and Jill* for a Christmas poem and an anthology of poetry printed in *The Farm Journal*, containing three of her own poems. The book *Who Tells the Crocuses It's Spring,* was illustrated by Gwen Frostic, an artist Jane had long admired and secretly wished for as the illustrator of her work. Now the wish had come true without her asking, and she was grateful.

A complimentary copy of the *Sunday Digest* for January 9, 1972, came with an article titled "Jane Merchant, First Lady of Poetry." The writer was Margaret Jean Jones, a friend-by-mail of several years, who also was bedridden and nearly immobile from a rare muscle ailment. She saw in

Jane's literary success proof of Jane's own words, that "despite the cramped routine of one's customary days, our minds may keep wide horizons and our hearts broad sympathies."[9]

Margaret Jean posed the question of "how [Jane] escapes the imprisonment of four walls to bring hope and happiness and inspiration to untold thousands." She found the answer in the opening lines of Jane's poem "Always with Wonder."

> Always with wonder I have looked at each
> Recurring commonplace of every day:
> At dawn skies deepening into luminous peach
> And turquoise radiance, serenely gay;
> At flash of wings across unclouded noons;
> At trees stirred tranquilly by winds' caressing,
> And fleecy clouds that nestle tiny moons,
> And stars bestowing their eternal blessing.
>
> These many days I've lived, perhaps I should
> Take daily commonplaces quite for granted;
> But it is God who granted them, these good
> And lovely sights at which I gaze, enchanted,
> Always with wonder widening my eyes,
> Always with gratitude and glad surprise.

The glad astonishments of the season could not dispel Jane's forebodings. "There's the undercurrent and the feeling of time running out," she confided to Pat on December 14. "But we're having many good surprises and enjoying them, and I trust we'll have a good Christmas."

Their small artificial Christmas tree was up and decorated, and the house looked festive with "ersatz holly and artificial pine"—mostly gifts from readers—though Jane missed the fragrance of *real* pine.

Ed Lee had come from West Tennessee with packages and homebaked cakes and cookies. Before leaving with Sara and Peggy, he installed their gift for Jane, an indoor-outdoor thermometer, on the wall beside her telephone. It was a wonderful surprise; she had never even thought to wish for it. Now she could tell the outdoor temperature without waiting for the weather report; she witnessed the astonishing climb of the mercury to a record high of 73° on December 15! A soft rain was falling over the garden. It looked more like spring than Christmas, with bright green grass under bare trees. It seemed more suitable to look for a crocus than for Santa, Jane observed to Frances.

Two days later she had an opportunity to type—the first time in

December—and was able to complete the Easter service, "amazing cause for celebration nowadays," she confided to Bruffie. "I've wondered sometimes if this Christmas might not be a match for the one when we four children were all abed with flu . . . or the one when Elizabeth was in nurses' training . . . and Nelson started thirty miles in our 'feeble flivver' to bring her home on Christmas morning, and it began snowing and they didn't come and didn't come, and Dad started out on foot to find them, and they came on foot, half frozen (they thought), the 'flivver' having broken down. . . . We've had something to talk about at Christmas ever since. I hope Nelson gets here this time without that much anxiety."[10]

Memories of past Christmases were especially vivid this year. In "Home Christmas Tree," from *Petals of Light* Jane had written:

> Our ways at Christmastime were simple ways
> With homemade gifts and homemade ornaments
> On some tree that had weathered the white blaze
> Of summer heat and storm, and the intense
> Assaults of winter tempests on our home.
> Our Christmas tree was always one that grew
> Along with us from our familiar loam,
> And shared the elemental tests we knew.
> It was a joyous thing for us to find
> A tree that had grown fitly straight and tall,
> To bring it home with singing, and to wind
> Our treasured chains and spangles over all.
> It was a joyous thing to find, not far
> From us, a tree to bear the Christmas star.

Often Jane's eyes sought the loblolly pine in the garden—their living Christmas tree. It seemed futile to hope she would be there to see it next year. But she was grateful that, at least, it would not belong to strangers. Elizabeth planned to stay in Knoxville when Jane moved to West Tennessee, after their mother—the thought was too painful to complete. Perhaps Donia would be at Ruth's for a while, too. It was a hope Jane did not cling to. Donia so loved their little home and garden. It would be best for her not to be transplanted.

The dark thoughts remained like a menacing shadow beyond the warm glow of the Christmas candles. But they could wait until January. Jane reminded herself that blessings from the Father of lights were often brought by dark winged messengers.

Together magazine for January 1972, with the "Calendar of Haiku," had arrived. The December verse was a distillation of hope and faith:

Bare trees, bare earth, bare
Room, where a new mother holds
Five rosebud fingers.

On December 21, Jane reported to Pat: "It seems we will have a good Christmas notwithstanding everything, if only Nelson gets here without causing Mother much worriment by being late. She *is* getting weaker almost daily, it seems, but she is eager for Christmas."

Jane's own gift doings were done, she wrote Bruffie the next day. She was reading again C. S. Lewis' *Letters to an American Lady,* reflecting on his words: " 'We are all fallen creatures and all very hard to live with.' Living with Mother I tend to forget the fallenness. . . . People are remembering when Mother's homemade jellies and preserves were a highlight of their Christmases, and are bringing her jellies and preserves. She is still convinced it is more blessed to give than to receive. . . . Prospects are good for Nelson to get here Friday before Mother starts out to find him, and for a time of rest and feasting."

Nelson knew his mother—and sister—well enough to arrive a day early, "before my worries got started," Jane confessed. So her fears of "a slightly catastrophic celebration" came to naught.

In fact, Christmas far exceeded her expectations. She was in the living room Friday and Saturday, enjoying the tree and drop-in visitors. Sunday, Christmas morning, Nelson handed out the gifts under the tree while the four of them had a joyous time together. "I wonder if *all* brothers are as good to have around as he is," Jane noted to Bruffie.

She was back in the bedroom by early afternoon, with time to rest and enjoy her paperback volumes of Winnie-the-Pooh, a gift from Eva. Pat would call at 5:00 P.M., and Jane was ready with her hand on the phone to feel it ringing. As soon as Elizabeth verified that it was indeed Pat, Jane began talking, telling of their Christmas. Elizabeth listened when it was Pat's turn to talk and relayed her message to Jane. The system worked.

Nelson left early Monday morning, Jane wrote to Pat the same day. Donia had done better than they had dared hope, even if she heard and saw little. Now, if she could only remain strong until Ruth's arrival on Friday! Temperatures continued to stay in the seventies, and Elizabeth had seen phlox in bloom! Two poinsettia plants—one white, one red—gifts from readers, brightened Jane's room, but she felt sleepy and tired. There were stacks of thank-you notes to write, "but I wanted to write you first. . . . Happy New Year, dear Pat, in case you don't get this before 1972."[11]

She wrote to Pat daily now, and two days later could report that Donia was still doing fairly well. They had decided that Elberta would come for a few days in January, if necessary, to give her a rest. "It really has been a rugged year, hasn't it? And '72 doesn't promise much to me. But I trust the necessary strength will be given me. I'm thinking of Whittier's 'I know not what the future hath of marvel or surprise/ Content to know that life and death His mercy underlies.' And there's my Pat to be grateful for, among many bleesings.''[12]

She tried to keep her anxiety for the future at bay. First there was Ruth's visit to look forward to. ''Then bang! Monday!'' she declared to Bruffie. ''Let's both stay away from junipers this January!''

Sunday afternoon, January 2, 1972, Jane reported to Pat on the happy family gathering. They had watched the Rose Parade and bowl game on television and tried something brand new for New Years: little meatballs cooked in Sara's new fondue pot on Jane's table and dipped in ketchup and mustard sauce. It was all very relaxed and enjoyable.

Ruth, Ed Lee, and Edwin had left Sunday morning. ''Now Sara and Peggy are waiting as patiently as they can for Elizabeth to get home and move their junk into the dormitory. It has stopped raining, but could start again as soon as they start moving. . . . Mother is asleep. . . .

''6:45 P.M. Elizabeth now has taken the girls to the dormitory. Tomorrow—Monday! Happy day, dear, whatever day you receive this!

''P.S. Eva came about 7:30.''

Eva had phoned to ask if she could come at such a late hour, and Elizabeth assured her it was fine. Monday began another work week, with little time for leisurely visits.

Snow flurries fell in the darkness outside when Eva arrived. A red candle burned on Jane's bedside table. She had a belated gift for Eva; a pair of warm mittens she had just finished knitting. The two friends exchanged pleasant news of their holiday doings and wished each other a Happy New Year.

In the pre-dawn darkness of a new day, Elizabeth brought coffee, toast, and the morning paper before leaving for work. She checked on Donia, who was sleeping restfully, and would call at noon to make sure all was well.

The night had been mild, and the windows were clear of steam. Jane watched the first gray light trace the familiar outline of her winter view before turning on her lamp to read while she waited for Donia to rise.

They had breakfast a little after seven and recounted the happy memories of their family Christmas. What a wonderful time it had been, much better than Jane had envisioned beforehand. Perhaps other worries were as unfounded. Donia seemed happier and stronger than she had been for weeks.

While her mother rested, Jane prepared the outgoing mail: her letter to Pat, several thank you notes, and the usual first-of-January batches of poems for editors, prepared between Christmas and New Years. The

Easter service addressed to Lucille Turner at David C. Cook was being sent now, "a little ahead of schedule, while I have time," Jane had noted in her cover-letter.

The mailman arrived in late morning. Donia brought the incoming correspondence to Jane, then went to the kitchen to prepare their lunch. The time was 11:30 A.M.

Minutes later she thought she heard a noise in the bedroom and went to investigate. She found Jane lying still, as if in peaceful sleep, but she knew instantly that her daughter was past waking.

Elizabeth answered the phone in her office and heard her mother calmly state: "Jane is gone."

Within minutes, she and Dr. Payne were at the Doll House. They could only ascertain that death had been instant, caused by sudden heart failure.

"It's the answer to her mother's prayer," the doctor added.

Donia had prayed to outlive her daughter and to care for her until the end. Now her task was done, and she could rest.

The burial was two days later in Bookwalter Cemetery, with a simple graveside service as Jane had wished it.

McCarty Mortuary, who had carried her to the mountains and on the dogwood trail, had charge of the arrangements. Gordon Sterchi and the Reverend Joe Dew, an old friend of the family, officiated.

Sterchi chose the words of Christ: "Well done, good and faithful servant; you have been faithful over a little, I will set you over much; enter into the joy of your master" (Matt. 25:23 RSV).

With the same quote Jane had introduced her poem "Rainbows" in *The Mercies of God*. Now the minister read it at her grave:

> Lying straight and proper in the impersonal bed,
> Fully occupied with her personal dying,
> She heard the nurse murmur, "What a dreary life
> She must have had!"
>
> And she, looking down as they did at her formal body
> With the thin hair tidy on the tired brow
> And the face pinched with nervous years of typing
> Statistics, and counting anxious dollars
> To keep a sister peaceful in a home for the retarded,
> Nodded without disarranging the tidy hair.
> "People usually thought it dreary," she agreed.
>
> They did not know that now, in her dying, she re-
>   membered
> Gathering violets one Christmas with her sister,
> And a doll in white Satin, and a Valentine

A boy gave her in grammar school.
"I'm glad to find dying isn't hard," she told them
  silently.
"Not hard for me or for the four-year-old
Who died at forty years.
And living was never so dreary as you suppose,
For there were elms in April, even for me,
And winter oaks, and many rainbows—"

The weary body faded from her sight in a midst of jubilee
  colors.
The nurse said, "Poor dear, she's gone."

EPILOGUE

All the New Year, may
Butterflies come to our thoughts
Even when blooms freeze.
             Haiku for January, 1972

"There's a great emptiness, isn't there?" Eva wrote to Bruffie after the funeral. "It's consoling though, to know that all was as Jane wanted it."

The absence was felt most in the Doll House, where Elberta had come to stay with Donia for a few days. The suddenness of Jane's death had added shock to the grief of all who loved her.

Several friends sought to comfort one another by mail. "I know full well your grief is as great as mine," Bruffie wrote to Pat. He quoted a line from one of Emily Dickinson's poems: "Indemnity for loneliness—that such a bliss has been."

Carl Arneson wrote to Eva of the "withdrawal pangs" from a friendship he had depended on to sustain him through difficult years. He quoted from Jane's poem "How Many Leaves," in *Petals of Light*: "How many million green leaves will it take/ To ease my heart a little of its ache."

Eva, Pat, and Shirley offered to help Elizabeth notify the nearly fifty regular correspondents listed in Jane's address book. No one had known just how extensive her network of friendships had been, spanning several continents, cities, small towns, and isolated farms. Her correspondents were of all ages, from young students to residents of nursing homes, and of such diversity of backgrounds and opinions that Jane had confided to Bruffie in 1968: "If numerous people with whom I correspond ever compare my letters they would probably think I'm several different people—not because I'm two-faced, I insist, but many sided. How fallacious the idea of immortality in the memories of friends; what friend can truly know, let alone remember, anyone as he *really* is? How necessary God is!"[1]

But as letters of grief and sympathy filled the Doll House mailbox, it became apparent that Jane's many friends had in common a sustaining memory of her steadfast love and understanding.

308

"She was a calm bulwark to me," wrote Webb Dycus, a correspondent of more than twenty years.

"Never before had I a friendship as selfless as hers for me," wrote Gurre Noble. "It's one of the most precious gifts I ever had."

"For forty years . . . I bathed in the warmth of her unfailing understanding," Carolyn Ruth declared. "I never imagined life without my friend. I took her extraordinary qualities quite for granted."

Carolyn Ruth had been in England on the day of Jane's death, and on the plane going home—still unaware—she wrote her last letter to her friend, "laying before her sights and sounds, tastes and smells, people and places, knowing . . . [that] in the glorious alchemy of that mind of hers, she would re-create the experience and relay it back to me through her artistry. Then I would be able to share *her* experience. This sharing became such a necessary part of my life that [now] there comes a fresh, specific loss with each thing . . . I know would have delighted Jane.

"All my 'firsts' I shared with Jane. My first at the University, my first at the ocean. . . . I still think, 'what would Jane say?' . . . I never gave thought to the possibility of the ceasing of that treasured flow of letters from Tennessee. Now the mailbox is a poor thing indeed."[2]

Jane had offered them all the gift of sharing their lives; their smallest concerns received her affectionate attention. Nothing was insignificant, and much of it became poetry.

"I am going to miss writing to her," said Frances. "I catch myself thinking, 'I must tell Jane about that,' for she was the one to whom I could write my innermost thoughts. But I have her books and many of her letters, which sometimes were better than the books, since they were directed to me particularly and often in answer to one of my problems."[3]

Pat had destroyed all but the most recent letters, and she would keep them as a treasured remembrance. "I just can't let her go," she confided to Shirley. . . . I'm so used to looking at everything carefully and storing up details to share . . . thinking. 'Oh, that's beautiful—I must remember to tell Jane,' or, 'That's funny—Jane will enjoy it.' I suspect you did the same thing. I wrote . . . nearly every day . . . even postage stamps or driving past a mailbox tears me up right now."[4]

But even with the wrenching pain of personal loss, Jane's friends acknowledged the timeliness of her death. "I found myself weeping," May Justus wrote to Eva, "but thought, 'How foolish—I should rejoice that Jane has entered into . . . the Presence of Him whom she loved and served all her life.' Surely He bestowed on her a special mark of His favor in taking her so gently from earth to Heaven!"[5]

Speaking before a women's gathering in her church, Frances said: "I cannot grieve for Jane. This is just as she would have planned it. . . . Perhaps [she] had said all that she had to say to us. Her last letter gave me the impression that she was weary with the effort to live and perhaps not too optimistic about the future."

Jane had begun to prepare for her move from the Doll House. She may have had a premonition that her destination was not to be West Tennessee. In a small red notebook placed on top of her personal papers in a box where Elizabeth knew to find it, she had written detailed instructions for the disbursement of her belongings. Bundles of special letters were marked "return to sender unread." Among them were Eva's and Bruffie's letters to her. Favorite books were inscribed with names of their intended recipients, often the original giver. Bruffie was to have the *Complete Letters of Emily Dickinson.* Shirley would get the Dickinson biographies she had given Jane. Pat's name was in the Amy Carmichael books and *The Complete Poems of Emily Dickinson.* Her niece Patricia was to have the carnelian ring, the small pillows from Jane's bed, and the well-worn read-aloud books. Even as a college student, Patricia had loved to snuggle against the pillows, listening for hours as Jane read aloud the old favorite tales. Each family member and close friend would have a special something Jane knew they would treasure.

All had her books of poetry. "They are a fine legacy to all of us who loved her, and to those who shall yet meet her through her inspiring lines," wrote Webb Dycus in January 1972. For many, her "Calendar of Haiku" seemed a final gretting, as if "she bequeathed us a poetic thought for each month of our first year without her, as though to diminish our loss gradually and gently," Kay Gudnason noted.

The haiku for June read:

> Always, shadows fall,
> But today we rest beneath
> Shadows of blossoms.

And for September:

> Storms wreck the old bridge;
> Today we adjust the past
> To fit the future.

In one sense Jane's writing had come full circle. She wrote her last poem for the Easter service mailed to David C. Cook Publishing Company the day she died. The editor, Lucille Turner, wrote to Elizabeth: "I have foggy recollections that . . . maybe Jane's first sales were made to publications which I edited."[6]

She was right. Jane's first direct sales (after first winning in the *Progressive Farmer* poetry contest) were to *Adult Bible Class,* a David C.

Cook publication edited by Mrs. Turner. They printed "Lazarus" in April 1946.

Jane's first and last sales were not only to the same editor, but also were poems written on the same topic: death and resurrection. In her last poem, "Christ Has Conquered," the beginning and ending stanzas read:

> On the darkness of our mourning
> For our Savior crucified,
> For a world of loss and anguish
> Wherein love and hope have died,
> See! The sun of Easter rises,
> Bright, with healing in its wings
> For distress and tribulation;
> Christ has conquered all these things.

> He has conquered death and evil,
> He has set us free to live,
> Free to love with cheerful courage,
> Free to give and to forgive.
> In all sorrow, need and hardship
> The divine assurance rings
> We have peace in Him who loves us;
> Christ has conquered all these things.

"Christ has conquered the very worst the world can do," she wrote in the text. "Whatever our hardships and sorrows we *can* be, as Paul triumphantly proclaimed, 'More than conquerors through Him that loved us.' "[7]

That triumphant theme had echoed in her writing and in her living, however much she felt a failure at times. Eva declared: "I never knew anybody else who could overcome everything the way Jane did. Marvellous spirit. She never acted as if she was 'just making the best of it.' That *was* her life. It *was* the best to her."[8]

Frances wrote to Pat a few weeks after Jane's death: "Today I saw jasmine blooming. It was encased in a film of ice from last night's freezing drizzle. Jane was like that. Bloomed through the darndest handicaps."[9]

Her writing and living had profoundly affected all who knew her. Robert Roy Wright, her first editor at Abingdon, wrote to Eva: "Knowing Jane was one of the real privileges of my editorial work. I never ceased to marvel at the fact that she was more alert to the real issues of living in today's world than many who are active in it. Through her writing she reached an amazing number of people, and added her own vitality to their lives."[10]

In the months after her death, many friends wanted to *do* something in her memory. Poets dedicated their works to her. Pastors read her poems from the pulpit. Gifts were made to the Osteogenesis Imperfecta Foundation, the East Tennessee Heart Association, the East Tennessee Children's Hospital, and to the organ fund of her church. The Poetry Society of Tennessee established a category in the Mid-South Poetry Festival Contest in memory of Jane Merchant, and several of her friends gave memorial readings of her poetry and wrote tributes.

The Knoxville Branch of the American Pen Women presented a memorial shelf of books to the University of Tennessee Extension Library. An "anonymous" donor (Shirley Kerr) gave one of Jane's books to each public school library and to several private schools in Knox County. Junior highs and high schools received copies of *The Mercies of God,* and elementary schools got *All Daffodils Are Daffy.*

In the months that followed, Eva, Bruffie, Pat, Shirley, Frances, Carl, and several others kept in close touch with Donia and Elizabeth at the Doll House, sending cards and letters of appreciation and encouragement. Donia was almost totally blind, but she wrote thank you notes with a large, clear hand, always signing herself "Jane's Mother."

Her strength gradually gave way, and in June 1973, eighteen months after Jane's going, Donia died peacefully at home, surrounded by her remaining children. Her body was laid to rest beside her husband and daughter in the family plot. Gordon Sterchi conducted the graveside service. He said of Donia: "I have never known a more gentle and gracious lady. I have never known a more Christlike person. We accept the fact of Christ's resurrection because—we see Him in the lives of radiant Christians and know that 'He Is Risen.'"

Jane had declared the same in her poem by that title, and Gordon Sterchi read it by her mother's grave:

> The Lord is risen indeed! We know it true,
> Since we, who cannot see him at our side,
> Have as abundant proof as had the two
> Who walked with him until the eventide.
> For we have witnessed fear-tormented men
> Transformed, like Peter, to men who boldly dare
> All things for Him, and women now, as then,
> Saved, even as Mary, from extreme despair.
>
> No surer proof than this could anyone
> Require. By every burden bravely borne,
> By every selfless act of service done,
> By every kindness in return for scorn,
> By every swift response to human need,
> We know that Christ the Lord is risen indeed.

312

Jane had written of God's mercy—so like a window in the stony walls of time, opening to his eternal love. She had seen it in God's creation, the seasonal wonders of nature outside her bedroom window. But she saw it clearest, perhaps, in the "windows" of humanity, God's love in the eyes of those who loved her, in the many acts of kindness she had lived by.

Patricia, her niece, said of her: "I always felt that Jane was immortal—ageless—that she . . . dwelt on a special plane—a world apart. But poets usually do . . . like having a window on heaven—a sneak preview of the world to come."[11]

Jane's own life and words have made "a little blessed window space" for many, a window with a view beyond stubborn walls of present circumstance or reflecting, as in a mirror, the secret of our inner rooms. There she may show us glimpses of God—and of ourselves.

And that is perhaps what it means to be a poet, a saint, and a friend.

NOTES

2. First Things *1936*

1. Letter to Carolyn Ruth Reynolds, May 2, 1948.
2. Letter to Eva Venable, March 21, 1951. Referred to as *Venable, March 21, 1951*.
3. Letter to Carolyn Ruth Reynolds, June 17, 1956. Referred to as *Reynolds, June 17, 1956*.
4. "By Strugglebuggy and Walking Man." Unpublished essay, 1960s.
5. "Two Scrapbooks." *Volta Review* (September 1952). Referred to as *"Two Scrapbooks."*
6. Letter to Eva Venable, March 21, 1951. Referred to as *Venable, March 21, 1951*.
7. Ibid.
8. "From Pond to Library." Unpublished essay, 1960s.
9. *Venable, March 21, 1951*.
10. Ibid.
11. Diary, July 1, 1964.
12. *Reynolds, June 17, 1956*.
13. *Venable, March 21, 1951*.
14. Ibid.
15. Ibid.
16. Letter to Bruffie Connor, Thanksgiving 1968.
17. Letter to Bruffie Connor, December 19, 1968.
18. *Reynolds, June 17, 1956*.
19. *The Portal*, 1936.
20. Interview with Carolyn Ruth Reynolds, Easter 1979.
21. Letter to Corrine Martin Erwin, July 8, 1936. Referred to as *Erwin, July 8, 1936*.
22. Letter to Corrine Martin Erwin, January 2, 1937.
23. Letter to Carolyn Ruth Reynolds, July 23, 1948.
24. Letter to Carolyn Ruth Reynolds, March 16, 1949.

3. Dimensions *1938–1944*

1. Letter to Eva Venable, March 21, 1951. Referred to as *Venable, March 21, 1951*.
2. Diary, July 1, 1964.
3. Comment on "Doom," unpublished poem, 1941.
4. *Scrapbook for Eva Venable*, p. 29.

5. Letter to Carolyn Ruth Reynolds, December 6, 1947. Referred to as *Reynolds, Dec. 6, 1947.*
6. Ibid.
7. Letter to Carolyn Ruth Reynolds, April 1949.
8. Letter to Jane from Carolyn Ruth Reynolds, December 31, 1942.
9. Letter to Eva Venable, December 31, 1950.
10. Letter to Frances Winter, August 30, 1961.
11. Interview with Elizabeth Merchant, September 1977.
12. Jane Merchant, *Every Good Gift* (Nashville: Abingdon Press, 1956), p. 66.
13. Diary, January 1947.

4. My Place on Earth *1944–1947*

1. Diary, 1948.
2. Diary, February 1947.
3. *Scrapbook for Eva Venable* (May 1945), p. 49.
4. "Two Scrapbooks," *Volta Review* (September 1952). Referred to as *"Two Scrapbooks."*
5. Letter to Corrine Erwin, October 6, 1945.
6. Letter to Jane from Carolyn Ruth Reynolds, August 19, 1946.
7. Letter to Jane from Peggy Dowst, *Saturday Evening Post.*
8. Letter to Carolyn Ruth Reynolds, March 28, 1947.

5. Intrinsic *1947–1949*

1. Letter to Carolyn Ruth Reynolds, July 5, 1947.
2. Letter to Carolyn Ruth Reynolds, October 1947. Referred to as *Reynolds, Oct. 1947.*
3. Letter to Carolyn Ruth Reynolds, Christmas 1947.
4. Letter to Carolyn Ruth Reynolds, December 6, 1947.
5. Letter to Carolyn Ruth Reynolds, January 29, 1949.
6. Letter to Carolyn Ruth Reynolds, July 12, 1947. Referred to as *Reynolds, July 12, 1947.*
7. Letter to Carolyn Ruth Reynolds, December 12, 1947.
8. Diary, June 2, 1947.
9. Letter to Carolyn Ruth Reynolds, February 17, 1947.
10. Bert Vincent, *Knoxville Sentinel,* April 23, 1947.
11. Diary, July 11, 1947.
12. Letter to Carolyn Ruth Reynolds, February 3, 1948.
13. Diary, Christmas 1947.
14. Letter to Jane from Carolyn Ruth Reynolds, July 14, 1948.
15. Jane Merchant, *In Green Pastures* (Nashville: Abingdon Press, 1959), p. 54.
16. Letter to Carolyn Ruth Reynolds, February 11, 1947.

6. Autumn of No Return *1949–1950*

1. Letter to Eva Venable, March 21, 1951. Referred to as *Venable, March 21, 1951.*

2. Letter to Eva Venable, February 24, 1951.
3. Letter to Shirley Kerr, January 5, 1966.
4. Ibid.
5. *Venable, March 21, 1951.*
6. Last line of "Departure."
7. Letter to Gurre Noble, Christmas 1961.
8. Letter to Eva Venable, February 1, 1951.

7. Meetings *1950–1951*

1. Jane Merchant, *The Greatest of These* (Nashville: Abingdon Press, 1954), p. 63.
2. Letter to Eva Venable, December 31, 1950. Referred to as *Venable, Dec. 31, 1950.*
3. Letter to Eva Venable, August 18, 1950.
4. Letter to Jane from Eva Venable, November 23, 1950.
5. Letter to Eva Venable, November 26, 1950.
6. Letter to Jane from Eva Venable, November 30, 1950. Referred to as *Letter to Jane, Nov. 30, 1950.*
7. Letter to Eva Venable, December 4, 1950.
8. Letter to Eva Venable, December 16, 1950. Referred to as *Venable, Dec. 16, 1950.*
9. Letter to Jane from Eva Venable, December 29, 1950. Referred to as *Letter to Jane, Dec. 29, 1950.*
10. Letter to Eva Venable, December 26, 1950.
11. Letter to Eva Venable, February 24, 1951.
12. Letter to Eva Venable, February 1, 1951.
13. Letter to Eva Venable, March 7, 1955.

8. Delight in Duty *1951–1952*

1. Diary, December 31, 1951.
2. Letter to Carl Arneson, April 5, 1962.
3. Diary, December 31, 1951.
4. Letter to Eva Venable, July 29, 1951. Referred to as *Venable, July 29, 1951.*
5. Letter to Eva Venable, January 22, 1951. Referred to as *Venable, Jan. 22, 1951.*
6. Letter to Jane from Dr. J. Wesley Hoffmann, January 24, 1951.
7. Letter to Eva Venable, July 15, 1951.
8. Letter to Eva Venable, July 15, 1952. Referred to as *Venable, July 15, 1952.*
9. Letter to Eva Venable, July 26, 1953.
10. *Venable, July 15, 1952.*
11. Letter to Eva Venable, July 13, 1952.
12. Letter to Eva Venable, May 10, 1954.
13. Letter to Carolyn Ruth Reynolds, December 15, 1952.
14. Letter to Jane from Eva Venable, August 18, 1951.
15. Letter to Eva Venable, July 22, 1951.
16. Jane Merchant, *Adult Bible Class* (New York: David C. Cook, 1950).
17. Letter to Carolyn Ruth Reynolds, September 18, 1952.

18. Letter to Eva Venable, October 9, 1952.

9. The Greatest of These *1953–1955*

1. Letter to Eva Venable, March 9, 1953.
2. Letter to Carolyn Ruth Reynolds, May 18, 1953.
3. Letter to Frances Winter, June 22, 1966.
4. Jane Merchant, *The Greatest of These* (Nashville: Abingdon Press, 1954), p. 60.
5. Letter to Eva Venable, July 19, 1953.
6. Letter to Sarah Jorunn Oftedal Ricketts from Robert Roy Wright, July 9, 1978.
7. Ibid.
8. Letter to Shirley Kerr, July 16, 1954.
9. Letter to Carolyn Ruth Reynolds, June 20, 1954.
10. Letter to Jane from Eva Venable, October 1954.
11. Merchant, *The Greatest of These*, p. 75.
12. Letter to Eva Venable, April 7, 1955.
13. Letter to Jane from James Waldo Fawcett, March 1955.
14. Jane Merchant, *Think About These Things* (Nashville: Abingdon Press, 1956), p. 82.

10. In Green Pastures *1955–1957*

1. Jane Merchant, *Think About These Things* (Nashville: Abingdon Press, 1956), p. 29.
2. Letter to Shirley Kerr, October 15, 1955.
3. Letter to Jane from Jean Mergard, April 11, 1956.
4. Jane Merchant, *Halfway Up the Sky* (Nashville: Abingdon Press, 1957), preface.
5. Letter to Kay Gudnason, May 29, 1958.
6. Letter to Eva Venable, October 14, 1956.
7. Letter to Carolyn Ruth Reynolds, March 23, 1957.
8. Letter to Carolyn Ruth Reynolds, April 15, 1957.
9. Diary, February 1957.
10. Jane Merchant, *In Green Pastures* (Nashville: Abingdon Press, 1959), p. 52.
11. Letter to Jane from Dr. Alwin Thaler, December 1957.
12. Letter to Kay Gudnason, November 1958.
13. Merchant, *In Green Pastures*, p. 73.

11. Through the Valley *1958–1959*

1. Letter to Shirley Kerr, February 11, 1958.
2. Letter to Eva Venable, July 5, 1953.
3. Letter to Gurre Noble, February 24, 1958.
4. Letter to Kay Gudnason, March 2, 1958. Referred to as *Gudnason, March 2, 1958.*
5. Letter to Kay Gudnason, Easter 1958.
6. Letter to Kay Gudnason, March 23, 1958. Referred to as *Gudnason, March 23, 1958.*
7. Letter to Kay Gudnason, May 18, 1958.

8. Letter to Kay Gudnason, November 3, 1958.
9. Letter to Shirley Kerr, January 3, 1959.
10. Letter to Kay Gudnason, March 10, 1959.
11. Letter to Gurre Noble, April 18, 1959.
12. Jane Merchant, *In Green Pastures* (Nashville: Abingdon Press, 1959), p. 78.
13. Letter to Kay Gudnason, May 2, 1959.
14. Letter to Gurre Noble, May 10, 1959.
15. Letter to Shirley Kerr, June 25, 1959.
16. Letter to Gurre Noble, September 20, 1959. Referred to as *Noble, Sept. 20, 1959.*
17. Letter to Kay Gudnason, September 16, 1959.
18. Letter to Frances Winter, September 22, 1959. Referred to as *Winter, Sept. 22, 1959.*

12. With Us *1959–1960*

1. Letter to Bruffie Connor, October 31, 1968.
2. Letter to Frances Winter, September 14, 1959.
3. Letter to Jane from Frances Winter, September 14, 1959.
4. Letter to Sarah Jorunn Oftedal Ricketts from Tess Hovde, May 1978.
5. Letter to Frances Winter, October 23, 1959. Referred to as *Winter, Oct. 23, 1959.*
6. Letter to Shirley Kerr, September 18, 1960.
7. Letter to Frances Winter, November 30, 1959.
8. Letter to Frances Winter, November 15, 1959.
9. Letter to Eva Venable, November 26, 1959.
10. Jane Merchant, *Blessed Are You* (Nashville: Abingdon Press, 1961), p. 82.
11. Letter to Frances Winter, March 5, 1960.
12. Letter to Jane from Gurre Noble, March 27, 1960.
13. Letter to Gurre Noble, April 1960.
14. Letter to Gurre Noble, May 1960.
15. Letter to Gurre Noble, August 10, 1961.
16. Letter to Frances Winter, April 12, 1961.
17. Letter to Frances Winter, July 14, 1960. Referred to as *Winter, July 14, 1960.*
18. Letter to Frances Winter, June 17, 1960.
19. Letter to Kay Gudnason, August 14, 1960.
20. Merchant, *Blessed Are You,* p. 108.

13. Boon *1960–1961*

1. Letter to Kay Gudnason, September 20, 1960.
2. Letter to Frances Winter, November 15, 1960.
3. Letter to Frances Winter, February 22, 1961.
4. Letter to Shirley Kerr, April 21, 1961.
5. Letter to Gurre Noble, March 1961.
6. Letter to Frances Winter, March 29, 1961. Referred to as *Winter, March 29, 1961.*
7. Lewis F. Ball, "Between the Book Ends," *Richmond Times Dispatch* (April 9, 1961): F13.

8. Jane Merchant, *Blessed Are You* (Nashville: Abingdon Press, 1961), p. 47.
9. Letter to Frances Winter, September 12, 1961.
10. Letter to Shirley Kerr, March 10, 1959.
11. Letter to Frances Winter, July 16, 1961.
12. Letter to Kay Gudnason, November 1, 1961.
13. Letter to Shirley Kerr, Christmas 1961.
14. Letter to Carolyn Ruth Reynolds, December 11, 1961.

14. Members One of Another *1961–1963*

1. Letter to Frances Winter, late July 1961.
2. Letter to Frances Winter, August 12, 1961.
3. Letter to Kay Gudnason, April 23, 1962.
4. Letter to Frances Winter, January 6, 1960.
5. Letter to Carolyn Ruth Reynolds, November 11, 1962.
6. Letter to Frances Winter, October 25, 1963.
7. Letter to Kay Gudnason, December 1963.
8. Letter to Betty Washer, December 3, 1963.
9. Letter to Shirley Kerr, December 11, 1963.
10. Letter to Kay Gudnason, December 1963.

15. By All the Radiance *1964–1965*

1. Letter to Shirley Kerr, February 9, 1964.
2. Letter to Jane from Shirley Kerr, February 11, 1964.
3. Letter to Frances Winter, May 3, 1964.
4. Letter to Carl Arneson, May 23, 1963.
*5. Letter to Jane from Carl Arneson, March 5, 1962.
6. Letter to Carl Arneson, March 9, 1962.
7. Letter to Carl Arneson, December 8, 1960.
8. Letter to Frances Winter, June 28, 1964.
9. Letter to Shirley Kerr, January 5, 1966.
10. Letter to Jane from Bruffie Connor, August 10, 1964.
11. Letter to Gurre Noble, September 1964.
12. Letter to Kay Gudnason, September 23, 1964.
13. Letter to Frances Winter, October 9, 1964.
14. Letter to Jane from Bruffie Connor, October 4, 1964.
15. Letter to Jane from Pat Lassen, October 18, 1964.
16. Letter to Shirley Kerr, March 31, 1965.
17. Letter to Kay Gudnason, December 13, 1964.
18. Letter to Kay Gudnason, November 20, 1964.
19. Letter to Frances Winter, December 30, 1964.
20. Letter to Carolyn Ruth Reynolds, January 3, 1965.
21. Alfred Mynders, *Chattanooga Times* (February 28, 1965).
22. Alfred Mynders, *Chattanooga Times* (March 19, 1965).

23. Jane Merchant, *The Upper Room Disciplines* (Nashville: The Upper Room, 1966).
24. Letter to Dorothy Brown Thompson, January 30, 1965.

16. Of Marred Creation *1965–1966*

1. Letter to Frances Winter, February 3, 1962.
2. Letter to Shirley Kerr, August 20, 1965.
3. Letter to Shirley Kerr, September 24, 1965.
4. Jane Merchant, *Every Good Gift* (Nashville: Abingdon Press, 1968), p. 55.
5. Letter to Shirley Kerr, October 17, 1965.
6. Letter to Jane from Gurre Noble, November 4, 1965.
7. Letter to Shirley Kerr, December 1, 1965.
8. Letter to Jane from Shirley Kerr, December 5, 1965.
9. Letter to Jane from Carl Arneson, November 27, 1965.
10. Letter to Jane from Shirley Kerr, November 10, 1965.
11. Letter to Shirley Kerr, January 5, 1966.
12. Jane Merchant, *The Upper Room Disciplines 1967* (Nashville: The Upper Room, 1967), Lenten meditations.
13. Letter to Kay Gudnason, February 23, 1966.
14. Letter to Kay Gudnason, April 12, 1966.
15. Jane Merchant, *In Green Pastures* (Nashville: Abingdon Press, 1959), p. 55.
16. Letter to Carolyn Ruth Reynolds, January 3, 1965.
17. Letter to Shirley Kerr, July 20, 1965.
18. Letter to Frances Winter, July 1, 1966.

17. For Becoming *November 1966–August 1967*

1. Letter to Shirley Kerr, November 10, 1966.
2. Letter to Jane from May Justus, June 23, 1966.
3. Letter to May Justus, July 3, 1966.
4. Letter to Jane from May Justus, October 10, 1966.
5. Diary, June 25, 1966.
6. Diary, June 27, 1966.
7. Letter to Shirley Kerr, July 15, 1966.
8. Diary, June 27, 1966.
9. Jane Merchant, *In Green Pastures* (Nashville: Abingdon Press, 1959), p. 110.
10. Letter to Pat Lassen, January 23, 1967.
11. Letter to Shirley Kerr, January 24, 1967.
12. *The Book of Worship for Church and Home* (Nashville: The Methodist Publishing House, 1965), p. 233.
13. Letter to Frances Winter, January 1967.
14. Letter to Shirley Kerr, February 16, 1967.
15. Letter to Frances Winter, March 29, 1967.
16. Letter to Jane from Edsel Ford, March 7, 1967.
17. Letter to Pat Lassen, April 10, 1967.

18. Letters to Frances Winter, April 17, 1967 and April 28, 1967.
19. Letter to Frances Winter, March 19, 1967.
20. Letter to Shirley Kerr, July 9, 1967.
21. Letter to Jane from Dr. Alwin Thaler, July 25, 1967.

18. Every Good Gift *September 1967–August 1969*

1. Letter to Jane from Ruth Northcott, September 9, 1967.
2. Letter to Bruffie Connor, January 22, 1968.
3. Letter to Shirley Kerr from Dr. Alwin Thaler, November 7, 1967.
4. Letter to Shirley Kerr from Dr. Rosemary Sprague, April 27, 1967.
5. Letter to Frances Winter, January 28, 1968.
6. Letter to Frances Winter, September 30, 1967.
7. Letter to Shirley Kerr, April 25, 1968.
8. Letter to Shirley Kerr, February 5, 1968.
9. Letter to Bruffie Connor, March 21, 1968.
10. Ibid.
11. Letter to Bruffie Connor, June 2, 1968.
12. Letter to Carolyn Ruth Reynolds, December 12, 1968.
13. Letter to Bruffie Connor, July 26, 1968.
14. Letter to Bruffie Connor, July 20, 1968.
15. Letter to Bruffie Connor, July 23, 1968.
16. Letter to Frances Winter, July 16, 1961.
17. Letter to Bruffie Connor, November 8, 1968.
18. Letter to Bruffie Connor, March 21, 1969.
19. Letter to Bruffie Connor, March 14, 1969.
20. Letter to Bruffie Connor, January 18, 1968.
21. Letter to Bruffie Connor, April 22, 1969.
22. Letter to Dorothy Brown Thompson, July 31, 1969.
23. Letter to Bruffie Connor, April 30, 1969.
24. Letter to Shirley Kerr, August 1, 1969.

19. Give Them to God *September 1969–December 1970*

1. Letter to Kay Gudnason, February 24, 1969.
2. Letter to Bruffie Connor, January 10, 1969.
3. Letter to Bruffie Connor, January 16, 1969 and January 18, 1969.
4. Letter to Bruffie Connor, January 28, 1969.
5. Letter to Bruffie Connor, September 26, 1969.
6. Letter to Jane from Bruffie Connor, September 29, 1969.
7. Letter to Carl Arneson, Thanksgiving 1969.
8. Letter to Bruffie Connor, December 4, 1969.
9. Letter to Kay Gudnason, February 4, 1970.
10. Letter to Jane from Bruffie Connor, March 30, 1970.
11. Letter to Bruffie Connor, April 17, 1970.
12. Letter to Pat Lassen, April 26, 1970.
13. Letter to Eva Venable, May 3, 1970.

14. Letter to Pat Lassen, May 1, 1970.
15. Letter to Frances Winter, June 17, 1970.
16. Letter to Jane from Carl Arneson, April 27, 1970.
17. Letter to Carolyn Ruth Reynolds, July 7, 1970. Referred to as *Reynolds, July 7, 1970.*
18. Letter to Bruffie Connor, October 16, 1970.
19. Letter to Jane from Rosemary Stevens, August 6, 1970.
20. Letter to Bruffie Connor, September 25, 1970.
21. Letter to Frances Winter, November 2, 1970.
22. Letter to Bruffie Connor, December 12, 1970.
23. Letter to Jane from Carl Arneson, December 27, 1970.
24. Letter to Carolyn Ruth Reynolds, December 12, 1970.

20. Bright Flowering *January–August 1971*

1. Letter to Carolyn Ruth Reynolds, February 26, 1971.
2. Letter to Bruffie Connor, March 19, 1971.
3. Letter to Jane from Shirley Kerr, September 5, 1970.
4. Jane Merchant, *The Mercies of God* (Nashville: Abingdon Press, 1963), p. 34.
5. Letter to Jane from Jaroslav Vajda, March 15, 1971.
6. Letter to Bruffie Connor, April 30, 1971.
7. Letter to Shirley Kerr, July 2, 1971.
8. Letter to Jane from Gemma Geismann, April 3, 1971.
9. Letter to Bruffie Connor, April 30, 1969.
10. Letter to Kay Gudnason, May 5, 1971.
11. Letter to Bruffie Connor, May 7, 1971.
12. Jane Merchant, *The Upper Room Disciplines* (Nashville: The Upper Room, 1973), pp. 131-37.
13. Letter to Bruffie Connor, May 21, 1971.
14. Letter to Bruffie Connor, May 25, 1971.
15. Letter to Carolyn Ruth Reynolds, June 8, 1971.
16. Letter to Bruffie Connor, June 11, 1971.
17. Letter to Bruffie Connor, June 25, 1971.
18. Letter to Bruffie Connor, August 20, 1971.
19. Jane Merchant, *Every Good Gift* (Nashville: Abingdon Press, 1968), p. 47.

21. One Gracious Time *September 1971–January 1972*

1. Letter to Dorothy Brown Thompson, October 15, 1971.
2. Jane Merchant, *The Greatest of These* (Nashville: Abingdon Press, 1954), p. 40.
3. Letter to Jane from Kathryn Robbins, October 11, 1971.
4. Letter to Bruffie Connor, October 22, 1971.
5. Jane Merchant, *Every Good Gift* (Nashville: Abingdon Press, 1968), p. 26.
6. Letter to Bruffie Connor, November 26, 1971.
7. Letter to Carolyn Ruth Reynolds, December 3, 1971.

8. Letter to Irma Lidner, December 14, 1971.

9. Jane Merchant, *In Green Pastures* (Nashville: Abingdon Press, 1959), p. 30.

10. Letter to Bruffie Connor, December 17, 1971.

11. Letter to Pat Lassen, December 26, 1971.

12. Letter to Pat Lassen, December 28, 1971.

Epilogue

1. Letter to Bruffie Connor, October 25, 1968.

2. Letter to Sarah Jorunn Oftedal Ricketts from Carolyn Ruth Reynolds, March 28, 1978.

3. Frances Winter in a speech to a women's group in January 1972.

4. Letter to Shirley Kerr from Pat Lassen, January 5, 1972.

5. Letter to Eva Venable from May Justus, January 12, 1972.

6. Letter to Elizabeth Merchant from Lucille Turner, February 9, 1972.

7. Jane Merchant, "Easter Service," in *Leader's Guidebook March-May 1972* (New York: David C. Cook, 1972), p. 9.

8. Eva Venable, in interview with Sarah Jorunn Oftedal Ricketts, September 1977.

9. Letter to Pat Lassen from Frances Winter, January 29, 1972.

10. Letter to Eva Venable from Robert Roy Wright, January 17, 1972.

11. Letter to Sarah Jorunn Oftedal Ricketts from Patricia Rogers, 1980.

POETRY INDEX

Index of Titles

Index of First Lines

INDEX

General index

ADDITIONAL COPYRIGHT INFORMATION

(Continued from copyright page)

335